Reflective Reader: Social Work and Mental Health

JOHN ARCHAMBEAULT

Series editor: Jonathan Parker

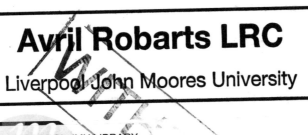

First published in 2009 by Learning Matters Ltd

British Library Cataloguing in Publication Data
A CIP record for this book is available from the British Library

ISBN: 978 1 84445 147 0

The right of John Archambeault to be identified as the Author of this Work has been asserted by him in accordance with the Copyright, Designs and Patents Act 1988

Cover design by Code 5 Design Associates
Project management by Deer Park Productions, Tavistock
Typeset by Pantek Arts Ltd, Maidstone, Kent
Printed and bound in Great Britain by Bell & Bain Ltd, Glasgow

Learning Matters Ltd
33 Southernhay East
Exeter EX1 1NX
Tel: 01392 215560
info@learningmatters.co.uk
www.learningmatters.co.uk

Contents

Extracts

Chapter 1

Reamer, F (1995) *Social work and ethics*. New York: Columbia University Press. Chapter 2, pp30–4.

Fook, J (2002) *Social work: Critical theory and practice*. London: Sage. Chapter 8, pp103–4 and pp108–9, reproduced with permission from Sage.

Mencap (2004) News. In *Viewpoint*, Nov/Dec. [online] **www.mencap.org.uk/download/ viewpoint_nov_dec_04.pdf p4**, reprinted with permission from www.mencap.org.uk/ viewpoint.

Department of Health (2004) *Advice on the decision of the European Court of Human Rights in the case of HL v UK (the 'Bournewood' case)*. [Gateway Reference 4269]. Crown copyright reprinted under Crown copyright PSI Licence C2006007372.

Chapter 2

Tilbury, D (2002) Determinants of practice: Defining mental health and mental illness. Chapter 1 in *Working with mental illness: A community-based approach*. 2nd edition. Basingstoke: Palgrave, pp1–3 and p10. Reproduced with permission of Palgrave Macmillan.

Prior, L (1993) Introduction: Social representations and social worlds. Chapter 1 in *The social organization of mental illness*. London: Sage, p3, reproduced with permission from Sage.

Allot, P (2004) What is mental health, illness and recovery? Chapter 1 in Ryan, T and Pritchard, J (eds) *Good practice in adult mental health*. London: Jessica Kingsley, pp17–19. Reprinted with permission from Jessica Kingsley Publishers (**www.jkp.com**).

White, P and Clare, A (2002) Psychological medicine. In Kumar, P and Clark, M (eds) *Clinical medicine*. 5th edition. Edinburgh: W.B. Saunders, p1225 and p1231.

Beresford, P (2005) Social approaches to madness and distress: User perspectives and user knowledges. In Tew, J (ed.) *Social perspectives in mental health: Developing social models to understand and work with mental distress*. London: Jessica Kingsley, p37 and pp43–4. Reprinted with permission from Jessica Kingsley Publishers (**www.jkp.com**).

Chapter 3

Bartlett, P and Sandland, R (2003) Conceptualising mental health law, Chapter 1, and An overview of the contemporary mental health system, Chapter 3, in *Mental health law, policy and practice*. 2nd edition. Oxford: Oxford University Press, pp71–2 and p26. Reprinted by permission of Oxford University Press.

Glover-Thomas, N (2007) A new 'new' Mental Health Act? Reflections on the proposed amendments to the Mental Health Act 1983. *Clinical Ethics*, 2 (1), 29–30.

Williamson, T (2007) Capacity to protect – the Mental Capacity Act explained. *Journal of Adult Protection*, 9 (1), 26–30, reprinted with permission from OLM-Pavillion.

Fakhoury, W and Wright, D (2004) A national survey of Approved Social Workers in the UK: Information, communication and training needs. *British Journal of Social Work*, 34 (5), 673–4, reprinted with permission.

Chapter 4

Kerfoot, M (2005) Children 'looked after' by the state. Chapter 22 in Williams, R and Kerfoot, M (eds) *Child and adolescent mental health services: Strategy, planning, delivery and evaluation*. Oxford: Oxford University Press, pp333–4. Reprinted by kind permission of Oxford University Press, **www.oup.com**

Walker, S (2003) *Social work and child and adolescent mental health*. Lyme Regis: Russell House, pp36–7, pp42–3 and pp48–9, reprinted with permission from Russell House Publishing Ltd.

Wright, J, Briggs, S and Behringer, J (2005) Attachment and the body in suicidal adolescents: A pilot study. *Clinical Child Psychology and Psychiatry*, 10 (4), 478–80, 483, 485, 487 and 488, reprinted with permission from Sage Publishers.

Honig, P (2007) Family approaches: Evidence-based and collaborative practice. In Lask, B and Bryant-Waugh, R (eds) *Eating disorders in childhood and adolescence*. 3rd edition. Abingdon: Routledge, pp215–16, pp219–20 and p226. Reprinted with permission from Routledge.

Chapter 5

Merritt, S (2008) My private hell. *Observer*, 6 April 2008 [online]. Extract from: Merritt, S (2008) *The devil within: A memoir of depression*. London: Vermillion, reprinted with permission from Random House UK and Bloodaxe Books.

American Psychiatric Association (2000) Mood disorders. In *Diagnostic and statistical manual of mental disorders*. 4th edition, text revision. Washington, D.C.: APA, pp349–51, p356 and pp422–3, reprinted with permission.

Cloutte, P (2003) *Understanding postnatal depression*. Revised edition. London: MIND, pp9–11.

Bird, A (2006) *We need to talk: The case for psychological therapy on the NHS*. London: Mental Health Foundation, p2. Reprinted with permission from the Mental Health Foundation/Foundation for people with Learning Disabilities.

Chapter 6

Redfield Jamison, K (1995) *An unquiet mind. A memoir of moods and madness*. New York: Alfred A. Knopf, p42, pp44–5, p91 and pp212–13.

Henderson, J (2001) 'He's not my carer, he's my husband': Personal and policy constructions of care in mental health. *Journal of Social Work Practice*, 15 (2), 149–52 and pp154–8.

Green, G, Hayes, C, Dickinson, D, Whittaker, A and Gilheany, B (2002) The role and impact of social relationships upon well-being reported by mental health service users: A qualitative study. *Journal of Mental Health*, 11 (5), 567 and 570–7. [online] Available at **http://dx.doi.org/10.1080/09638230020023912**.

Chapter 7

Golightley, M (2008) *Social work and mental health*. 3rd edition. Exeter: Learning Matters, pp139–40.

Pollard, K, Sellman, D and Senior, B (2005) The need for interprofessional working. In Barrett, G, Sellman, D and Thomas, J (eds) *Interprofessional working in health and social care: Professional perspectives*. Basingstoke: Palgrave Macmillian, pp9–10. Reproduced with permission of Palgrave Macmillan.

Wood, S and Green, B (2006) Integrated care pathways and integrated working. In Hall, J and Howard, D (eds) *Integrated care pathways in mental health*. Edinburgh: Churchill Livingstone Elsevier, p57. Reproduced with permission of copyright © Elsevier.

Norman, I and Peck, E (1999) Working together in adult community mental health services: An inter-professional dialogue. *Journal of Mental Health*, 8 (3), 225–7.

Chapter 8

Brockbank, A and McGill, I (2007) Reflection and reflective practice. Chapter 5 in *Facilitating reflecting learning in higher education*. 2nd edition. Maidenhead: Open University Press, pp85–7. © Reproduced with the permission of Open University Press. All rights reserved.

D'Cruz, H, Gillingham, P and Melendez, S (2006) Reflexivity, its meanings and relevance for social work: A critical review of the literature. *British Journal of Social Work*, 37 (1), 74–5, 80–1 and 83, reprinted with permission.

Hughes, L and Pengelly, P (1997) *Staff supervision in a turbulent environment: Managing process and task in front-line services*. London: Jessica Kingsley, pp83–5. Reprinted with permission from Jessica Kingsley Publishers (**www.jkp.com**).

About the series

The *Reflective Readers* series supports the *Transforming Social Work Practice* series by providing relevant and topical theory and research that underpins the reflective learning and practice of social work students.

Each book includes extracts from classic and current publications and documents. These extracts are supported by points to consider, comments, links to the National Occupational Standards, academic benchmarks, links to other titles in the *TSWP* series and suggestions for further reading.

Integrating theory and practice, the *Reflective Reader* series is specifically designed to encourage students to develop the skill and habit of reflecting on their own practice, engaging with relevant theory and identifying opportunities to apply theory to improve their professional practice.

In this series, the emphasis is on theory and research. The authors guide the student to analyse practice within a theoretical framework provided by a range of texts. Each book provides focussed coverage of subjects and topics and each extract is accompanied by a *points to consider* section which helps students and lecturers to engage with the extract, draw out the implications for professional practice and to develop as a reflective practitioner.

Whilst the series is primarily aimed at undergraduates, as practitioners return to undertake post-qualifying awards in social work, they will find these texts useful to refresh and update their knowledge.

About the series editor

Professor Jonathan Parker is Associate Dean for Social and Community Work at Bournemouth University, UK, and director of the Centre for Social Work and Social Policy. He is co-editor of the highly successful *Transforming Social Work Practice* series and has published widely in social work education, practice learning, theories for social work and dementia and palliative care, including ten books and over 50 journal articles. He is a past chair of the Association of Teachers in Social Work Education and vice-chair of the Joint University Council Social Work Education Committee in the UK. He is currently engaged in research into effectiveness in practice learning, mental capacity and dementia care.

About the author

John Archambeault is a senior lecturer in social work at Kingston University, contributing to undergraduate and graduate qualifying courses. He has over 16 years of health and mental health social work experience in hospital, community mental health and specialist mental health settings. The majority of his work has involved psychotherapeutic practice in the United States and work in therapeutic communities in the UK, including at the Henderson Hospital and the Cassel Service. He holds a Master of Social Work degree from the University of Maryland at Baltimore. He is also a qualified acupuncturist with a special interest in treating persons with substance misuse problems, emotional difficulties and stress.

Introduction

Mental health: Concepts, services and practice

A companion piece to Golightley's (2008) *Social work and mental health*, the *Reflective reader: Social work and mental health*, also part of the *Transforming Social Work Practice* series, will facilitate your deeper consideration of social work practice in mental health services. Using extracts from relevant titles in social work and mental health, journal articles, government policy, non-statutory responses and service user viewpoints, the text will offer an opportunity for you to review and analyse the material provided and, through this, develop a critically reflective appreciation and understanding of the multiple perspectives and systemic nature of mental health social work practice. Moreover, you will be invited to remain mindful of a variety of influences that may affect decision-making at local, regional and national levels. Further, the book supports you to consider the implications of such decision-making not only for yourself but also for service users, their significant others and carers and the agencies – both statutory and voluntary – that deliver mental health services. Throughout, you will be encouraged to question your own perceptions of mental health, of mental illness, of service users or clients, and of the naming of terms in mental health practice.

As part of this exploration, you will be invited to think, too, about the treatment of people with distressing mental health problems and to consider the legitimacy of the divide between those who may be considered to possess 'good' mental health and those who are experiencing mental illness. Central to this consideration is the voice of service users. It seems fitting to introduce this book with its emphasis on reflection by describing a piece of work commissioned by the National Institute for Mental Health for England (NIMHE, 2003) to conduct a national inquiry into the treatment of personality disorder. Initially a group of mental health professionals was brought together to do this work; however, this work was soon amended to include service users. Part of the inquiry included service users' contributions to a series of focus groups. In the following excerpt, a service user describes her experience in relation to social work and her diagnosis.

> In 1996 my children were taken away from me. A social worker arrived on my doorstep saying she had received a phone call from a friend stating she was concerned that I'd harm the children. Since then my son has remained in the custody of his father, who has a history of violence, and whose parenting abilities have never been assessed by the Local Authority. I did not need help from Social Services on that day. It was forced on me. Previously, when I had asked for assistance, they had placed the children twice at my request. The point being that when I felt I needed help I had always asked for it. I love my children, I would never harm them, and have never self-harmed when they have been in the house. I saw a TV programme about Munchausen's Syndrome by Proxy. It seems it is considered to be a way in which Personality Disordered mothers respond to their children. I wonder if this explains why Social Services were so ready to take away my children. Anon.
>
> (Haigh, 2006, p164)

Haigh (2006, p164) subsequently comments on the above quote by writing that *mental disorders all carry stigma, and personality disorder more than most – in the field of mental health, it has parallels to the public and professional perception of cancer in general health services half a century ago*. This is a powerful statement to which readers may either be able to relate or to which you feel called to respond. In this quote, stigma is associated with a particular disorder; yet, stigma still seems to permeate the perception of and response to mental health needs as characterised in individual beliefs and societal responses.

Reading and responding to this perspective are integral to the work you are invited to do with this book. For instance, the previous quote represents one person's voice which deserves to be heard. In the learning approach advocated in this text you are encouraged to consider this account and similar material alongside research, academic writing and policy guidance. By incorporating a variety of source materials highlighted as extracts, the book offers an opportunity for you to engage with multiple perspectives. Through these extracts and accompanying reflections, we offer a respectful enquiry into a variety of sources hoping to provide a comprehensive consideration of the meaning of social work and mental health.

In one of my first encounters with a service user in England after practising social work in the United States, I recall speaking with a man in his late 50s who at first impression appeared older. His family was hopeful that he might be offered supported housing to stimulate him to provide better care for himself. He did not accord this the same priority as his family. In describing his life story, his history – *his story* – he spoke about his initial experience of mental health symptoms which took place in university. He was the first person in his family, an Irish immigrant one, to attend university. His account was poignant as he related how mental health problems had interfered with and brought to an end his hopes of attending university. He found himself losing this opportunity, the first goal of his adult life, due to the presence of intrusive thoughts or delusions which affected his ability to study and later to work. These problems also affected his ability to maintain relationships outside his family and ultimately interfered with his ability to take care of himself. As he described how mental health symptoms, for him those of paranoid schizophrenia, had affected his life, he seemed to be describing a crushing loss.

Though both this and the earlier account suggest the difficulty of living with mental health symptoms, this text will also explore scenarios of relief and recovery. It will also consider varying perspectives on treatment, recovery and care by considering terminology, service delivery and the responses offered by both the social and medical fields in relation to mental health practice. While reading this book, you are encouraged to remain aware of the impact of mental health difficulties for people living with them and consider how to prioritise the self-identified needs of service users.

I have also included these accounts to encourage you to place yourself in the shoes of those in the accounts. If you are in university, you may be able to easily imagine the blow that difficult, unforeseen circumstances might have on you and your studies. As someone practising social work, you may imagine how you might respond similarly or differently to the female service user and mother quoted above. And as persons, we all need to imagine the impact of great stress on our abilities to cope and ask for help. These stories also lead us to question whether we will be treated fairly and with respect by society's helping institutions when in need.

A student recently commented that she was pleased to have a placement in a community mental health team because *mental health underpins everything we do as social workers* (personal communication, 2007). Some of you will agree, and some will argue the opposite. This student seems to have based her conclusion on the realisation that understanding mental health needs may prove an important foundation from which to think about and understand people and their lives in a variety of social work settings. As you know, social work practice involves engaging with individuals of all ages, with families, with groups and in communities at times of need to begin a process of intervention that will hopefully lead to improvement in the person's or family's quality of life. At times of need, people will certainly have feelings about their circumstances, and it is likely that their feelings will affect how they behave and how they consider their problems and develop solutions. Having the capacity to understand what is happening in people's lives and to be able to talk to them about their mental health needs will be helpful in any social work setting.

This reflective reader will support you as you embark on social work practice in a contemporary mental health context and will begin with a review of the role of ethics and values in social work. By presenting multiple perspectives alongside one another – for instance, government policy and a non-statutory service provider's commentary – readers are stimulated to develop a research-minded, reflective and critical perspective in relation to policy, system changes and practice delivery. Chapter 1 both reviews the value base of professional social work and urges consideration of one's personal values in relation to professional values required in work experiences. Using extracts written by social work ethicists and academics linked to the practice of critically reflective social work, we look at value conflicts and the role of power in social work practice.

In Chapter 2, we explore the links and divisions that exist in the fields of social work practice and mental health services. By considering the differences between understanding mental health from a social perspective and the more medical approach commonly taken in mental health services, we highlight the potential for conflict that such divisions may promote. Historically, social work has taken a social, practical approach, whereas mental health has been informed by a medical model that seeks to respond to symptoms and 'unwellness' or mental ill health. In this text, it will be essential to consider these, at times, divergent perspectives and reflect on their approaches while highlighting more integrated work. As social work practice is primarily offered within statutory parameters, we consider the legislative aspects of social work in relation to mental health practice. Extracts in Chapter 3 include an overview of the history of mental health legislation and introduce changes brought by the Mental Health Act 2007 and the Mental Capacity Act 2005.

Chapters 4, 5 and 6 focus on the implications of living with mental health difficulties throughout the life course. Chapter 4 highlights the mental health needs of children and adolescents and addresses how to approach assessment when working with this group. Additional extracts prompt thinking about working with suicide and eating disorders. Chapter 5, by exploring the topic of postnatal depression, addresses service use during acute presentations of mental distress. Chapter 6 expands on this and considers the role of services for those who may need ongoing mental health support to improve quality of life and to promote safety and respond to risk. Central to these chapters are narratives from service users about their experiences of living with mental health distress along with critical consideration of issues of diagnosis, crisis response and the terms 'user' and 'carer'.

Chapter 7 focuses on working in partnership in mental health services and explores the development of integrated team work as a reality for service users and practitioners when working across organisations and agencies. Finally, the reflective nature of your development as you accrue additional theoretical and practice knowledge is considered in Chapter 8. This includes a focus on clinical supervision and the concepts of reflexivity and reflection in mental health practice. Throughout the book, learning is linked to the profession's National Occupational Standards (Topss, 2004).

Chapter 1
Social work values and ethical practice

A C H I E V I N G   A   S O C I A L   W O R K   D E G R E E

This chapter will contribute to helping you to meet the following National Occupational Standards.
Key Role 1: Prepare for, and work with individuals, families, carers, groups, and communities to assess their needs and circumstances.
Key Role 3: Support individuals to represent their needs, views and circumstances.
• Advocate with, and on behalf of, individuals, families, carers, groups and communities.
Key Role 5: Manage and be accountable, with supervision and support, for your own social work practice.
Key Role 6: Demonstrate professional competence in social work practice.
• Work within agreed standards of social work practice and ensure own professional development.
• Manage complex ethical issues, dilemmas and conflicts.

It will also introduce you to the following academic standards as set out in the social work subject benchmark statement.
Nature and extent of social work

3.9
• ... In providing services, social workers should engage with service users and carers in ways that are characterised by openness, reciprocity, mutual accountability and explicit recognition of the powers of the social worker and the legal context of intervention.

5.1.3 Values and ethics
• The nature, historical evolution and application of social work values.
• The moral concepts of rights, responsibility, freedom, authority and power inherent in the practice of social workers as moral and statutory agents.
• The complex relationships between justice, care and control in social welfare and the practical and ethical implications of these, including roles as statutory agents and in upholding the law in respect of discrimination.

Introduction

Practising social work involves engaging, as the Key Roles emphasise, with individuals, families, groups and/or communities to have an impact on problems of living. Social work has been defined internationally as a

profession which promotes social change, problem solving in human relationships and the empowerment and liberation of people to enhance well-being. Utilising theories of human behaviour and social systems, social work intervenes at the points where people interact with their environments. Principles of human rights and social justice are fundamental to social work.

(IASSW/IFSW, 2002)

When you engage with someone to offer social work services, you are becoming involved in *problem solving* (IFSW, 2002, n.p.) among other tasks and will *intervene* at points of interaction between people and between people and systems or structures, like schools, mental health centres or hospitals. Intervening as a social worker in mental health involves working with service users to respond to problems that may have arisen from experiencing mental distress or when their well-being has been compromised by mental or emotional distress. Offering this support may occur in specific mental health settings, but it is just as likely that social workers in a wide range of, if not all, social work settings will meet with clients whose circumstances are causing difficulties, such as stress, anxiety or emotional upset, which are having a depleting effect on their mental health. As you read through subsequent chapters in this book, you will be invited to think and learn about the impact of mental health needs and the services available across the life course for people in need. In this chapter, the foundation of social work practice will be considered, and your reflections will cover concepts such as values, ethics and power and authority.

Values and ethics are at the core of the key roles of social work practice as outlined in the National Occupational Standards (NOS) (Topss, 2004). The NOS recommend that you have an *awareness of your own values, prejudices, ethical dilemmas and conflicts of interest and their implications on your practice* (Topss, 2004, p20). Part of the work you will be invited to do in this chapter will involve reflecting on your own values. You will also have an opportunity to read an extract from the work of Reamer (1995), a social work academic who has written frequently on social work values and ethics. In this extract, you are invited to think about the potential conflict between personal and professional values.

Since mental health social work may involve providing services to service users who are not asking for help or support, we will also consider an extract on the topics of power and authority. Fook (2002), the author of the extract, has contributed to a developing discourse on social work practice and encourages social work students and practitioners to reflect critically on their roles and power affiliations. Finally, the chapter provides two extracts with differing perspectives. The first recounts the outcome of a legal case about forced hospitalisation taken from a non-governmental organisation's newsletter; the second reviews government guidance developed in response to the same case. In the commentary that follows, you will have an opportunity to think about value conflicts and authority in relation to care, human rights and compulsory services.

As you work through this chapter, keep in mind the following questions for reflection.

1. Am I aware of and able to apply social work values that are expected of me as a student and a practitioner in mental health work?

2. How do I consider and work with any value conflicts I experience between my personal beliefs and what is expected of me as a practitioner?

3. How does my identity as a professional affect the work I do with service users in the field of mental health?

Values

Practitioners need to recognise the influence of values in their work. The value base for social work provides a context for practice and stimulates a sense of conviction in practitioners when facing difficult and challenging practice experiences. As a contextual container, values ideally support the role we occupy as social workers, guide the approach to our work and influence decision-making. In mental health practice, there may be times when we work with persons whose mental distress, emotional upset or misperceptions of reality contribute to problems of living that may necessitate intervention to protect their or others' safety and well-being. In this context, we especially need to be mindful of our value base and also judicious and balanced in our approach to offering help or stimulating the personal resources of those using services. In such situations, we need to become aware of power differences between practitioners' and service users' experiences and between social work and the wider society. As a preliminary step to developing and enhancing this awareness, it is necessary to consider the personal values that you hold and values that relate to your professional or occupational role. Subsequently, you need to consider the potential influence of your personally held values on your social work practice. The British Association of Social Workers (2002), in its Code of Ethics, sets out five basic values, namely:

- human dignity and worth;

- social justice;

- service to humanity;

- integrity;

- competence.

These are in line with the International Federation of Social Workers' (IFSW) definition and compare favourably to the four values identified by Clark (2000):

1. *Respecting the worth and uniqueness of every person.*

2. *Ensuring just responses to situations requiring control and the fair distribution of resources or services.*

3. *Supporting individual freedom and liberation from problems of living.*

4. *Highlighting the importance of interdependence which comes from being part of a community.*

I suspect that you have entered social work training or the profession with a personal conviction to be helpful and make a difference; however, it would seem presumptuous of me to assume that you as an individual will have such a congruent personal value system that your values and those of the profession would entirely agree. In this book, your values are being considered in relation to studying and practising social work; however, I would maintain that becoming aware of your own values and prejudices is an essential task. Knowing something about yourself and your preferences will help you to distinguish between your personal opinions and conclusions and your professional response where you will be expected to apply social work values and engage in a thoughtful and measured approach to problem-solving and decision-making. The ethical dilemmas to which the NOS refers may stem from a conflict between your personal and professional values or between your values and those espoused by a service user, a colleague, a manager or another person or entity involved in your training or work.

The following extract from Reamer (1995) offers initial insights into the potential conflict that may arise in social work practice. Reamer (1995) begins his text with a comprehensive historical overview of social work ethics and values. He develops this further by offering case material that summarises a range of value orientations. Within the chapter excerpt that follows, he explores the dilemmas which arise when personal and professional values conflict. As you read, consider the implications for you, for your practice and your value orientation.

EXTRACT ONE

Reamer, F (1995) **Social work values and ethics.** *New York: Columbia University Press. Chapter 2, Social work values, pp30–4.*

Reconciling personal and professional values

Several issues related to social work values deserve special emphasis. First, social workers occasionally face tension between their own personal values and those held by clients, employers, or the social work profession itself. Inevitably, social workers will face such conflicts.

With regard to clients, social workers sometimes encounter clients whose values and behaviours seem immoral and abhorrent (Goldstein, 1987; Hardman, 1975). Social workers may have strong reactions to the ways in which some clients parent their children, violate the law or treat spouses or partners. How social workers respond in these situations – whether they share their opinions with clients or withhold any form of judgment – depends on practitioners' views about the role of their own personal values and opinions ...

In some instances the social worker's principal goal is to recognize that clients are struggling with their own value and ethical dilemmas and to help clients address them (Siporin, 1992, p77). Examples include clients who are overwhelmed by the moral aspects of decisions or actions related to having an affair, caring for an elderly parent, aborting a pregnancy, divorcing a spouse, and dealing with domestic violence (Goldstein, 1987). As Goldstein (1987) argues, social workers must learn that clients' difficulties often contain an important moral dimension, that clients are often wrestling with the moral aspects of problems in their lives: The conflict and anguish that clients experience frequently result from the consequences of serious moral and ethical dilemmas and from the absence of dependable solutions. Such dilemmas are related to critical choices that need to be made about special problems of living, including obligation and responsibility to others (pp181–2). Thus to be helpful to clients, social workers must learn to view problems through an ethical lens – as well as a clinical lens – and to speak the language of ethics.

Cultural and religious values

Value conflicts can arise especially when a social worker is providing services to a client whose cultural or religious beliefs support behaviours or activities (for example, concerning health care or the treatment of children) that run counter to the profession's or the worker's personal values (Hardman, 1975, Hollis, 1964, Loewenberg and Dolgoff, 1992, Reamer, 1990, Rhodes, 1986, Timms, 1983). Thus it is important for social workers to recognize the influence of their own and clients' religious and cultural values and beliefs ...

EXTRACT ONE *continued*

Social workers must also be mindful of possible conflicts between their personal values and clients' cultural or ethnic norms. This sort of conflict can be particularly troubling …

Social workers disagree about the extent to which they should share their own opinions and values with clients. Some practitioners argue that the worker's role is to provide a neutral sounding board for clients who are struggling with issues in their lives. From this perspective, the worker's values should not bias clients' efforts to resolve problems in their lives. A competing view, however, is that social workers should acknowledge with clients their own personal values, so that clients have a full understanding of the practitioner's possible biases. In spite of this enduring debate, there is considerable support in the profession for the sentiment enunciated years ago by Hollis (1964):

> Despite the fact that the concept of acceptance has been emphasized in casework for many years, it is still often misunderstood. It has to do with the workers' attitude – and hence communications – when the client is feeling guilty or for some reason unworthy of the worker's liking or respect. It is sometimes mistakenly assumed that the worker must be without an opinion about the rightness or wrongness, the advisability or inadvisability, of the client's activities. This would be impossible even if it were desirable … Certainly the worker's *personal* values must not be translated into goals for the client. His *professional* norms and values, on the other hand, inevitably and quite appropriately become a factor in treatment objectives. (pp85, 208, italics in original)

POINTS TO CONSIDER

Having read the extract from Social work values and ethics, *please think about your values using the definition below.*

- A value is an enduring belief that a specific mode of conduct or end-state of existence is personally or socially preferable to an opposite or converse mode of conduct or end-state of existence *(Rokeach, 1973, p5, emphasis in original, cited by Reamer, 1995, p28).*

- *Make a list of your values using Rokeach's definition of value. Consider what values you hold or, in other words, what you have believed in for a long time as a way of doing something or as a way of being that you prefer over the opposite way of doing something. Be frank and honest – try to avoid censoring or cleaning up your values and beliefs to make them acceptable to the outside world. This reflection is for your use and your development.*

- *Consider how your values are similar or dissimilar to social work's values and what impact your and the social work profession's values have on ethical social work practice.*

Comment

As you considered your personal values, what have you identified as being significant to you?

You might have talked about trust, honesty, taking care of others, maintaining religious traditions, treating others with respect, pleasure, having a good time, saving money. The list and possibilities will be lengthy and varied. In doing this, you may have recognised similarities between your values and those of the profession; you may, too, have found some conflict between the two. This may be an area of further inquiry, self-reflection and development for you.

Reamer's writing highlighted the potential for tension and the need for reflection in relation to a social work practitioner's personal and professional values. In several examples within the extract, there are potential conflicts: a service user might be involved in something *immoral or abhorrent* (Goldstein, 1987 and Hardman, 1975, cited in Reamer, 1995, p31), or there might be the revelation of an affair. If your value is incongruous with the value of a service user, what might be the outcome? It may be difficult to refrain from making a conclusion that there is a right and a wrong position. If you support the service user's position, you may feel badly for compromising your personal values; however, if you assert your own value, you may risk discarding the belief of a service user and potentially disempowering him or her.

Working in mental health means considering what it means for people to be living with mental health distress. Such an experience – in and of itself – may affect how people feel about themselves and whether they perceive themselves to have power to make changes in their experience or their lives.

> **POINTS TO CONSIDER**
>
> *In thinking about people with mental health needs, how do you feel? Is this a client group with which you would like to work? Do you have experience of this through voluntary or paid work? Or might you know something about this from the context of your family?*

By reading this book, you are engaging in a process to help make the difficulties of mental health need less pervasive, which is commendable. However, we must be aware that in many communities, people with mental health needs may not be treated with dignity and respect. Perhaps you have noticed this and wondered what is wrong either with that person or with the way a community responds to this need. Here we have an essential dilemma – we need to see the humanity in the people with whom we work and from that point begin to make sense of those individuals' problem(s) of living.

At times, such problems may inhibit or interfere with seeking help. In these situations, mental health social work may involve the difficult task of compelling individuals to take part in mental health services, perhaps through an involuntary hospital admission. Clearly social work values promote social justice, integrity and service to humanity. As Clark (2000) noted, a social work value should also free people from their problems of living. Difficult decisions arise when a person's problem of living – perhaps strong beliefs that they are not worthy of living which compel them to hurt themselves or attempt to take their life – conflicts with society's expectation of offering help and valuing life. In such a scenario, it may be a service to humanity and integral to social work values to force help on someone who is unable to seek it voluntarily. These issues are more complex and multi-layered than this brief introduction suggests, and they will be revisited later in this chapter

---

The National Framework of Values for Mental Health

The work of the National Institute for Mental Health in England (NIMHE) on values in mental health care is guided by three principles of values-based practice:

1) **Recognition** – NIMHE recognises the role of values alongside evidence in all areas of mental health policy and practice.

2) **Raising Awareness** – NIMHE is committed to raising awareness of the values involved in different contexts, the role/s they play and their impact on practice in mental health.

3) **Respect** – NIMHE respects diversity of values and will support ways of working with such diversity that makes the principle of service-user centrality a unifying focus for practice. This means that the values of each individual service user/client and their communities must be the starting point and key determinant for all actions by professionals.

Respect for diversity of values encompasses a number of specific policies and principles concerned with equality of citizenship. In particular, it is anti-discriminatory because discrimination in all its forms is intolerant of diversity. Thus respect for diversity of values has the consequence that it is unacceptable (and unlawful in some instances) to discriminate on grounds such as gender, sexual orientation, class, age, abilities, religion, race, culture or language.

Respect for diversity within mental health is also:

- *user-centred* – it puts respect for the values of individual users at the centre of policy and practice;

- *recovery oriented* – it recognises that building on the personal strengths and resiliencies of individual users, and on their cultural and racial characteristics, there are many diverse routes to recovery;

- *multidisciplinary* – it requires that respect be reciprocal, at a personal level (between service users, their family members, friends, communities and providers), between different provider disciplines (such as nursing, psychology, psychiatry, medicine, social work), and between different organisations (including health, social care, local authority housing, voluntary organisations, community groups, faith communities and other social support services);

- *dynamic* – it is open and responsive to change;

- *reflective* – it combines self monitoring and self management with positive self regard;

- *balanced* – it emphasises positive as well as negative values;

- *relational* – it puts positive working relationships supported by good communication skills at the heart of practice.

NIMHE will encourage educational and research initiatives aimed at developing the capabilities (the awareness, attitudes, knowledge and skills) needed to deliver mental health services that will give effect to the principles of values-based practice.

(National Institute for Mental Health in England, 2004)

Figure 1.1 *The NIMHE Values Framework*

and in later chapters. However, in bringing these issues to your mind, it is to stimulate your discussion and thinking about the myriad value conflicts that may arise in practising social work in mental health contexts. To address the value base unique to mental health service delivery, the National Institute for Mental Health in England (NIMHE, 2004) has produced the framework presented in Figure 1.1.

This framework gives us greater detail in relation to mental health practice than the social work code; yet, in some ways it does not address the difficult challenge in mental health practice of offering care to the smaller proportion of service users who experience symptoms or make decisions that might mean they resist services or support. More successfully, it highlights the critical need for respect for a service user's input into the decision-making process.

Power and authority

As we think about practitioners and service users working together, we must acknowledge the influence that both parties may have on each other. Social workers and social work students will often be perceived by service users as part of the system even when we embrace a more inclusive and collaborative value base. We may be considered to be agents of or represent power perceived to be held or actually held by statutory bodies. Like other areas of social work practice, mental health social work generally involves working in agencies and institutions deemed to hold power – community mental health teams, mental health trusts operated by the NHS, and children and adolescent mental health programmes. In these settings, social workers may work with service users who have sought help themselves for their problems. However, as we have touched on, mental health social work will, at times, involve working with *unwilling recipients of social work services*, as phrased in the Social Work Benchmark statement (QAA, 2008, p5), who may benefit from urgent intervention to prevent injury, harm or risk and hopefully to promote safety. As we revisit the idea that some service users may require help that they do not choose, we are able to emphasise that mental health practice requires sensitivity and an understanding of legal parameters as well as the ability to make decisions ethically. In addition, thinking about service users who are unwilling recipients also highlights the importance of thinking about our power, authority and professional role in delivering services and how this factor is either congruent or incongruent with our value base.

Fook (2002, p52) emphasises that *power is both a good and bad thing* and that the social structures providing services can be both empowering and disempowering. She is suggesting that social service providers or helping agencies may simultaneously offer opportunities for service users to have a sense of autonomy and control over their lives but may also take away these opportunities, as in engaging service users in mandatory treatment. Chenoweth and McAuliffe (2005, cited in Bowles, et al., 2006) note that service users *coming into contact with social workers have been disempowered by experiences and systems* [they have previously encountered and that] *social workers need to understand the dynamics of power in their working relationships* [as there is an] *unavoidable power imbalance between practitioners and clients* (p15). Remaining aware of this dynamic will support our work as we recognise the dilemma of working with service users who, at times, may reject services.

In the extract that follows, Fook (2002) proffers a multi-textured discussion of power as a dynamic that influences social work systems, social work practice and the working relationships that we, as social workers, have with our clients and in turn how clients and service users relate to us. As a background to this, it may be helpful to revisit ideas about empowerment theory which Payne (2005) describes in Chapter 14 of *Modern social work theory*. You may also need to familiarise yourself with some philosophical concepts and philosophical frameworks. Websites listed at the end of the chapter provide a conceptual overview of modernism, post-structuralism and postmodernism which are referenced in the extract.

EXTRACT TWO

Fook, J (2002) Social work: Critical theory and practice. *London: Sage.* Chapter 8, pp103–4 and pp108–9.

New notions of power and empowerment

We criticised modernist conceptions of power because they tend to see power as being invested in particular people, often by virtue of their position in the social structure. It is 'possessed' rather than 'exercised' and thus is more fixed and less accessible to change. Empowerment of one person or group might automatically mean disempowerment of another, thereby unwittingly setting up binary conflicts. Also, because power is attributed from 'outside', that is, by virtue of position in the social structure, efforts to empower people and groups who are marginalised might actually be experienced as disempowering, since this may not be their own understanding of their experience. The act of empowering involves defining a person or group as 'disempowered', and this process is in fact potentially disempowering. Such blanket definitions also dilute differences between people and situations and do not allow for different identities at different times and in different contexts. Without a complex analysis of how power works in relation to different people and contexts, and a corresponding vision for how it should work in social justice terms, there is a danger that empowerment can simply become a tool to preserve existing power imbalances. In reformulating the concepts of power and empowerment we need to take into account:

- *the contextual and changing nature of power;*
- *how power operates at different levels, often simultaneously and in contradictory ways;*
- *how power is experienced by different people;*
- *the creative, as well as controlling, possibilities power entails.*

Empowering people therefore involves a complex (multilayered) understanding (which includes their own perspective as well as those of other players) of how power is exercised and how it affects them, but also of how they exercise and create their own power. This includes an understanding of how they might participate in their own powerlessness as well as their own powerfulness ...

> ### EXTRACT TWO continued
>
> #### Common constructions of power in social work practice
>
> *... how do workers actually construct power in their everyday practice situations?*
>
> *Many social work students I have taught over the years construct themselves as powerless in relation to their field supervisors, other professional workers on place-ment, or university teaching staff. Over the last decade I have also been involved with many different groups of workers conducting seminars, workshops and ses-sions in which we have presented and reflected upon instances in our practice. One of the most burning issues which is always present, particularly as it poses a dilemma in people's practice, is the issue of power. For instance, Napier and Fook (2000) included a number of workers' reflections on their practice and the theme of power was paramount. People were particularly concerned about how much power workers have and should have, and whether it can be exercised to bring about enough change. Many were concerned that what they perceived as their powerless-ness meant they could not achieve what they took to be the ideals or values of social work, such as social justice or anti-discrimination ...*
>
> #### Social workers' constructions of themselves
>
> *It is widely acknowledged that social workers feel ambivalent about power or, more accurately, about their own power (Laragy, 1997). While our textbooks write clearly about the use and abuse of structural and personal power by professionals (e.g. Hugman, 1991), the more informal culture within social work in relation to power is much more complex. Accounts from social workers seem to indicate that they feel uncomfortable with the idea of having power and often, therefore, construct them-selves as relatively powerless.*
>
> *In my experience I have found this idea of powerlessness is almost universal in accounts of practice in which workers feel they are caught in a dilemma or impasse. For example, in a group of ten workers with whom I conducted a series of critical reflection workshops, this idea was paramount (Fook, 2000d). Workers felt caught underneath the power of a manager or supervisor, the power of bureaucratic rule, or even of agency or community culture ...*
>
> *A major assumption therefore was that other people had the power, workers did not. There was almost a sense in which workers saw themselves as victims.*
>
> *This construction of ourselves as powerless is noted elsewhere. For instance, Laragy (1996) notes that caseworkers often identify with their clients, feeling powerless in the same way ...*

As you reflect on Fook's (2002) extract, please consider the themes of power and authority. You may have an immediate reaction to the concepts of power, authority, power imbalances, voluntary participation in service and mandatory service participation. You may also be questioning the implications of power and what you know about the social work role whether you are a student, newly qualified practitioner or someone in practice. You might even be thinking: What power would I have as a social worker or as a student? *Using this sense of inquiry, reflect on and respond to the following tasks. If some of the following terms are unknown to you or unclear, please do some research and obtain necessary information before you proceed.*

1. *Jan Fook writes,* People were particularly concerned about how much power workers have and should have, and whether it can be exercised to bring about enough change. *Thinking about social work in mental health, some social workers who have authorised power under the Mental Health Act 1983, 2007 contribute to mandatory hospital admission. What do you think about that? Would you be comfortable with that role?*

2. *In the mental health system, consider how service users and/or their friends and family may experience a sense of disempowerment.*

Comment

In the reflection, you were encouraged to think about how social workers may exert their power in securing compulsory treatment for service users. You may, as I inferred in the directions for the task, have found this a difficult concept to grasp. If you did, you would have a lot in common with the social workers described by Fook (2002) in the extract. Her findings and the writing of Laragy (1997) which she cites suggest that social workers often feel powerless in relation to some other. By 'other' I mean any individual, group, organisation or system with which social workers may be engaged. For example, a social worker may feel powerless in relation to a client – even a client with very limited emotional and financial resources – if the social worker is finding it difficult or is unable to provide a solution or help for the problem the person is describing. Social workers also may feel powerless in relation to managers, particularly if managers are implementing changes that have been decided elsewhere in an agency.

The experience of being disempowered, then, is one to which social workers may be able to relate. In point 2 above, imagining the experience of service users may have highlighted the difficulty of getting timely help for a problem or the frustration of repeatedly getting an answering service instead of a personal contact. Similarly, service users in trying to secure help may face a fixed appointment system which restricts them from choosing when to attend an appointment or, more seriously, may find themselves placed in hospital without consent. Such experiences represent structural problems, resource issues and possibly dehumanising interventions if not clinically appropriate. Significantly, we need to be mindful of our power and its impact on others. Fook, furthermore, is asking us – as individuals and a profession – to challenge often automatic beliefs about power. She highlights some of the assumptions made about power in the philosophical approach called modernism which assumes that power is held by certain individuals. With this type of thinking, it generates two fixed positions – one powerful and one powerless. This relates to one of Fook's points in relation to formulating power and perhaps other things, like possessing money or being right, as either one or the other. In a binary conflict such as this, there will only be two options. And yet there are other approaches to power or decision-making, to give power a practical focus. Power could be shared; decisions could be made by consensus.

Exploring ways of challenging routinely held assumptions about power and authority are essential in social work practice. Efforts to improve service delivery may improve the experience for service users if they are offered appointments in line with their schedule, if they have some choice about what to speak about in appointments, if they are involved in the decision-making about their participation in services, and if they are able to identify personal goals and objectives to make improvements to their lives.

Responding to oppression

A further significant issue to keep central to your work is the experience of oppression. As Chenoweth and McAuliffe (2005) note, service users often have historical experiences that are disempowering. It is particularly important to acknowledge this set of experiences for persons from different ethnic or racial groups or those whose identities are not part of the dominant culture. Within mental health practice, there are incidences and case material that suggest a differential treatment and diagnosis of people of colour. Such accounts emphasise the need to consider the role of oppression in responding to mental health distress and the service delivery system. The Department of Health (2005) produced a document titled *Delivering race equality in mental health care* as part of an inquiry into the death of David Bennett, a black man who died while being restrained in a medium-secure unit; the document also offered recommendations to improve mental health service delivery and access to it for people of colour.

Depending on your own personal ethnic or cultural background, you may have experiences of cultural, ethnic or other difference. Being able to access this experience of difference may be a powerful and useful means of confirming a service user's experience of having restricted access to or being denied services. For those of you without this frame of reference, you will need to consider how best to gain an understanding of oppression and discrimination. As part of working in a just way that acknowledges human worth and dignity, social workers need to consider how to work in culturally responsive ways so that service users have experiences that are validating.

To summarise, the extract demonstrated a prominent sense of powerlessness among social work students and practitioners, some of which may stem from how practitioners get alongside service users and so take up a position which society may invest in service users and professional helpers of lack and disadvantage. However, this leaves us with a dilemma in that we may feel powerless and yet society and service users may relate to us as if we are powerful. Appreciating the complexity of this dynamic is as relevant to understanding mental health social work as is understanding the impact of oppression for service users.

Rights, freedom and care

The difficulty in maintaining an empowering approach emerges in relation to needing to provide mandatory services, either in mental health or other fields. This brings us back to Clark's (2000) list of values, one of which – supporting individual freedom – may conflict with a related value of freeing someone from problems of living. Thinking about individual freedom and what is just and unjust introduces dilemmas in relation to mandatory versus voluntary treatment. In such a scenario, we may be faced with what seems to be a binary conflict – that is, it involves either freedom or restricting freedom. Before concluding that it is, we would need to explore the facts and circumstances of the situation in order to draw a firm conclusion.

Building on the theme of service users and choice, it is relevant to consider the roles of various bodies in setting up service systems and service agendas. The government is both perceived to be and realistically is an agent of power and authority within most modern societies. In the United Kingdom, members of the electoral roll are enfranchised with a vote that may be used to make choices about whom we select as representatives in government. Other bodies, such as charitable organisations or non-governmental organisations, seek to represent citizens and service users by putting forward other, perhaps competing, views about service need and service provision. As we continue to think about social work practice from an ethical and value-orientated perspective, we need to explore the rhetoric and process of government's policy recommendations and the counterpoint offered by non-governmental agencies.

The following extracts highlight this. These extracts relate to a finding by the European Court of Human Rights in the case of *HL* v *UK* that an individual's liberty was restricted when hospitalised under complex circumstances. The first extract is drawn from Mencap's (2004) newsletter, *Viewpoint*, which offers the perspective of a charity working to protect and promote the human rights of those with learning disability. The extract following this is a portion of the guidance produced by the Department of Health (2004) in response to the ruling. As you read both extracts, you are asked to consider the two sources of information and their relative authority in society. It is important to be mindful of the government's agenda as well as the mission and goals of Mencap to be able to develop your own objective understanding of these perspectives.

EXTRACT THREE

Mencap (2004) 'News'. In **Viewpoint**, *Nov/Dec, p4. [online] Available at* **www.mencap.org.uk**

Bridging the Bournewood gap

The European Court of Human Rights has ruled that the detention of a man with autism and learning disabilities at a Surrey hospital was a breach of his human rights. The hearing, which took place in Strasbourg, was the culmination of seven years of legal wrangling between the man concerned and the hospital in which he was confined.

EXTRACT THREE *continued*

'HL', who cannot be named for legal reasons, had been successfully living with carers for a number of years. In 1997, after becoming agitated at a day centre he was admitted to Bournewood Hospital's psychiatric unit. HL was classed as an 'informal patient' and was not officially sectioned under the Mental Health Act 1983. This meant that he had no right to apply for release through a review tribunal and was denied the right to be visited in hospital. HL was not released to his carers for nearly four months.

The case went to the High Court where a judge ruled that the hospital had not acted unlawfully. The Appeal Court overturned this decision, but in June 1998 the House of Lords finally ruled in the hospital's favour. The Bournewood case is significant because it highlights the existence of a large number of patients – possibly up to 50,000 – with a severe learning disability, dementia or other conditions, who are in hospital or residential care, and receive treatment without being able to agree to being there or to being treated. This shortcoming in the Mental Health Act has become known as the 'Bournewood gap'. The European Court of Human Rights ruling, announced at the beginning of October, has been welcomed by Mencap and those campaigning for a greater level of freedom for people who lack the capacity to give their consent to be kept in a particular place ...

EXTRACT FOUR

Department of Health (2004) Advice on the decision of the European Court of Human Rights in the case of *HL v UK* (the 'Bournewood' Case) [Gateway Reference 4269]

37. Elements of good practice which are likely to assist in this, and in avoiding the risk of legal challenge, may include:

– ensuring that decisions are taken (and reviewed) in a structured way, which includes safeguards against arbitrary deprivation of liberty. There should, for example, be a proper assessment of whether the patient lacks capacity to decide whether or not to accept the care proposed, and that decision should be taken on the basis of proper medical advice by a person properly equipped to make the judgment

– effective, documented care planning (including the Care Programme Approach where relevant) for such patients, including appropriate and documented involvement of family, friends, carers (both paid and unpaid) and others interested in their welfare

– ensuring that alternatives to admission to hospital or residential care are considered and that any restrictions placed on the patient while in hospital or residential care should be kept to the minimum necessary in all the circumstances of their case

– ensuring appropriate information is given to patients themselves and to family, friends and carers. This would include information about the purpose and reasons for the patient's admission, proposals to review the care plan and the outcome of such reviews, and the way in which they can challenge decisions (e.g. through the relevant

complaints procedure). The involvement of local advocacy services where these are available could be encouraged to support patients and their families, friends and carers – taking proper steps to help patients retain contact with family, friends, carers, with proper consideration given to the views of those people. If, exceptionally, there are good clinical reasons why that is not in the patient's best interests, those reasons should be properly documented and explained to the people they affect

– ensuring both the assessment of capacity and the care plan are kept under review. It may well be helpful to include an independent element in the review. Depending on the circumstances, this might be achieved by involvement of social work or community health staff, or by seeking a second medical (or other appropriate clinical) opinion either from within the organisation or elsewhere. Such a second opinion will be particularly important where family members, carers or friends do not agree with the authority's decisions. But even where there is no dispute an authority must ensure its decision making stands up to scrutiny.

38. If it is concluded that there is no way of providing appropriate care which does not amount to deprivation of liberty, then consideration will have to be given to using the formal powers of detention in the Mental Health Act 1983. However, it is important to remember that:

- nothing in the judgment changes the requirements in the Mental Health Act which must be met before patients can be detained. It should not therefore be assumed that all patients who are to be subject to restrictions which may amount to deprivation of liberty can be detained under the Act. (For example, it would be unlawful to detain patients under the Act if their mental disorder does not warrant detention in hospital, although reception into guardianship under the Act might be appropriate in some cases.)

- there are dangers in using the Act simply to be 'on the safe side'. Although it provides procedural safeguards, the use of the Mental Health Act will not necessarily be welcomed by patients themselves or by their family, friends or carers, given the 'stigma' that is often (wrongly) perceived to attach to it. Moreover, a significant increase in the use of the Mental Health Act will inevitably put considerable further pressure on local authority approved social workers, the availability of second opinion appointed doctors (SOADs) and on the operation of Mental Health Review Tribunals (MHRT).

Comment

In reading the perspective offered by Mencap alongside the DOH's recommendations, you have the opportunity to consider how a society and its institutions develop meanings and discourse about important social issues. You also gain a sense about how the legal system is used to redress and revise issues of human rights violation. In this case, a man who was diagnosed with severe autism and had profound communication impairment to the point that he did not speak was hospitalised. He was unable to give consent and would not have met the standard of having mental capacity. His carers were not contactable at the time of the admission into hospital. However, subsequent to his admission, his carers with whom he had lived for approximately three years were restricted from contact for four months. The Mencap article documents that the legal process took seven years to gain some redress for depriving the service user of his liberty; in so doing it highlighted a deficiency in law that is described as the Bournewood gap and is being addressed in revised mental health legislation. It also highlighted that up to 50,000 persons may be in similar situations, unable to make informed decisions as to treatment in their best interest. Such scenarios clearly require us to reflect on our value base and our role in challenging authority when it seems unjust even if we feel powerless.

The Department of Health eager, no doubt, to avoid any further legal challenges has offered advice to practitioners and institutions in managing similarly complex cases. Such complex cases reinforce the centrality of value-laden dilemmas in complex mental health care. This case also highlights the many variables involved in social work practice in mental health, particularly in the advice to work in collaborative ways with service users, family and partners, and colleagues to ensure a robust and user-centred treatment response. Also the DOH guidance identifies social work as an objective perspective to consult when faced with similar case dilemmas. Efforts to respond to legislative gaps are addressed by government in the revised Mental Capacity Act 2005 and Mental Health Act 2007 (see Chapter 3). Engaging service users in discussions about their requests and expectations through documents known as advanced directives will be explored further in subsequent chapters. Such documents, though, are one means of working to ensure that service users' needs and interests are central in joint efforts to promote safety and well-being.

Open-mindedness and multiple perspectives

In response to this discussion, you may be left with a sense of the profundity and importance of the social work role in mental health care. There is both the need to value the autonomy of the service user while simultaneously working to clarify issues of safety. While engaged in this, you may note conflicts between the service user and his or her family and friends or you may experience disagreements between yourself and colleagues. As in this legal case, you will need to appreciate the multiple perspectives that are involved in working with complex case scenarios in mental health social work practice. In the complexity of practice in mental health you will need to think reflectively and objectively so as to adhere to social work's values and to engage in ethically informed practice.

The following discussion about open-mindedness helps to contextualise several themes in this chapter in relation to values, ethical practice and power dynamics as well as encouraging us to develop a critically reflective mind capable of considering multiple viewpoints and evaluating the relative merits and problems of a perspective:

> *If we are to change from having our perceptions of reality being completely shaped by the dominant discourse, if we are to be open to seeing how to work with our environment instead of despite it we need to cultivate an open mind ... We will always be enslaved to our prejudices, enculturated values, old habits and environments unless we can consider alternatives and try to see things from the perspectives of others. Perspective ... means imaginatively occupying the position of others ...*

(Bowles, et al., 2006, pp22-3)

In the outcome of the legal case just noted, securing the viewpoints of all of those involved, including the carers, the medical personnel, the other healthcare practitioners and data about the service user, was necessary for the European Court to reach its decision. You will, as social work students or practitioners, recognise the value and integral part that comprehensive inquiry and multiple perspectives, including those of service users, play in our learning. Appreciating and understanding multiple perspectives will be an important means of working professionally in the field of social work and mental health.

C   H   A   P   T   E   R   S   U   M   M   A   R   Y

In summary, this first chapter of *Reflective reader: Social work and mental health* focused on social work values and ethical social work. Values that frame the delivery of social work services were reviewed with particular emphasis on working in ways to honour human dignity and to empower service users. You were able to consider the role of your personal values in relation to practice. Central to this overview was a consideration of the issue of power and authority as it applies to professional practice. The issue of oppression, either from societal pressures or social structures, was emphasised. Social work, as a profession involved in working with human beings, needs to ensure that its practice has clear ethical standards. Ethical principles urge people to act in ways that protect others, do no harm and consider the impact of their actions. In practising social work, you will be working with people who may require help to consider the decisions they make and potential risks that could develop. By developing your self-awareness, cultivating an open mind and working to consider multiple viewpoints, you will be able to successfully develop your social work practice. As you read through the rest of this book, you will be expected both in reading and in your practice to consider how mental health distress and upset may affect how service users engage with and participate in services. By integrating a values framework into your practice, you will be able to ensure that service users will have a voice that will contribute to service use and service delivery.

FURTHER READING

Banks, S (2006) *Ethics and values in social work*. 3rd edition. Basingstoke: Palgrave Macmillan.

Targeted for social work learning, Sarah Banks's book is updated and helps readers think about values in relation to their practice.

Department of Health (DoH) (2005) *Delivering race equality in mental health care*. London: The Stationery Office. www.doh.gov.uk.

The government's strategy to provide more culturally responsive mental health services.

Kramer, R (2002) The Bournewood case. *Tizard Learning Disability Review*, 7(4) 21–5.

A journal article which provides greater detail regarding the Bournewood case and its impact for practice.

Parrott, L (2006) *Values and ethics in social work practice*. Exeter: Learning Matters.

An additional title in Learning Matters' *Transforming social work practice* series which offers a focus on values and ethics.

Payne, M (2005) *Modern social work theory*. 3rd edition. Basingstoke: Palgrave Macmillan.

Payne's text offers an overview of various social work theories including more detail regarding empowerment theory.

WEBSITES

www.philosopher.org.uk

plato.stanford.edu

www.nimhe.csip.org.uk

Chapter 2
Social work practice and mental health

This chapter will contribute to helping you to meet the following National Occupational Standards.

Key Role 1: Prepare for, and work with individuals, families, carers, groups, and communities to assess their needs and circumstances.

- Prepare for social work contact and involvement.
- Assess needs and options to recommend a course of action.

Key Role 2: Plan, carry out, review and evaluate social work practice, with individuals, families, carers, groups, communities and other professionals.

- Interact with individuals, families, carers, groups and communities to achieve change and development and to improve life opportunities.

Key Role 4: Manage risk to individuals, families, carers, groups, communities, self and colleagues.

Key Role 5: Manage and be accountable, with supervision and support, for your own social work practice.

- Work within multidisciplinary and multi-organisational teams, networks and systems.

It will also introduce you to the following academic standards as set out in the social work subject benchmark statement.

Defining principles

4.3

- There are competing views in society at large on the nature of social work and on its place and purpose. Social work practice and education inevitably reflect these differing perspectives on the role of social work in relation to social justice, social care and social order.

4.7 ...Involves learning to:

- think critically about the complex social, legal, economic, political and cultural contexts in which social work practice is located.

5.1.2 The service delivery context, which includes:

- The significance of interrelationships with other social services, especially education, housing, health, income maintenance and criminal justice...

5.1.4 Social work theory, which includes:

- The relevance of sociological perspectives to understanding societal and structural influences on human behaviour at individual, group and community levels.
- The relevance of psychological, physical and physiological perspectives to understanding individual and social development and functioning.

5.1.5 The nature of social work practice, which includes:

- The factors and processes that facilitate effective inter-disciplinary, inter-professional and inter-agency collaboration and partnership.

Introduction

In this chapter, we consider social work practice in a mental health context. A social work approach to mental health need would address problems of living for individuals, families and/or communities by seeking to understand how social forces have both contributed to mental health distress as well as how mental health difficulties affect service users' social circumstances and relationships. Through seeking to shore up the capacity of individuals to cope by providing links to services to respond to gaps in care and through intervening in service users' social and care networks, social work practitioners offer help at individual and systemic levels. At a broader conceptual level, social work with its aim to foster development and well-being may question naming a situation, such as living with mental health needs, as a 'problem', preferring to question limiting and disabling terms and to introduce alternatives. To this end, we may reject the idea of problems of living and prefer 'challenges' of living as noted by a recent social work text (Hutchison, et al., 2007). A strictly mental health approach based on medical factors would not disregard social forces; however, from a health perspective, practitioners responding to mental health distress may focus on individual biomedical aspects of the problem; identifying the disorder that a person seems to be experiencing, such as major depression, and providing treatment, such as prescribing a course of counselling, group support or medication.

I pose these two responses and their related points of view – the social and the medical – in some stark separateness to emphasise the potential for dichotomy between the social approach to understanding human distress and the health or biomedical perspective's conclusions about a problem. The dilemma for us and for all professions, whether aligned more with the medical or social approach, is that we may become engaged in a split way of thinking about human problems. Split in the sense that a problem may be seen to have its roots in one cause predominantly rather than being understood as an effect of multiple influences and contributing factors. Such a dichotomy may lead to trying to understand mental health need as a debate between social forces and the medical approach when it is more likely that a multiplicity of factors, some sociocultural and some physical, will influence how we develop and respond to mental health need.

Developing and considering an integrated understanding to identifying mental health need and responding to mental health distress is essential. However, in highlighting the social and medical perspectives toward mental health distress and care in this chapter, it is less to reinforce this distinction and more to acknowledge it and engage you in thinking about how to approach mental health care with greater integration. A holistic approach to identifying, understanding and responding to mental health distress would involve a bio-psychosocial framework, one that acknowledges and considers the interconnected impact of biological, medical and genetic influences along with the psychological, emotional, social and spiritual aspects of an individual. Interventions from this perspective would both treat psychological upset and offer support to respond to practical needs and deficits. As you work through this chapter and the book, you are invited to consider this more comprehensive and holistic framework and thesis through reading and reflective exercises. This approach also serves as a prompt to consider how best to acknowledge social exclusion and to promote social inclusion of mental health service users.

Mental health and mental distress

As part of your learning and development, you will be asked to think about the very nature of concepts such as mental health and mental distress and terms like symptoms, diagnoses, and treatment interventions. Tilbury (2002), in the first extract, provides an overview and summary of elements of mental health developed over several decades. By contemplating what is meant by 'mental health', we are then able to reflect on the state outside of mental health – or what is variously described as mental disorder, mental illness or mental distress. The presence of different perspectives in defining and responding to mental health needs compels us to highlight the development and change in these perspectives over time. Prior (1993) offers a sociological perspective of mental distress in the chapter's second extract and introduces his inquiry into the changing social structures and understanding surrounding efforts to deal with mental distress. Following this, Allott (2004) discusses the impact of social and cultural forces on mental health functioning, particularly considering the influence of poverty and the meaning of mental distress in different cultures, specifically less techno-logically advanced communities. In contrast to this, the fourth extract is taken from a medical students' textbook written from what may be considered a dominant discourse – that is, the medical perspective – in the current approach to understanding mental health issues and their classification. Reflecting on the contrast between these two extracts offers an opportunity to explore how different groups in society contribute to the social construc-tion of an issue which in this case involves defining mental health need and what is classified as a mental health problem. Finally, Beresford (2005) introduces the perspective of service users as formulators of knowledge in relation to mental health both in policy considerations and in how mental health support is delivered. The voice of service user experience will help-fully offer a counterpoint to the previous extract's medical perspective and may also stimulate your thinking about the longstanding hierarchical dynamic that persists in doctor–patient interactions and relationships.

Identifying mental health need

Service users may seek help and relief in relation to their mental health needs. This will prompt them into contact with the broad range of providers who offer mental health care. The first part of this equation involves service users' mental health needs. According to a survey of psychiatric morbidity among adults living in England, *one in six (16.5%) of the population surveyed ... exhibited symptoms in the week prior to interview sufficient to warrant a diagnosis of a common mental health problem* (London Health Observatory [n.d.]). This finding suggests that mental health need is perhaps more widely present than expected. Thinking about our family, work colleagues and social networks, it would be pos-sible – using this statistic of one in six – to imagine the prevalence of mental health need. Realising this, I wonder if you thought about yourself as these figures were introduced. If you have not personally experienced mental health need, you may be able to relate to having 'down days' or being constantly active as a means of avoiding troubling feelings. You may have friends or family members who have experienced mental health difficulties. Keeping this in mind will be helpful so that you may be supportive to clients and others in tending to their mental health needs. As part of this reading and your related training, you will develop greater understanding of the range of mental health needs and services that are available and needed so that you will be able to share your understanding. In becoming a source of information and support, you will be able to help educate people about the importance of being open to considering or asking for help. By educating others, you will promote well-being as highlighted in the IFSW's (2002) definition of professional social work. In the following extract, Tilbury introduces ideas about mental health, mental health's parameters and thoughts about how mental distress is defined.

EXTRACT ONE

Tilbury, D (2002) Determinants of practice: Defining mental health and mental illness, Chapter 1 in Working with mental illness: A community-based approach. 2nd edition. Basingstoke: Palgrave, pp1–3 and p10.

What constitutes mental health

What constitutes mental health is difficult to define. Most attempts at definition (Jahoda, 1958; Maslow, 1969; Vaillant, 1970; McCullogh and Prins, 1978; Hershenson and Power, 1987) appear to group around three elements:

1. *The idea of the mature self – the sort of people we are. Mentally healthy people will be satisfied with and enjoying their lives. They will have a positive self image but be realistically aware and accepting of their limitations. Their self identity will be linked to an underlying philosophy or value system which forms the basis of their integrity and their internalised standards for behaviour. They will have a capacity to learn and develop, factors worthwhile in themselves and necessary if they are to maintain their mental health as their life circumstances change.*

2. *Self-management in social relations – Some literature suggests that our most important capacity is the ability to make and sustain intimate relationships. The number and nature of such relationships may not be specified, but the inference is that close relations with one's parents, one's children and at least one friend are very significant. The epitome of a healthy capacity to relate would appear to be a successful marriage or cohabitation: an ongoing relationship with a member of the opposite sex which includes physical intimacy. Where this leaves stable homosexual relationships is not quite clear.*

With this ability to make and sustain intimate relationships is the notion of the ability to retain one's autonomy: the 'one flesh, separate persons' concept of Skynner (1976). Despite the intimacy, the partner is not essential for survival. This idea of autonomy links to another, of being in control of oneself and one's circumstances. A mentally healthy person is not at the mercy of their inner needs, desires or feelings but can control, express and direct them in a socially constructive way. Nor are they at the mercy of other people: they can resist emotional demands, pressures and manipulations without either meekly submitting or angrily rejecting. They can tolerate frustration and postpone gratification as necessary. They can read and respond to social situations with realism and appropriateness; exercise choice and make decisions with objectivity and a greater chance of a successful outcome. Even when engaged in 'non-intimate' relations of the day-to-day kind, they will interact with interest, sensitivity and receptivity to others' messages, conscious of what they are communicating, aware of its effects and modifying matters where this is called for.

3. *The discharge of social roles, whether these relate to home-based life within family, kinship and neighbourhood groups, to work-related functions, or to recreation/interest activities. To discharge any social role involves a realistic understanding of what general social expectations accrue around that particular role as well as the more particularised ideas of one's immediate social groups. Effective role performance will depend on one's capacity to meet the obligations of that role, together with the ability to adjust that performance, since many roles, such as parent, are developing, not static. Other role performances may have unexpected challenges thrown up within them, from new technology at work to a friend becoming seriously ill, which demand adjustment.*

Adjustment is to be distinguished from conformity. Mentally healthy people will be able to choose whether they conform. They have the capacity to evaluate and weigh the social and personal consequences of conforming or not. Most societies and groups will tolerate, in varying degrees, some flexibility in the way roles are executed; but there can be times when individuals are faced with painful, even dangerous choices. To be mentally healthy is not always comfortable, as the records of Amnesty, to name but one organisation, demonstrate.

The discharge of social roles will call for qualities such as a sense of responsibility and a reasonable self-reliance, but will also require the associated technical and social skills. Modern living is making increased demands in technical terms (domestic appliances, computers, cars, form-filling and so on) and in the social sphere (negotiating with bank managers, resisting sales pressures, holidaying abroad, meeting neighbours from different ethnic backgrounds and so on). These represent routine demands: the literature goes on to suggest that the really mentally healthy will also be able to cope with emergencies. They will need problem-solving skills, the ability to handle crises and manage stress, to recognise where to find help when it is needed and a willingness to use it.

Approaches to defining mental illness

The widest stance regards as mental health problems all breakdowns in coping and the associated pain ...

Though the range is still wide, Hershenson and Power (1987), for example, limit what they consider mental ill health to four broad areas of problem: (a) social behaviour (disabilities in social skills, making relationships, handling aggression and coping with social expectations); (b) emotional behaviour (where problems give rise to depression, anxiety, phobias and so on); (c) health-related issues (a diverse group including insomnia, pain control and destructive behaviours from smoking to drug abuse); and (d) work-related issues (another extensive group ranging from boredom to burnout; from unemployment to 'workaholicism').

Having read Tilbury's (2002) summary of attributes of mental health and the broad definitions of mental health need, what are your criticisms or comments about these ideas?

Comment

As social work students or practitioners invited to engage in critical thinking, you may have wondered about the utility of providing discrete classifications of either mental health or mental distress since they may be too limited to provide specificity and sensitivity in describing the lived experiences of most people. Tilbury (2002) also questioned these definitions by summarising a review of literature critical of these mental health definitions and highlighting that research often overlooks two significant groups: children and young people and older adults. He also challenges lists meant to define mental health, as they suggest that mental health is an absolute without taking into consideration people's changing life circumstances, their abilities to cope and their varying tolerance of change or distress.

You may have noted the difficulty in segmenting mental health and mental distress or you may have simply posited that mental health was the absence of mental distress. In some ways, it may be easier to think about the state of mental distress than to think about mental health. How do we define what many of us might take for granted, particularly if we or those close to us have not experienced intrusive emotional or psychological difficulties? Tilbury cited the work of Jahoda (1958), who offered a variety of definitions related to mental health, including:

- the absence of mental illness;
- the ability to introspect with clarity of action and reason;
- the capacity for growth, development and self-actualisation;
- integrating internal drives or achieving ego identity;
- the ability to cope with stress;
- having autonomy;
- seeing the world as it really is;
- satisfaction in love, work, leisure and interpersonal connection

(cited in Gross, 2001).

Suggesting that mental health is *not* having a mental health problem as noted above should engage your critical thinking because such a formulation highlights a point made in the first chapter in relation to power which emphasised that there are rarely two polarised concepts or binary positions. Mental health and mental distress do not need to be considered as two dichotomies. Remaining conscious of this dilemma is essential as the concepts of mental health are fluid and will inevitably be influenced by society and culture. What is considered mentally healthy in one society or culture, such as being assertive or sticking up for oneself, may be considered abnormal in another. The challenge involves offering distinctions about normality and abnormality while both respectfully striving to make sense of the struggles of persons with serious and intrusive mental health symptoms and offering treatment and intervention that prove helpful. Further challenges exist as changing ideas about these concepts and even definitions will occur over time and with societal influences.

Societal perspectives on mental health

Delineating what is mental health or what is mental distress is influenced by changing perspectives within society which encompasses the medical or professional field as well as changing views espoused by individuals – who may or may not need mental health support – and institutions, such as provider groups and government. In the following extract, Prior (1993) introduces his sociological inquiry of mental illness. His book, *The social organization of mental illness*, is a review of evaluative work he did investigating the experiences of two groups: patients within a psychiatric hospital in the late 1980s, and those who had been discharged and were living in the community. The extract makes mention of these two social experiences; he also highlights other significant variables, like work roles, types of therapy and diagnosis. As a prelude to this extract, it may be helpful to review the work of a seminal theorist, Emile Durkheim, whose writing on the changing social conditions in the early part of the twentieth century led to the birth of the field of sociology. Durkheim (1964, p7, cited in Prior, 1993) writes that *the collective aspects of the beliefs, tendencies and practices of a group ... characterise truly social phenomena*. When reading Prior's (1993) work and Allott's subsequent piece, you will want to keep in mind the Durkheimian precept about collective aspects in relation to beliefs and practices. Thinking about how the United Kingdom collectively considers mental health needs and responds to the diversity of mental health need may stimulate your thoughts.

EXTRACT TWO

Prior, L (1993) Introduction: Social representations and social worlds. Chapter 1 *in* The social organization of mental illness. London: Sage, p3.

The lives and worlds of the patients and ex-patients ... were, of course, structured both in terms of the practical contingencies of everyday interaction, and in their terms of a system of concepts, ideas, and theoretical frameworks ... Thus, both the concept of the psychiatric hospital and the actual physical structure in which patients were treated and cared for had come into existence during the first decade of the present century (i.e. twentieth century). In addition the official diagnostic system by means of which most of the patients' disorders were recognized and described had been emerging since 1911, whilst the forms of therapy to which patients were and had been subject – occupational therapy, shock therapy, drug therapy, and in some cases, surgical intervention – had been woven into psychiatric theory and practice at quite diverse points of the twentieth century. And when one reflects on such facts it becomes evident that just as abstract theory requires reference to essential detail, so the study of personal biography and social worlds requires cognizance of larger conceptual and ideational contexts. Indeed, it is plain that such personal detail cannot be fully understood by restricting oneself to the immediate empirical context of action in which patients commonly find themselves. Thus, when a social worker talks to a 'schizophrenic patient' in a hospital ward about how that patient would consider the possibility of living in the community, we can legitimately ask a whole series of sociological questions about the entities and processes which underpin the entire conversational transaction. Why, for example,

---

EXTRACT TWO *continued*

are the interactional roles structured in terms of social worker and patient in a hospital environment? Why is it only during the latter quarter of the twentieth century that the question of living 'in the community' adopts a new meaning and a new significance? And what in any case is a schizophrenic patient?

POINTS TO CONSIDER

- *Considering Prior's (1993) final questions, what do you think he means by the roles of social worker and patient?*

- *Since 1993, what changes have happened in the terminology we use to define roles in the field of mental health?*

Comment

Prior helpfully ends with a series of difficult, and unanswered, questions about the then changing nature of society's contract with its members – those with mental health difficulties and those without them – in terms of care provision. In the late 1980s when this work was being done, many countries were continuing a process of discharging persons from psychiatric hospitals where they had been living for long periods of time. Prior, further along in his book, asks what changed. Did these individuals suddenly no longer have mental health needs? Did their needs no longer require hospitalisation? Did mental health providers begin to question the ethical nature of long hospital admissions? Certainly some of these factors contributed to this change, as did several others, including advances in medical treatments and more recognition of the rights of those living with presumably mental health problems.

You were invited to reflect on the terminology of the piece and to comment on the idea of roles within the mental health context that Prior (1993) described. In your reflection, we have the benefit of living 14 years following the publication of his book and can compare our current understanding with his findings. In relation to roles, Prior is acknowledging the idea of role theory, which notes that the roles we take up in an interaction will influence how we behave and how we are perceived. At a basic level, the first question notes the difference between a social worker and a patient, which recalls some thinking from Chapter 1 in relation to power and authority. It also highlights the change in terminology as well as a shifting trend in service use to reject assigning a 'patient' role to people with mental health needs but rather to identify people as 'service users'. By changing this term, we attempt to acknowledge not only illness but health in people. This provides an example of an ongoing and still evolving social construction in relation to delivering and seeking mental health help in the contemporary UK social context. As we work further through this chapter, this discussion will re-emerge.

Mental health and social exclusion

Allott (2004), whose extract follows, considers the impact of poverty on the development of mental health problems; he also fosters a useful discussion about cultural implications in terms of how people perceive and respond to mental distress, which further emphasises the influence of society on naming and understanding phenomena.

EXTRACT THREE

Allott, P (2004) What is mental health, illness and recovery? In Ryan, T and Pritchard, J (eds) (2004) Good practice in adult mental health. *London: Jessica Kingsley, pp17–19.*

Mental health, poverty, culture and social justice

Prilleltensky (2001a, p. 253) defines mental health as a state of psychological well-ness characterised by the satisfactory fulfilment of basic human needs. Prilleltensky highlights that some of the basic human needs for mental health include a sense of mastery, control, and a sense of efficacy; emotional support and secure attachment; cognitive stimulation; sense of community and belonging; respect for personal identity and dignity; and others identified by the Basic Behavioural Science Task Force of the National Advisory Mental Health Council (1996a, 1996b).

Given the above it is not surprising that the experiences we identify as 'mental illness' are closely connected with poverty and social injustice and what might more accurately be referred to as 'disempowerment' or 'losing control over one or more aspects of one's life.' Prilleltensky (2001a, p. 254) highlights the importance of cultural assumptions on mental health, particularly cultural assumptions about poverty and social justice, the way this is framed and society's response to it. He summarises his view that:

> Cultural assumptions exert a direct influence on mental health through definition of the good life and the good society and through psychological definitions and solutions to problems. Notions of the good life derived from competition and individualism lead to social isolation and psychological stress. When these problems are defined in individualistic terms, the person is viewed as responsible for her or his suffering. But cultural assumptions also exert an indirect influence on mental health via society's definitions of social justice. The way we frame justice determines how we allocate resources, and the way we allocate resources has a direct impact on the mental health of the poor and the vulnerable.

Psychiatry is part of the Western medical science and as such has developed within the context of Western cultures. When one considers, in addition to the cultural assumptions identified above, the cultural differences between nations including differences of ethnicity and race and the way these issues are dealt with in a multicultural society, concepts of mental illness become very much more complex. Until relatively recently the significance and importance of differences in cultural meanings of mental health have gone unrecognised, or been ignored, and this has led to considerable social injustice; in particular the fact that many more people from African Caribbean backgrounds in the UK experience considerably greater levels of coercion both on entry to and within the mental health system.

The importance of culture has been recognised since the beginnings of psychiatric classification (Kraepelin, 1904), but the Western societies in which we now live and our ability to travel and communicate around the world easily have created a very different context to that experienced by Kraepelin. Culture within these societies has become very much more complex. Marsella and Yamada define culture as:

> Shared learned meanings and behaviours that are transmitted from within a social activity context for purposes of promoting individual/societal adjustment, growth, and development. Culture has both *external* (i.e., artifacts, roles, activity contexts, institutions) and *internal* (i.e., values, beliefs, attitudes, activity contexts, patterns of consciousness, personality styles, epistemology) representations. The shared meanings and behaviours are subject to continuous change and modification in response to changing internal and external circumstances. (Marsella and Yamada, 2000, p12)

They highlight the work of Murdock (1980), an American anthropologist, who separated Western views from non-Western views of disease causality. He reported that Western models were based on naturalistic views of disease causation, including infection, stress, organic deterioration, accidents and acts of overt human aggression. In contrast, among many non-Western societies, disease models were based on supernatural views (i.e. any disease which accounts for impairment of health as being a consequence of some intangible force) including:

1. *theories of mystical causation because of impersonal forces such as fate, ominous sensations, contagion, mystical retribution.*

2. *theories of animistic causation because of personalised forces such as soul loss and spirit aggression.*

3. *theories of magical causation or actions of evil forces including sorcery and witchcraft.*

It is considered significant that many people in the United Kingdom who are 'experts by experience' (people who experience mental illness/distress, their families and friends) and have been diagnosed as 'mentally ill' have adopted a mixture of Western naturalist models of disease – including stress, accidents and acts of human aggression, including abuse – and non-Western models that are more supernaturally or spiritually based, while rejecting naturalist biological concepts of infection and organic deterioration.

Comment

Allott's (2004) extract cited Prilleltensky's (2001a) straightforward definition of mental health and relates this to a series of descriptors of mental health, similar to those previously listed. He positions mental health within a context in which 'basic human needs' are met. Allott (2004) argues that poverty and social deprivation undermine the capacity to possess mental health, which challenges us to think as practitioners and social work students how we work to support people's basic needs as an impetus to improving mental health.

Connected to this is his contention that Western society tends to view the individual who suffers from mental health distress as someone responsible for his or her suffering; whereas a similar but non-Western culture may implicate a wider set of factors. He also introduces cultural concepts about causes of mental distress which from an anthropological viewpoint have been divided along Western and non-Western lines. Similar cultural distinctions are echoed by Fernando (1995), who discusses psychiatry's development in the Western world from a philosophical foundation of a mind and body duality based on the ideas of the French philosopher, Descartes. The culture of psychiatry Fernando (1995, p13) describes includes a *mind-body dichotomy … a segmental approach to the individual* and stipulates that illness requires biomedical change. Through this approach mental distress is primarily understood as an illness model.

Yet, significant to this excerpt are the differing perceptions about the causes of mental distress based on culture of origin which might either conclude that causes stem from natural or supernatural forces. Illness, linked to more natural constructs, seems to represent a more Western approach to understanding mental distress. The effect of spiritual forces may relate more closely to a supernatural understanding about mental distress. As noted in Allott's (2004) excerpt, understanding persons' perceptions of the cultural and societal influences on themselves and others in relation to their mental health or distress will define mental health. This is pertinent to responding to mental distress in the UK as the cultural context increasingly reflects diverse multi-ethnic and multicultural communities.

Also significant in this piece is Allott's (2004) introduction of the moniker, *expert by experience*, which highlights the recognition by traditional mental health providers of the importance of consulting with those who use services to enhance the field's knowledge base. This term, 'expert by experience', stands in stark contrast to the earlier term of 'patient' and highlights the magnitude of this change.

Psychiatry and classification

Another strand that is relevant to the discussion of mental health relates to how and if mental health distress is labelled or categorised. Prior (1993, p3) wrote about an *official diagnostic system … [that had] been emerging since 1911*. Classification systems have been developed by the medical profession, usually by physicians, psychiatrists and, in some cases, nurses, to provide a label for behaviour, symptoms and client functioning; this label is considered a formal diagnosis (see Chapter 5 for related discussion). Classifying mental disorders or illness dates back to the early 1900s when Kraepelin (1904), as cited in Prior (1993), proposed terms to describe mental distress. This approach to naming mental distress has been refined over a century. The point at which mental distress becomes categorised as a diagnosis depends on multiple factors such as severity of symptoms, duration of distress and types of symptoms being described by the person seeking or in need of help. Developing a system of classification has been proposed to facilitate communication between providers and to make judgements on treatment. As you will see in the following extract, there are two classification systems attempting to classify and distinguish psychiatric diagnoses.

The use of such classification systems has not been without difficulty, prejudice and oppression. As Tilbury (2002) noted in his inquiry into mental health, previous thinking in psychiatry would have labelled homosexuality or affectional relationships between members of the same sex as a pathology needing hospitalisation or treatment. Such beliefs within the medical and mental health system were officially in place as recently as three decades ago. Golightley (2008), Allott (2004) and Fernando (1995) among many others have highlighted the ongoing inequity in treatment of African-Caribbean and black persons within the mental health and forensic systems in relation to diagnosis, treatment and restraint. This reality emphasises that a classification system, which may be useful, is still not objective; its application is influenced by the thoughts and feelings of the person who by nature of role and training has the authority to make the diagnosis as well as by the prejudices and biases that may be dominant in society at any given time. Please keep this in mind as we consider psychiatric classification.

The following extract includes sections about psychiatry and classification from a textbook, *Clinical medicine*, used by medical students. Through this, you have a brief entrée into the learning of another profession as it introduces a specific type of psychiatry working with people with physical health problems.

EXTRACT FOUR

White, P and Clare, A (2002) Psychological medicine. In Kumar, P and Clark, M (eds) (2002) Clinical medicine. 5th edition. Edinburgh: W.B. Saunders, p1225 and p1231.

Introduction

Psychiatry is the branch of medicine that is concerned with the study and treatment of disorders of mental function. Psychological medicine, or liaison psychiatry, is the discipline within psychiatry that is concerned with psychiatric and psychological disorders in patients who have physical complaints or conditions. This chapter will primarily concern itself with this particular branch of psychiatry.

Many doctors believe that psychiatric disorders imply that the cause or even the disorder itself is psychological. All your tests are negative so it must be 'all in your mind'. But absence of evidence is not the same as evidence of absence. The last 10 years has seen an explosion of research which has consistently shown that the brain is functionally or anatomically abnormal in most if not all psychiatric disorders. This evidence is breaking down long-held beliefs that diseases are either physical or psychological. We now know that doctors must consider both physical and psychological factors, and their interaction, in order to understand and thus help their patients. This philosophical change of approach rejects the Cartesian dualistic approach of the mind/body medical model and replaces it with the more holistic biopsychosocial model …

Classification of psychiatric disorders

The classification of psychiatric disorders into categories is mainly based on symptoms, since there are currently few diagnostic tests for psychiatric disorders. The fourth edition of the Diagnostic and Statistical Manual of the American Psychiatric Association *(DSM-IV) provides descriptions of diagnostic categories in order to enable clinicians and investigators to diagnose, communicate about, study and treat people with various mental disorders. This scheme has five axes:*

I *Psychiatric disorders.*

II *Personality disorders, learning difficulty.*

III *General medical conditions.*

IV *Psychosocial and environmental problems.*

V *Overall level of functioning.*

Another classification system – the International Classification of Mental and Behavioural Disorders *(ICD-10) has been published by the World Health Organization.*

Comment

Reflecting on the ideas present in Allott's (2005) writing about causes of mental health symptoms and responses to address them is usefully juxtaposed with the overview of the psychiatric perspective introduced by White and Clare (2002). The latter is heavily couched – as one would suppose – in medical terminology in relation to symptoms and diagnoses and also introduces the growing evidence that solidifies the link between brain chemistry and mental health symptoms. This emphasis on medical causes and physiology is somewhat tempered by advocating a bio-psychosocial approach. Allott's perspective, in the previous extract, offers an argument that social deprivation and poverty need to be recognised more clearly as a potential cause of mental distress in contrast to purely physiological and organic causes, and needs to be addressed more successfully in prophylactic strategies to reduce deprivation and poverty thereby reducing damaging or limiting psychological or mental health difficulties. The ideas from both of these extracts need to be considered critically; physiological causes of mental distress, psychiatric labelling and the very issue of diagnosis would be usefully scrutinised.

The table presented as Figure 2.1 offers a more detailed list of mental disorders with main terms and key symptoms. The ICD-10, which was developed across several continents at the behest of the World Health Organisation (WHO), is most commonly used in the United Kingdom.

Service user perspectives

Beresford (2005) writes eloquently about the growing foundation of service user involvement in the development of knowledge in relation to mental health. This would stand in contrast to the areas of policy, research, and practice being dominated and influenced by professional and academic bodies that may not incorporate service user perspectives. The following extract is a chapter drawn from a text that seeks to promote and develop social perspectives in responding to mental distress. Beresford (2005) highlights some of the contradictions in governmental policy on mental health between its embrace of service users as socially inclusive and its seemingly contradictory stance of increasing the powers of compulsory mental health treatment. In the latter part of the extract, Beresford (2005) relates service users' contributions to this developing discourse.

Psychiatric diagnoses and conditions	Key symptoms[1]
Mood (affective) disorders	
● Depression	Pervasive sadness, apathy, fatigue, suicidal ideation, hopelessness as well as appetite and sleep disturbances
● Mania/Bipolar disorder	Elevated or irritable mood, mood lability, excessive energy, decreased need for sleep, racing thoughts, grandiosity
Schizophrenia, schizotypal and delusional disorders	
● Schizophrenia of various types, delusional disorders and substance-induced psychotic disorders	Sensory hallucinations, delusions, thought disorders and loose associations as well as flattened or grossly inappropriate affect. Negative symptoms including social withdrawal and lack of motivation
Neurotic, stress-related and somatoform disorders	Emotional distress, nervousness and apprehension, heightened arousal, intrusive anxiety-provoking thoughts, sleep disturbance, breathing difficulties, and palpitations
Adjustment disorders	Depression and/or anxiety of less severity which is directly related to an identifiable stressor in the recent past
Disorders of adult personality and behaviour	Persistent, maladaptive life behaviours that interfere with interpersonal relationships and interactions
Mental and behavioural disorders due to psychoactive substance use	Excessive misuse of alcohol, narcotics, stimulants, cannabis or other illicit or prescription drugs leading to physiological and psychological dependence
Disorders of childhood including intellectual development, psychological development and behavioural or other emotional disorders	
● Learning or intellectual disability and developmental disorders	Delay in emotional, social or intellectual functioning based on generally prescribed developmental milestones
● Conduct or behaviour disorders	Pervasive and intrusive problems related to lying, stealing, and verbal and/or physical aggression
● Attachment disorders	Excessive anxiety and fearfulness that precludes social development
● Disorders of attention and hyperkinetic behaviour	Extreme and persistent restlessness, sustained and prolonged movement and activity and difficulty maintaining attention
Organic disorders	Dementia involving severe problems of memory loss and impaired problem-solving and planning as well as brain trauma, delirium and other problems of thinking with adult onset.

[1] This is not an exhaustive list of mental health or behavioural diagnoses. Symptoms and order of table have been adapted from McDaniel, S (1999) incorporating terms used in the DSM-IV-TR (APA, 2000) and the ICD-10 (WHO, 1992).

Figure 2.1 *Key symptoms of selected mental health diagnoses*

EXTRACT FIVE

Beresford, P (2005) Social approaches to madness and distress: User perspectives and user knowledges. In Tew, J (ed.) Social perspectives in mental health: Developing social models to understand and work with mental distress. London: Jessica Kingsley, p37 and pp43–4.

User involvement became one of the guiding formal principles of mental health policy. Requirements for it have been built into mental health guidance and processes. It is meant to operate at individual and collective levels. Provisions for user involvement have been at the heart of assessment procedures established with community care 'care management' and the 'care programme approach'. State interest in user involvement led to a massive expansion in market research and consultation initiatives in mental health as in other areas of health and social care (Beresford and Croft, 1993). The consumerist commitment of former Conservative administrations to user involvement became embedded in New Labour managerialist/consumerist 'third way' variants which have followed (Beresford, 2002; Giddens, 1998).

Thus the emphasis on user involvement in mental health policy and practice means that we should be hearing from other voices and accessing different viewpoints and understandings. To some extent this has happened. But mostly people as mental health service users have internalised the dominant mental illness/health model of understandings. They are often under enormous personal pressure to do so. It offers some kind of explanation which, at times of great individual difficulty and pain, may seem helpful. It is likely to be the only framework for understanding that many people are offered or can access. Service users also express concerns that much user involvement has only been able to operate within existing frameworks of policy, analysis, organisations, 'treatment' and so on, thus restricting the opportunities service users have had to generate their own ideas on equal terms …

New survivor-led understandings of madness and distress

While mental health service users/survivors may not have developed an agreed and discrete theory or philosophy so far, there is no doubt that they and their organisations have developed different ways of understanding their experience, feelings and perceptions and, as a result, different approaches to and understandings for support and services. There can be little question that these are based on a thought-through ideology, albeit one that is frequently not articulated in any depth. This ideology follows from their own experiential knowledge and is strongly suggestive of an implicitly social approach.

For example, as long ago as 1987, Survivors Speak Out, the pioneering organisation of psychiatric system survivors, at its founding conference in Edale, produced a 'Charter of Needs and Demands' which were agreed unanimously. These demands prioritised the provision of non-medicalised services and support, the value of people's first-hand experience, the rights of service users and the ending of discrimination against people with experience of using mental health services (Survivors Speak Out, 1987).

EXTRACT FIVE *continued*

Significantly, the understandings that mental health service users/survivors have developed about their 'illnesses' have generally followed less from knowledge production through research, than from knowledge production through collective action and reflection.

Such survivor understandings have developed from people trying to make sense of their own experience by sharing, collecting and analysing it. This has been reflected in discussions of their individual experience, their history and their 'treatment' (Campbell, 1996; Chamberlin, 1988; Craine, 1998; Mental Health Media, 2000; Read and Reynolds, 1996). Most important, perhaps, it has also emerged from efforts to reinterpret and make better sense of their experience than they feel that the psychiatric system and the predominant medical model have done. This is a common theme, in all the key areas where mental health service users/survivors have renewed thinking about the psychiatric categories into which they have been placed. They have challenged (and rejected) medicalised understandings of the experience as pathological and only negative. They have implicitly challenged the 'illness' model.

Instead they have placed an emphasis on people's first-hand understandings of themselves and their situation. This is exemplified by the development of the international hearing voices movement and in the UK of the Hearing Voices Network. Instead of accepting the diagnostic category 'schizophrenia' and victim status as a sufferer, the emphasis has been on trying to make sense of hearing voices both at a personal and at a societal level. There is no denial of the phenomenon or attempt to minimise the difficulties it may cause individually or socially. Instead the accent is on acknowledging and exploring the experience, recognising its power relations and learning to comprehend and deal with it better (Coleman, 1999; Coleman and Smith, 1997; Romme and Escher, 1993).

POINTS TO CONSIDER

Turning back to the beginning of this chapter, re-read the Key Roles and responsibilities that are listed there or look at the full list of the NOS. Reflect on the roles and responsibilities of social workers while taking into account Beresford's thoughts about contradictory aspects of government policy in relation to mental health.

- *How would you work to ensure that you follow social work tasks as framed by the Key Roles while incorporating service user perspectives?*

- *Would you notice any contradictions in this work – perhaps in relation to managing risk, for example, or other contexts?*

Comment

Clearly evident in the benchmark statement was a reference to *competing views in society ... on the nature of social work and ... differing perspectives on the role of social work in relation to social justice, social care and social order* (QAA, 2008, p6) These competing views seem evident in Beresford's (2005) writing. As social workers, we are often working within statutory parameters and compelled by legislation to take actions that may include acts of social control; in mental health this particularly involves social workers who work as Approved Social Workers (ASWs) and must make decisions about compulsory hospitalisation. (The term Approved Social Worker and the role will change with the implementation of the amended Mental Heath Act 2007. The role will include additional mental health providers from the fields of nursing, occupational therapy and psychology, so the term will change to Approved Mental Health Professional. See Chapter 3 for further information.) A task like this, linked more to Key Role 4, may seem to sit uneasily next to a facilitative and collaborative social work approach that actively includes service users in identifying goals and fosters person-centred goal planning. Perhaps you also wondered about how as a social worker you may advocate for responses to mental health distress that do not necessarily incorporate medical interventions solely, such as medication, but identify and work towards improving a service user's social experience and thereby their mental well-being. Tasks like this, more aligned with Key Roles 1 and 3, might include the use by a service user of direct payments to engage in a weekly art therapy group or to attend an evening class in photography. Incorporating these ideas and interventions when aligned with a service user's own goals contributes to working within a bio-psychosocial framework in your social work practice.

C H A P T E R   S U M M A R Y

Mental health distress may prove a very troubling and intrusive experience for people living with such distress and for those surrounding them as friends, family and partners. Such distress may also be felt by providers who work in this field, though it may be assumed that they are removed from it. With statistics showing that one in six persons reports experiences that could be classed as a definable mental health problem, it appears that a sizeable percentage of us either have an experience of mental distress or are close to someone who may. The concepts of mental health and mental distress brought us to a variety of definitions of these two states and conflicting viewpoints; usefully, it prompted reflection about the very nature of mental health. The impact and influence of society featured in two extracts as we considered the changing perspectives of mental distress and the impact of culture. One cultural impact is the role of psychiatry in responding to mental health needs and, as noted by Beresford (2005, p36), the dominant trend *to interpret ... madness and distress in predominantly medicalised individual terms,* both of which influence understanding and treating mental health difficulties. However, the psychiatry perspective clearly addressed its sense of a change in philosophy from a mind–body dichotomy represented in earlier Cartesian thinking to a more holistic bio-psychosocial approach. Finally, the tension between a facilitative social work practice and a practice that is legitimated by social policy and legislation was noted. As we embark in the next chapter on considering the policy and legal aspects of mental health, it is helpful to keep this in mind. Having read several differing and, at times, contentious perspectives on the matter of mental health, you will have a broad overview to consider the diversity of your social work role in a mental health context, striving to maintain an integrated and bio-psychosocial understanding of a person's experience.

Pritchard, C (2006) *Mental health social work: Evidence-based practice*. Abingdon: Routledge. Pritchard explores the philosophical and historical foundation of these concepts in Chapter 2. Subsequent chapters describe categories of psychiatric disorder.

Ray, M, Pugh, R with Roberts, B and Beech, B (2008) *Research briefing 26: Mental health and social work*. July. London: Social Care Institute for Excellence.

SCIE has a focus on disseminating good practice in the field of social care. This recent research document succinctly captures the relevance for social work to be a part of a socially inclusive and holistic approach to mental healthcare.

Chapter 3
The legal and policy context

This chapter will contribute to helping you to meet the following National Occupational Standards.

Key Role 1: Prepare for, and work with individuals, families, carers, groups, and communities to assess their needs and circumstances.

- Assess needs and options to recommend a course of action ... taking into account legal and other requirements.

Key Role 2: Plan, carry out, review and evaluate social work practice, with individuals, families, carers, groups, communities and other professionals.

- Respond to crisis situations ... identify(ing) the need for legal and procedural intervention.

Key Role 5: Manage and be accountable, with supervision and support, for your own social work practice.

- Manage and be accountable for your own work ... within organisational policies and procedures.

Key Role 6: Demonstrate professional competence in social work practice.

- Manage complex ethical issues, dilemmas and conflicts.

It will also introduce you to the following academic standards as set out in the social work subject benchmark statement.

Defining principles

4.6 Social work is a moral activity that requires practitioners to recognise the dignity of the individual, but also to make and implement difficult decisions (including the restriction of liberty) in human situations that involve the potential for benefit or harm ... This means ... learn(ing) to:

- Recognise and work with the powerful links between intrapersonal and interpersonal factors and the wider social, legal, economic, political and cultural context of people's lives ...

5.1.2 The service delivery context

The significance of legislative and legal frameworks and service delivery standards (including the nature of legal authority, the application of legislation in practice, statutory accountability, and tensions between statute, policy and practice).

5.1.3 Values and ethics

- The moral concepts of rights, responsibility, freedom, authority and power inherent in the practice of social workers as moral and statutory agents.
- The complex relationships between justice, care and control in social welfare and the practical and ethical implications of these, including roles as statutory agents and in upholding the law in respect of discrimination.

Introduction

The legal and policy context of social work is dynamic. Guidance from the government, policy developments in the form of White or Green papers, consultations in relation to proposed introductions of or amendments to legislation, and court judgements or changes to statutes will each contribute to and refine the practice of social work. This is evident in the case *HL* v *Bournewood* (see Chapter 1). The significance of that case prompted the Department of Health to revise its guidance. A further outcome stimulated changes to protecting service users' liberty in relation to hospitalisation and institutional care. In addition, this court case also highlighted deficiencies in mental health law, particularly in relation to human rights' protections following the introduction of the Human Rights Act 1989. Consequently, these deficiencies compelled the governments of England and Wales to foster changes to the Mental Health Act 1983 and the Mental Capacity Act 2005. Through this sequence of events, both knowledge and practice dynamically change.

In legislative and policy matters, we also expect change. Changes in law and policy signify that a society is adapting to the needs of its citizens. Legislation that is undermining liberty and human rights will hopefully be amended to adhere more justly to its remit. Considering whether this is routinely the case and forming judgements about the just and accurate interpretation of the law is a matter for reflection in this chapter. Legal parameters and policy initiatives are in flux, affected by government leaders, public opinion and the findings of higher courts. In light of this, the material in this chapter is likely to be subject to further and ongoing refinement. Mental health legislation has been under review for nearly a decade, and recent developments and enactments mean that some legislative change is in place; while further changes will ensue (Department of Health, 2007).

The recently amended Mental Health Act received Royal Assent in July 2007; it amends the Mental Health Act 1983. Additionally it provides for the 2007 amendment of the Mental Capacity Act 2005. The Mental Capacity Act 2005 has been in place since April 2007. A section of the Mental Health Act 2007 is in effect; however, the bulk of the sections remain in draft form. In fact, some conditions of the Act will not be expected to come into force for perhaps several years while capacity (DoH, 2007, n.p.) and the infrastructure to provide the changes in services authorised by the Act are developed. As this is a work in progress, your reflections on the legislative and policy aspects of mental health will not only apply while reading this chapter but will represent an ongoing task for you as a student and as a social work practitioner. Being prepared to accommodate and incorporate newly revised policy recommendations and legal mandates is a cornerstone of your role in social work. This is perhaps most evident in the application of law and its interpretation in practice, so I encourage you to be aware of both dominant and alternative perspectives in relation to mental health law.

As ethical principles and values provide internal guidance about how social work practitioners need to conduct themselves in their professional tasks, laws and statutes provide an external framework to respond to situations of need in our lives. In this text, we principally consider legislation related to mental capacity, mental health and human rights as the areas of law to shape and provide oversight to social work practice in mental health. As social work students and social work practitioners, you would be expected to adhere to statutory expectations such as in the protection of children from abuse or neglect or adults from financial exploitation or other abuse, for instance. Laws offer the container in society to establish expectations and boundaries in relation to mutual respect, safety and security.

Reflecting on legal developments

The crux of this chapter involves reflecting on the changes that characterise mental health and mental capacity law, particularly its effect on social work practice and its concomitant impact on service users. To do this, a number of current and recent extracts are provided to highlight the process and pace of change. Focusing on the Mental Health Act (MHA) 1983 as the primary legal framework for mental health practice, in the first extract Bartlett and Sandland (2003) write about the history of changes in the law and provide a service delivery context for this legislation. Their work, drawn from a prior edition of the text – *Mental health law, Policy and practice* – offers a measured, thoughtful and comprehensive appreciation of the benefits and limitations of this piece of legislation. Following this, you are able to read about the 2007 changes to the Act in an excerpt from a journal article by the Reader in Law, Nicola Glover-Thomas (2007).

In the subsequent extract, Toby Williamson (2007), writing as a member of staff at the Department of Constitutional Affairs, describes the Mental Capacity Act 2005 and its role in protecting persons from harm or exploitation. This extract also usefully describes new mechanisms to safeguard choice and support advocacy. Finally, extract four includes findings and recommendations from a survey of Approved Social Workers (ASWs) which was published in 2004. Though the amended MHA expands the professions beyond medicine and social work responsible for assessing persons for compulsory hospitalisation, this article offers useful recommendations for improvement in this task with its overarching goal of providing more containment for those with more serious and intrusive mental health distress.

The spectrum of control and care

The concepts of mental health and mental distress were introduced in Chapter 2, while the experience and personal meaning of living with mental health need will be explored in the subsequent three chapters. However, bearing in mind the lived experiences of those with mental health needs is just as important when considering the legislative and policy context of mental health practice. In this chapter, thinking about legislation and policy means that we consider the role of these in exerting control and containment. As a practitioner, you may need to act to provide control, but by thinking about the service user's experience you may be able to understand the dilemma for someone who may need control but, at times, may resist and resent it or may feel ambivalent about it. As a social work practitioner, you may question your comfort level in exerting more coercive and controlling interventions when working with service users. The parameters and boundaries of legislation and policy are points for debate. In the following quote, Bartlett and Sandland (2003) address the dilemma that arises when confronting the conflicting matters of liberty and containment through legislative intervention.

Whether as the liberal right to be free from intervention, or the more paternalist question of who should or should not be protected, the issue involves the deployment of power over individuals. This is most easily seen in the overtly legal context: civil confinement under the MHA is obviously the deployment of power. The development of social policy is also the deployment of power, however, for it involves the structuring of society and the creation of social programmes in which the participants will be

> *expected to fit. Even naming individuals as mentally disordered is an exercise of power, since it changes their perceptions of themselves, and the perception of them by other people.* (p41)

This quote passionately suggests a dynamic tension between someone who holds power and – in relation to them – someone who may feel without power. This dynamic may also occur in relationships between entities and systems. Though we challenged the idea of making easy distinctions between power and powerlessness in Chapter 1, there seems to be a real demarcation when deploying power legislatively. As we know, the government with input from its citizens has the power to enact legislation. In MHA legislation, professions and their roles and responsibilities are defined to carry out the law's duties. Challenging this power dynamic is one layer. In addition, the law also highlights another power dynamic, as it suggests a dichotomy between people who have mental health problems and those who do not. Bartlett and Sandland (2003) emphasise this when they express gratitude to students with whom they have worked who have shared their experience of the mental health system as either users or providers. For these authors, it reinforces the belief that there is an illusory line that divides 'us' and 'them' – with perhaps 'us' signifying the providers of mental health services or the ones with 'good' mental health, and 'them', signifying those in need of help. Certainly, depending on your experience, you may interpret this differently. No matter your interpretation, I encourage you while reading this chapter and engaging in the reflective tasks to strive to inhabit the experiences of persons on the receiving end of more intrusive and containing services delivered as part of mental health legislation, and thereby keep a picture of the humanity in each of us.

Control as care

Control and containment services involve compulsory detention in hospital in relation to mental health law. In the prior chapter, we grappled with defining concepts of mental health and mental distress as a way of understanding both personal and societal perspectives. In the legal context, definitions of certain concepts are enshrined in legislation and will be applied in real life; one of those real-life situations involves detention or compulsory hospitalisation. Circumstances requiring intervention to prevent harm and to promote care will at times seem clear but generally offer complexity and prompt uncertainty or disagreement among colleagues about whether or how to act, and may generate conflicting perspectives in oneself. Beckett and Maynard (2005) consider the concepts of care and control, arguing that they may be, depending on situation and circumstance, the same thing. They write:

> *Many texts speak of social work's dual roles of 'care' on the one hand and 'control' on the other, as if they were different, even opposite things. Thus, the International Federation of Social Workers speaks of helping and controlling as being opposite aspects of social work (IFSW, para 2.3.1 (2), www.ifsw.org) while Pamela Trevithick refers to conflicting responsibilities (Trevithick, 2000, p140). But in fact in social work, as in other areas of life, care and control are not necessarily in conflict at all … In situations where people are unable to take full responsibility for their own safety because of lack of understanding (as is the case with small children and roads) a*

professional duty of care may well extend to exercising some control over them. Similarly, in situations where people are at risk due to their own lack of power, professionals with a duty of care may need to exercise control over others in order to protect them ... 'Control', used appropriately, is not the opposite of care, but on the contrary is an expression of care ...

(Beckett and Maynard, 2005, pp119–20)

Beckett and Maynard's (2005) quote suggests that on the continuum of care, control is a manifestation of care and that decisions regarding the use of control as care permeate social work practice. With this perspective, they reframe the offering of care so that it also encompasses control when more restrictive options are needed. Related to this is the role that further legislation – especially the Human Rights Act 1989 – plays in ensuring that control is not so restrictive that human rights are violated.

POINTS TO CONSIDER

What might you consider to be the risks of providing restrictions on people's liberties in mental health care? What might be the benefit of control? Methods of restriction or control might relate to being compelled to go into hospital, being compelled into seclusion or held in a safety hold.

Comment

Beckett and Maynard (2005) are not commenting specifically on mental health law; yet their thesis that control is a manifestation of care offers a valid perspective. It also helps to reframe actions that social work practitioners may need to take that would likely be perceived as coercive. By conceiving of interventions that are more coercive as a means of care, they help us to think about our roles and urge us to be reflective and objective about tasks requiring more control. In the preceding reflective point, you were asked to think about situations in which exerting control may be helpful and/or risky. You may have found it difficult to cite situations falling neatly into one or the other category but may have considered such situations requiring control to possess both benefit and risk. Some situations that may have greater benefit would be exerting control to prevent risk of death or injury to the service user or someone else though, even in such situations, risk may not necessarily be imminent. A further benefit may occur when a service user – who feels out of control – experiences the imposition of a service or a restriction to be containing and reassuring. Examples when exerting control would be problematic would involve imposing control to allay your or a colleague's anxiety or when more coercive action is proposed when an alternative such as developing a supportive and containing network would require effort and resources. Beckett and Maynard (2005) emphasise that practitioners need to get to know themselves – particularly to avoid the unconscious or possibly conscious application of coercive powers as a means of punishment. They note that scenarios which may call for compulsory hospitalisation will likely be fraught with conflict and evoke difficult and upsetting emotions. Being able to work in a controlled way will require significant resources to cope with threats, anxiety and potential risk either for yourself, for your clients or for others.

Control, care and issues of oppression

The provision of compulsory mental health services would naturally seem more fraught in working with people and in communities where there have been experiences of racism, sexism and oppression. This would be the case in working with women, with people of colour, with persons who have been subject to forced migration or those exploited or coerced in other ways. To appreciate the complexity of our work, it is necessary to consider the social and political context of our practice also. In the following two passages developed by the Department of Health (2003 and 2005a), there is an effort to acknowledge and respond to mental health need for black and minority ethnic (BME) persons. Issues of control are noted and extremely relevant. The first is a passage from the document, *Inside outside: Improving mental health services for black and minority ethnic communities in England.*

> *We must begin by acknowledging the problems of mental health care as it is experienced by black and minority ethnic groups:*
>
> - *that there is an over-emphasis on institutional and coercive models of care;*
> - *that professional and organisational requirements are given priority over individual needs and rights;*
> - *that institutional racism exists within mental health care.*
>
> *To change this it is essential to place progressive community based mental health at the centre of service development and delivery. Those who use mental health services are identified, first and foremost, as citizens with mental health needs, which are understood as located in a social and cultural context.* (DoH, 2003, p7)

This passage ends emphasising that all persons accessing mental health care are considered 'citizens'. This reinforces human rights and the themes of enfranchisement and membership in society. By emphasising this, the authors highlight the importance of respecting these rights and the effort to limit more coercive actions while developing more culturally responsive community services.

The second passage offers recommendations for improved delivery of mental health services to BME service users and was published in the policy document, *Delivering race equality [DRE] in mental health care.* As you read it, you will note the significant themes related to fear, compulsory admission and seclusion.

> *The five year vision for DRE is that by 2010 mental health services should be characterised by:*
>
> - *Less fear of mental health services among BME communities and service users.*
> - *Increased satisfaction with services.*
> - *A reduction in the rate of admission of people from BME communities to psychiatric inpatient units.*
> - *A reduction in the disproportionate rates of compulsory detention of BME service users in inpatient units.*
> - *Fewer violent incidents that are secondary to inadequate treatment of mental illness.*
> - *A reduction in the use of seclusion in BME groups.*

- *The prevention of deaths in mental health services following physical intervention.*

- *More BME service users reaching self-reported states of recovery.*

- *A reduction in the ethnic disparities found in prison populations.*

- *A more balanced range of effective therapies, such as peer support services and psychotherapeutic and counselling treatments, as well as pharmacological interventions that are culturally appropriate and effective.*

- *A more active role for BME communities and BME service users in the training of professionals, in the development of mental health policy, and in the planning and provision of services.*

- *A workforce and organisation capable of delivering appropriate and responsive mental health services to BME communities.*

(DoH, 2005a)

These recommendations emphasise the challenge to improve mental healthcare in BME communities to ensure safety in care and the need to expand psychotherapeutic support and training.

Mental health law: History and application

Bartlett and Sandland's (2003) writing is both comprehensive and to the point as they consider and explore mental health legislation. The extract that follows provides a succinct socio-political context of mental health law, highlighting the coercive powers of the MHA as well as the changing ethos related to legislation and the perception of risk arising from mental health concerns.

EXTRACT ONE

Bartlett, P and Sandland, R (2003) Conceptualising mental health law, Chapter 1 and An overview of the contemporary mental health system, Chapter 3 in Mental health law, Policy and practice. 2nd edition. Oxford: Oxford University Press, pp71–2 and p26.

3.1 Introduction

The study of any area of law will be deficient unless the legal rules and procedures in question are studied in their operational context. This truism is, if anything, especially applicable to mental health law, the study of which can never pretend to be an end in itself. This is because law functions here, in the arena of mental health, not as an abstract discourse to be evaluated solely in terms of its internal coherence (although this is obviously an important question), but variously as the most formal and the most coercive expression of policy of the state towards persons with mental disorder; as permission and limitation; as the authorisation of a hierarchy which licenses some to invade or significantly curtail the freedom of others, possibly indefinitely. Mental health law is at once a mere tool, a function of policy in the same way

---

that a decision to build a new hospital or fund an out-reach programme is a function of policy; at the same time as it (as with other things) is an expression of values, or of compromise between competing values or considerations, which can themselves be unpacked to reveal an untidy conglomeration of political, economic, moral, professional, systematic, as well as legal and other forces.

Moreover, law must be seen as a source of the mental health system in its own right (Fennell, 1986). Law, in terms of discourse, ideas, structures, and so on, has had a constructive influence on the contemporary system, a point which has been underscored with the coming into force of the Human Rights Act 1998, and the various (if so far limited) changes in practice which litigation under that Act has brought. Thus, it can be said that a psychiatric facility is both a physical structure and a legal entity. There is little point in studying the operation of one without reference to the operation of the other. The same, it must follow, is true of those who enter the system. The patient, or client, is in some sense a product of the legal regime, just as he or she is a product also of social and medical policy and practice. The tradition in some of the literature has been to see these approaches as conflicting, This is not necessarily appropriate. As Roger Smith (1981) has shown, legal and medical discourses have had considerable similarity in the past. The mutual reliance of these discources in both the past and present will be a theme of this chapter, and indeed a recurring theme in this volume.

Crucial to understanding the contemporary system is an awareness of its history. The intimacy of the relationship between past, present, and future in the delivery of mental health services cannot be overestimated. Mental health policy over the last two and a half centuries or so has tended to be reactive, and as a consequence has had continually to live with ghosts, in terms of physical plant, professional discourse, vested interest and, to a greater or lesser extent, public perceptions. To provide an example, it has been (although the picture has become more complex in recent years) the policy of successive governments since at least 1960 that the preferred mode of delivery of mental health services, all things being equal, should be in the form of 'care in the community'. Yet throughout the entirety of that period mental health law, in the form of the Mental Health Acts of 1959 and the current Act of 1983, has been predicated on the view that that 'confinement' is the norm; a view which is an inheritance from earlier legislation that gave expression to such policies. In consequence, the 5–10 per cent or so of patients who are detained in hospital are administered under a relatively developed (albeit controversial) legal regime; but for the majority of hospital inpatients, and the many more who are treated in the community, the relevant law is sketchy and must be pieced together from any number of sources, many of which give expression to a different order of policy imperatives – concerned for example with the housing benefits and general health care systems – in addition to a hotch-potch of overlapping legislation, caselaw and other forms of guidance dealing specifically with community care for mental disorder. The result is both that the policy on care in the community is incoherent and that law and policy are out of kilter …

EXTRACT ONE *continued*

In the 1995 (Act) ... significant amendments were made to the Act regarding control of patients released into the community. The 1983 Act already made the provision of aftercare in the community mandatory for people who were released from civil confinement in psychiatric facilities (s 117). The 1995 amendments allowed service providers in the community to be appointed, who would ensure that the patient live in a specific place, attend a specific place for treatment (although there is no power to require that the person consent to the treatment), and could require access to the individual by other service providers (ss 25A-25J; ...). The particular relevance of these provisions in an historical context is the blurring of control between the institution and the community and, perhaps more significant, the debate surrounding the introduction of these provision(s) turned from a language of rights, the predominant discourse in the 1983 debates, to a language of risks. That latter language has proven central to the government's thinking regarding mental health reform in the last few years.

POINTS TO CONSIDER

- *What might have prompted a shift from thinking about rights to an emphasis on risks?*

- *Since 1995 there have been new amendments to the Mental Health Act. Review this topic at the Department of Health's website in the section devoted to policy and guidance where you will find* mental health *under* health *topics: www.doh.gov.uk. An overview, changes to the legislation and further information are available by clicking,* 'Reforming the Mental Health Act' *or at:* www.dh.gov.uk/en/Policyandguidance/Healthandsocialcaretopics/Mentalhealth/ DH_077352

Comment

Your thoughts might have instinctively considered a real or imagined question of safety by the media or the public which often leads to a clamp-down and greater control. As this extract ends, the authors note that the government, although it has emphasised rights in relation to mental health, has shifted more significantly to an understanding of mental health legislation in relation to risk. In 1995, this included aftercare provisions which were part of s 117. This will no longer be part of the newly amended Act, but the issue of managing risk remains an ongoing feature. In the new legislation, the Act introduces Compulsory Treatment Orders (CTOs) in the form of Supervised Community Treatment (SCT). Offering compulsory treatment outside of an institution is a relatively new means of care along the care–control continuum and was first developed in Australia in the mid-1980s. By offering treatment in the community as opposed to the hospital, there is an attempt to offer less restrictive and non-institutional services while maintaining a mandatory treatment component. These options do still represent coercion and the restriction of individual choice. Campbell, et al. (2006) reported that using SCTs in the UK may *lead to more coercive powers for mental health social workers and other professionals* (p1110). This article also highlighted that earlier amendments to the MHA included control in the community options, such as guardianship orders and supervised discharge orders, which achieved varying levels of success. Bartlett and Sandland (2003) noted that policy is not only a written statement but is manifested through service development and funding choices. They note that the government's position seems contradictory – particularly in relation to care in the community – as its policy supporting care in the community may be nullified through later funding decisions which do not provide monies to support treatment options in the community. Their contention that legislation seems to prioritise or favour institutional treatment undermines the policy of supporting community-based care. This contradiction may also be relevant in the policy of SCT, which extends care beyond an institution yet still preserves a coercive approach to treatment.

The updated Mental Health Act

The amendments to the Mental Health Act took effect in November 2008. One of these, the provision of SCTs, has been noted. The following extract, written by Nicola Glover-Thomas (2007), a reader in law, provides some context to the update of the MHA in an article which contrasts current and proposed legislation. As a background to the proposed changes, the article highlights the level of debate and consternation put forward by many groups, including user groups; providers, such as psychiatrists; and   independent-sector representatives. She also notes that amendments do not even reflect the desired outcomes of the groups – giving as an example the opposition from user groups to SCT. As you read, note the changes in relation to the definition of mental disorder and the parameters of detention prescribed in the Act.

EXTRACT TWO

Glover-Thomas, N (2007) A new 'new' Mental Health Act? Reflections on the proposed amendments to the Mental Health Act 1983. Clinical Ethics, 2 (1), pp29-30.

Definition of mental disorder

Current

Section 1 of the 1983 Act contains a general definition of mental disorder: mental illness, arrested or incomplete development of mind, psychopathic disorder and any other disorder or disability of mind. *Four specific categories of mental disorder are then described: mental illness, severe mental impairment, mental impairment, psychopathic disorder. Exclusions to the definition are also listed including immoral conduct, drug and alcohol dependency.*

Proposed

The Government intends to simplify this definition so that it applies throughout the Act. The four separate categories of mental disorder will be abolished as, in the past, these have prevented some individuals from being detained and compulsorily

---

treated. The removal of these categories may mean that some people who cannot now be brought under compulsion could be in the future, including those diagnosed with a personality disorder. A new provision will be included dealing specifically with learning disabilities. Learning disabilities will only be treated as a mental disorder for the purposes of the Act when it is associated with abnormally aggressive or seriously irresponsible conduct on the part of the person concerned.

The use of compulsion will be used in the future, as now, when the needs and risks associated with a patient make it appropriate rather than simply on the basis of a diagnostic label. The current exclusions within the MHA 1983 will be removed – it is now clearly recognized that immoral conduct and promiscuity are irrelevant to any definition of mental disorder ... The exclusion for sexual deviancy will also be removed because this has resulted in some patients who require compulsory care not receiving it because the disorder exhibits sexually deviant behaviour. The drug and alcohol dependency exclusion will be retained although reworded – merely being a drug addict or an alcoholic is not enough to be compulsorily detained. However, for many with mental disorders a dependency of some kind is also common. Where a dual diagnosis is indicated this will not prevent use of the legislation.

Criteria for detention

Current

Civil criteria to detain are separated into two [categories] – detention to assess under section 2 and detention to treat under section 3 of the 1983 Act. Assessment may take place for 28 days if an individual is suffering from a mental disorder which warrants detention and is necessary for the individual's own health or safety or the safety of others. Detention for treatment may take place initially for 6 months where an individual is suffering from one of the four specific categories of mental disorder which makes it appropriate for medical treatment in hospital to take place, for those with a psychopathic disorder or mental impairment, treatment is likely to alleviate or prevent a deterioration in the condition, and treatment is necessary for the health or safety of the individual or of others.

Proposed

As with the definition of mental disorder the Government proposes to simplify the process by introducing a new, appropriate treatment test which will apply to all longer-term powers of detention. The appropriate treatment test will require consideration of both clinical and associated factors, including whether treatment in hospital is culturally appropriate and what impact hospitalization may have on the patient and her ability to maintain contact with the family. The appropriate treatment test is said to strengthen the detention criteria by ensuring that:

- *... [p]ractitioners are required by law to consider an holistic assessment of whether appropriate treatment is available before detaining someone, and*

- *clinicians have to decide what is clinically appropriate in the same way as for any other patient.[3]*

It is intended that the appropriate treatment test will apply to all patients equally irrespective of diagnosis, as focus will be placed upon the needs of patients and the risk that is posed by the disorder.

The fundamental revision which arises from proposed changes to the detention criteria is the removal of the 'treatability test' as it is customarily known. This test has traditionally been used to ensure only those individuals who could benefit from treatment would be compulsorily detained under the 1983 Act, i.e. that there was a clinical purpose to detention. The Government views the treatability test as being counter to both the wider public's interests and those of mentally disordered individuals. In the past some patients have been labelled 'untreatable' and have, therefore, been denied treatment and care within the Act, most notably those with severe personality disorders. It is argued that the treatability test focuses too much on the potential outcome of treatment rather than the beneficial aspects of the treatment process as a whole. The holistic approach adopted by the proposed appropriate treatment test is intended to respond to these difficulties.

Much of the basic legislative structure within the 1983 Act will remain unchanged. It is hoped that this will enable the transition and incorporation of these amendments to be relatively straightforward while enabling practitioners to work with essentially familiar legal frameworks.

[3] *Department of Health (2006)* The Mental Health Bill, Plans to amend the Mental Health Act 1983: Briefing sheet, Criteria A2, Gateway ref: 6420, *p. 2.* www.dh.gov.uk

Comment

The extract begins by noting the change in definition in the amended MHA. You may need to read the earlier definition and its exclusions as well as the proposed definition to note the changes, since this article does not include those details. However, Glover-Thomas (2007) relates that the updated definition incorporates a broader picture of mental disorder which will not involve excluded diagnostic categories such as personality disorder. Whether this is a good thing or problematic is still uncertain; yet it does seem to offer an opportunity to respond to distress rather than to impose categories on certain distress.

Similarly, in the removal of the concept of treatability, the amended Act attempts to remove barriers to intervention. The idea of 'treatability' to some meant that those in distress, needing containment, may have been routinely excluded based on a decision by a provider that the intervention would not improve the outcome. This may have been perceived as a prejudicial view towards types of mental distress or the behaviours of those suffering. It also may mean that more coercive powers may now be applicable to groups of persons who would have to this point been free from them.

Following the thoughts expressed by both Bartlett and Sandland and Glover-Thomas, we are able to appreciate the flow of ideas into policy and legislation. The incorporation of ideas – to change the definition of mental disorder – further reinforces earlier arguments about the social construction of mental health concepts. This process of amending the

MHA also suggests how essential it is for practitioners to continually refine their knowledge base to remain current in their practice.

Mental capacity

Mental capacity refers to the mental processes of making decisions following a reasoned and deductive process that evaluates the benefits and problems of a given decision. To gain better perspective on how mental capacity is defined, Hotopf (2005), a professor of general hospital psychiatry, relates the law's wording which states that someone with mental capacity would be able to:

- *Understand information relevant to a decision.*
- *Retain that information.*
- *Use or weigh the information.*
- *Communicate a decision.*

(p580)

Those who lack these abilities are considered to lack mental capacity as a result of *an impairment of, or a disturbance in the functioning of, the brain or mind* (Mental Capacity Act 2005, cited by Hotopf, 2005, p580). The Mental Capacity Act 2005 as amended incorporates changes to the legal and practical concept of mental capacity. Its amendments have been implemented as of 2007; guidance for adhering to this Act is available from the Office of the Public Guardian, a new entity, and the Ministry of Justice. Prominent in understanding and working with the issue of mental capacity is the task of assessing it. Legislation, however, does not prescribe this; rather, it provides a definition and with its amendments attempts to provide safeguards and parameters for honouring the wishes of and delivering optimum service to individuals deemed to lack mental capacity.

As we have seen with the amended MHA, legislation is able to alter definitions and parameters. By refining how we assess mental capacity and amending legislation, there is an attempt by society to respond to the needs of those with problems in decision-making. As this illustrates, *mental capacity legislation has … been developed to deal with the needs of people with cognitive difficulties – either due to learning disability or dementia* (Hotopf, 2005, p581). Though this specifically links to conditions such as learning disability or dementia which involves loss of memory, problem-solving and other cognitive abilities such as planning, there are other circumstances which may require an evaluation of capacity. In Hotopf's (2005) article, this is noted in medical settings when persons are admitted, treated as outpatients or seen in A & E departments, and may involve either permanent or temporary cognitive difficulties. Hotopf in research with colleagues (Raymont, et al., 2004, cited by Hotopf, 2005) conducted a study in which 159 inpatients being treated for an acute medical condition were interviewed. Findings revealed that *31%...were judged according to English legal standards to lack mental capacity*. Significantly, they found that only 25% of those deemed to lack mental capacity were assessed *as such by their treating clinical teams* (Raymont, et al., 2004, p582 cited by Hotopf, 2005). As this is one study, it is not fair or appropriate to generalise this finding; however, it does offer an important consideration as it highlights that practitioners may not be accurately identifying the true numbers of persons lacking capacity.

The following extract by Williamson (2007) offers some context to the revised and amended Mental Capacity Act 2005. Several important changes have been made to the Act, including changes to how persons choose a representative to make decisions for them in advance and the development of advocacy services to support people whose capacity is diminished. Williamson (2007) is writing to identify how the Mental Capacity Act 2005 will be used to protect individuals deemed to lack mental capacity. It is also important to note that he is writing as a stakeholder and communications manager based in the Mental Capacity Implementation Programme of the Department for Constitutional Affairs.

EXTRACT THREE

Williamson, T (2007) Capacity to protect – the Mental Capacity Act explained. Journal of Adult Protection, 9 (1), 26–30.

Principles of the Act

The first principles in the Mental Capacity Act reinforce the importance of the autonomy of the individual to make decisions for themselves, always starting from the presumption that individuals have the capacity to make decisions for themselves, providing as much support as possible to enable people to make decisions for themselves and not assuming someone lacks capacity because they make an 'unwise' decision. The third principle could prove particularly important in the context of adult protection because it allows people to make decisions that their carers or professionals may fundamentally disagree with, but would have to accept, providing that it could be shown that the person had the capacity to make the decisions (him or her)self.

The fourth and fifth principles of the Act relate to people who lack the capacity to make a particular decision. Decisions or actions taken on behalf of a person who lacks capacity must always be done in the person's best interests and such decisions or actions must restrict the person's rights and freedoms as little as possible ...

Determining best interests

Where someone is found to lack capacity to make a particular decision, such as consent to care or treatment, the Act allows that to be provided to the person as long as it is in their best interests. The process of establishing a person's best interests is carefully defined in the Act, in the form of a non-exhaustive list of factors that provides a starting point. As much effort as possible should be made to find out the person's views regarding the decision to be taken, taking into account their known wishes and feelings, beliefs and values, and any written statements they may have made. Family members and others involved in their care must be consulted if practicable and appropriate – thereby creating the legal right for families to be consulted in these situations. In addition, it must always be in the best interests of the person who lacks capacity, not what the decision-maker would want to do if they were the person who lacked capacity ...

Other safeguards

Although the Act does not create a formal procedure for assessing capacity or determining best interests it does create a number of organisational safeguards for dealing with mental capacity issues. It creates a new Court of Protection that will replace the existing one, and has a jurisdiction to cover all issues concerning mental capacity ... The Court will be the final arbiter in dealing with disputes and disagreements, including being able to rule on whether someone has capacity or not, and dealing with both financial and personal welfare/health decisions involving someone who lacks capacity. The Court will be able to make rulings on such matters, as well as being able to appoint 'deputies', particularly where a series of decisions needs to be made on behalf of a person who lacks capacity, but there is no agreement among the parties involved in the decision-making processes. Deputies will replace the existing system of 'receivers' who currently make decisions relating to the property and financial affairs of someone who lacks capacity. The Court will have specially trained staff and judiciary, and will be able to hold hearings in a number of locations around the country ...

A concern that some supporters of the Act expressed when it was still in draft form was that it contained insufficient provision to both assist and protect people who lacked capacity, particularly where important decisions were involved. This has been addressed by the inclusion in the Act of a new Independent Mental Capacity Advocate (IMCA) service – the first time that there has been a statutory right to advocacy. IMCAs will support people who lack capacity and have no family or friends with whom it is appropriate to consult regarding their best interests, when important decisions need to be made regarding serious medical treatment or the provision of residential or hospital accommodation. An IMCA must be involved in these situations although their role is to ascertain and represent, as far as is possible, the views of the person, not to make the actual decision. NHS bodies and local authorities have also been given powers to extend the use of IMCAs to include decisions involving care reviews where someone is in hospital or residential care, and also in adult protection cases involving someone who lacks capacity. For the latter, the local authority or NHS body could involve an IMCA irrespective of whether or not they have family or friends who could be consulted ...

Using your access to the internet, download and read this PDF file which has been developed by the Office of the Public Guardian in relation to mental capacity. www.publicguardian.gov.uk/docs/making-decisions-opg603-1207.pdf

- How would you approach assessing someone's mental capacity?

- How would you discuss making a lasting power of attorney with someone?

- Would you feel comfortable addressing and inquiring about a client's advanced directives?

Comment

The development of and recent revisions to the Mental Capacity Act respond to the growing need to deliver an appropriate level of service to those lacking capacity. A further motivation from the government to amend this Act was the identified gap in ensuring service users' rights to liberty as highlighted by the Bournewood case (see Chapter 1). As part of your reflection, you were asked to consider your possible role in assessing someone's capacity; in addition, you were asked to consider how you might address the delicate issues of lasting power of attorney and forward planning by an individual in relation to future care needs. I wonder if you feel skilled or competent enough to consider the matter of capacity. You may figuratively draw back from engaging in this, concluding that it is a medical colleague's responsibility. In some ways this is the case; yet, as noted by Hotopf (2005, p581), mental capacity is a *legal, clinical, ethical and social construct* and, as such, needs to be understood in the context of social work practice. The matter of mental capacity will more likely arise in certain service contexts, such as learning disability or working with older adults. I mention the latter owing to the greater incidence of cognitive decline in that group of service users, but it is critical that practitioners who work with other client groups do not disregard this information or consider it irrelevant. Dementia is possible in earlier life and may be associated with certain diseases, such as later-stage human immunodeficiency virus (HIV) infection, or with head or brain trauma from accidents. Significantly, loss or diminishment of capacity may be transient or fixed. When we think more broadly about the variety of factors that could contribute to loss of capacity, it becomes apparent that these conditions or factors could affect broader numbers of individuals. As a result, becoming familiar with this will support your practice.

Significant in this extract and in the policy document is the inclusion in law of an advocacy service. The IMCA is considered an innovation and a means of protecting the rights of those with mental incapacity. The further helpful feature in refining this legislation is the option for persons to make choices proactively about selecting an individual or party to act for them through a lasting power of attorney. The benefit of this for those who develop mental incapacity is that it offers a written means of documenting wishes regarding health or financial decisions. Also it will be immeasurably helpful to practitioners to be able to work to honour the wishes and plans of individuals rather than needing to speculate about how to proceed or to rely on the wishes of a third party.

As part of your reflection, you were invited to consider how it might feel if you were to engage in this discussion. Clearly, it is often difficult for most people, if not all of us, to engage in thinking about a future when we will not be able to function. We would prefer to avoid this, or we believe that our clients would prefer to avoid this. We may think that it would be macabre or rude to speak about illness, or that it would impinge on someone's hope by mentioning the possible future lack of health and the expectation of disability. Certainly this is a delicate area, as suggested; however, it is an area that you may need to consider understanding more fully to enhance your level of comfort in discussing these matters with clients, as there will be clients who want and need to talk about this. It is important to gain skill in discerning when this topic is appropriate to consider. By helping others to think about their ability to make decisions, you will be offering an opportunity for individuals to ensure that their wishes and rights are respected if or when their capacity is diminished.

Roles and responsibilities

The MHA as amended involves several significant changes. One of these will expand the types of professions that will be involved in the application of the law's compulsory powers. As a student or qualified social worker, you may be familiar with the term Approved Social Worker, commonly known as an ASW, which is an agent of the local authority. This role involves assessing persons under the MHA and making conclusions about mandatory assessment or treatment in the context of a hospital. Approved social workers would need to be in possession of specialist knowledge about the impact of mental health for individuals in need and in the application of the MHA.

Fakhoury and Wright (2004) completed a postal survey of ASWs in the UK to investigate their needs in relation to training and up-to-date information and their interaction with other professionals. Such a study is useful for you to read in full as it will help you to appreciate how researchers identify an area of inquiry, devise a research strategy and pursue data gathering before reviewing the data and reporting findings. The following extract is limited to their findings, but you may wish to seek out the whole article.

EXTRACT FOUR

Fakhoury, W and Wright, D (2004) A national survey of Approved Social Workers in the UK: Information, communication and training needs. British Journal of Social Work, 34 (5), 673–4.

Although ASWs play an important part in the delivery of care to people with mental health problems, their role is not separate from the role of other community mental health professionals. They are placed in specialist multidisciplinary mental health teams whose success in community care depends on elements such as information sharing, successful co-ordination of services, and effective communication with other members of the team. Our findings indicate major problems with these elements, with reported lack of time and resources, and bureaucracy, as barriers to the successful co-ordination of services. Communication with other professionals is also another problem, especially when it comes to co-ordinating with GPs. The respondents indicated that GPs were the most difficult to be accessed and the least likely to have been helpful when accessed. These results are worrying, not least because ASWs and GPs are supposed to be working closely together as members of the community care team. Evidence in the literature suggests that primary care professionals involved in mental health care have problems in collaborative working and effective communication, and need more training in mental health (Ford et al., 1997). These may have negatively impacted on the relationship of these professionals with members of the CMHT including ASWs. However, particular problems seem to exist between GPs and social workers. Differences in perception regarding duties for compulsory admissions and collaborations between the two were reported in the literature, as were problems of attitudes and relationships (appearing when differences arose between ASWs and GPs on the nature/seriousness of a case) and problems of procedures (appearing when knowledge of legal procedures is needed for sectioning) (Quinn, 1992). Thomas and Corney (1993) reported that inadequate feedback and difficulty with contact were the major problems affecting the relationship between GPs and ASWs. Given this, one would therefore recommend joint ASW/GP training about their respective roles under the Mental Health Act legislation, about increasing ASWs' access to GPs, and about enhancing communication between these two professions. Strategies to achieve better working relationships should be developed, while taking into account the heavy workload and the time restriction under which ASWs' and GPs work, and probably in consultation with GPs' practice managers who could play a role in reducing the barriers (bureaucracy in particular) for ASWs access to GPs.

In conclusion, this national UK survey showed that ASWs, like other members of the community care team, have communication, information and training needs that should be investigated. A proper discussion with a nationally representative sample of ASWs on how to address these needs is recommended. Input from other mental health professionals, particularly those operating at the community level, on how to reduce bureaucracy and increase contact and communication among the community care team members is encouraged. In short, ASWs are valued professionals whose needs should be addressed if we are to maintain their competence.

Comment

The findings from the survey of ASWs present a bleak, perhaps too real, picture of the difficulty of professional demands and interdisciplinary collaboration. In the survey, there is a finding of problems in both attitudes and relationships between ASWs and GPs as well as difficulty in interpretation of the legislation. Fakhoury and Wright (2004) hypothesised that working with mental health need may represent a challenge in primary care. This may explain some of the difficulty in this interaction; however, further contributing factors may be structural problems, inadequacies and time pressures required under the MHA to respond to psychiatric crisis and to assess under the MHA, which would undoubtedly prompt anxieties due to time pressure.

Under the MHA 2007, the professions that will perform this task – which has heretofore been completed by specially trained ASWs – will expand and include clinical psychologists, registered mental nurses and occupational therapists. Persons from these professions will also undergo more specialised training in mental health and the application of the MHA that social workers have historically completed. After this, with appropriate registration, they will be given the rubric of Approved Mental Health Professional (AMHP).

There will no doubt be repercussions for the social work profession – might this be considered an attack on social work or is it an appropriate development to respond to the dearth of ASWs in many jurisdictions, particularly in London? Will the multidisciplinary nature of the AMHP group help to facilitate a greater understanding and response to acute mental health distress? Critics of the change suggest that the medical perspective is all too prominent in psychiatric treatment currently, and suspect that this widening of professions will serve to reinforce this. Alternatively, the perspectives of occupational therapists and clinical psychologists may stimulate greater awareness about alternatives to hospitalisation, medication and medical intervention. The current proposed draft in relation to defining the authorisation of persons to act as AMHPs includes several key competencies which include the application of values, knowledge and skills. Practitioners will need knowledge in relation to legislation, policy and mental distress while being able to apply skills in working in partnership and in communication of informed decisions. The following relates the value orientation of those working in the AMHP role.

- *The ability to identify, challenge and, where possible, redress discrimination and inequality in all its forms in relation to AMHP practice.*
- *Understanding and respect for diversity and the ability to identify and counter any decision which may be based upon oppressive practice.*
- *Respect for individuals' qualities, abilities and diverse backgrounds, enabling them to contribute to decisions which affect their quality of life and which may affect their liberty.*
- *Promotion of the rights, dignity and self determination of individuals consistent with their own needs and wishes.*
- *Sensitivity to individuals' needs for personal respect, choice, dignity and privacy while exercising the AMHP role.*

(The Mental Health (Approval of Persons to be Approved Mental Health Professionals) Regulations 2007. Order 2007, p4)

The value statements suggest an appreciation of working across culture and of the need to ensure self-determination. By incorporating specific values material into the work of the AMHP, the competence structure seems to be embracing social work values and acknowledging the necessity for humane, culturally responsive and informed service even when needing to provide compulsory care.

C H A P T E R   S U M M A R Y

As the last extract indicates, there is often conflict and discomfort in considering taking and in taking coercive action in relation to the lives of others. This was evident in the inquiry into the dimensions of care and control which Beckett and Maynard (2005) questioned as distinct concepts, preferring to consider the more coercive and constraining tasks of control as care. Such a conceptualisation represents a useful way of thinking about care in the context of working with acute mental distress which stems from mental health need, or mental disorder as enshrined in the Mental Health Act 2007, or working with those lacking or needing to consider the loss of mental capacity in relation to the Mental Capacity Act 2005. These new developments and new amendments are meant to capture the changing elements of society; yet the changes create difficulties for practitioners in relevant work contexts. They, perhaps, also create conflict between professionals in needing, but finding it difficult or onerous, to take professional responsibility in relation to these two pieces of legislation.

Prominent in this discussion was the adoption of the Human Rights Act 1989, which stimulated a review of practice and moreover prompted a review of legislation in the UK following multiple legal challenges. New amendments and developments in both the Mental Health Act 2007 and the Mental Capacity Act 2005 will undoubtedly need challenge and refinement in order to respond to those living with mental health need, the practitioners involved in delivering services, and the public. The prospect of challenge and revision to the law represents the most reassuring aspect of this chapter because it suggests that inequity and the imposition of abusively coercive actions will be held in check. Social work practitioners have been among those challenging the imposition of control and coercion and will need to remain involved in this important role to ensure that care is never too controlling.

FURTHER READING

Brown, R (2009) *The Approved Mental Health Practitioner's guide to mental health law*. Exeter: Learning Matters.

Brown, R and Barber, P (2008) *The social worker's guide to the Mental Capacity Act 2005*. Exeter: Learning Matters.

Johns, R (2006) *Using the law in social work*. Exeter: Learning Matters.

White, R, Broadbent, G and Brown, K (2007) *Law and the social work practitioner*. Exeter: Learning Matters.

The previous texts represent both entry-level and more advanced reading on this topic.

Brayne, H and Carr, H (2005) *Law for social workers*. 9th edition. Oxford: Oxford University Press.

The previous text provides a detailed overview of legislation across all specialisations; Chapter 17 specifically considers the role of legislation for adults in relation to hospitalisation and guardianship and, though not fully current, offers a thorough foundation to this complex topic.

WEBSITES

www.doh.gov.uk

www.nimhe.csip.org.uk – The site for the National Institute for Mental Health in England.

www.publicguardian.gov.uk

www.opsi.gov.uk/acts/acts2007/ukpga_20070012_en_1 – The online site for the text of the Mental Health Act 2007.

Chapter 4
Mental health needs of children and adolescents

Introduction

Development in early life and through adolescence is marked by periods of rapid change, learning and identity formation. In this period of the life course, problems that affect learning, behaviour and social and emotional development will present challenges for both individual children and adolescents and their family systems immediately and, if not resolved, may have ongoing consequences for a child's continued development. The government's approach to children's health and well-being is represented by the policy guidance, *Every Child Matters* (Department for Education and Skills, 2003), and ensuing service changes, such as the delivery of integrated care through Children's Trusts, introduced by the Children Act 2004. In the policy, the government sets out five aims to support young people's development. The five aims each have implications for mental health and well-being.

- *Be healthy.*
- *Stay safe.*
- *Enjoy and achieve.*
- *Make a positive contribution.*
- *Achieve economic well-being.*

(DCSF, 2005, n.p.)

With these highlighted, we are all called to be aware and informed of these outcomes for children's development.

In a more specialised response to the mental health needs of young people, the government produced the *National Service Framework for Children, Young People and Maternity Services* (NSF) (Department of Health and Department for Education and Skills, 2004), devoting Standard 9 to the *Mental health and psychological well-being of children and young people*. The framework represents a comprehensive attempt to address mental health needs from early years through adolescence, to consider the involvement of young people and their families or carers and to address the learning and training needs of providers of services. In its vision statement, it sets out the following.

We want to see:

- *An improvement in the mental health of all children and young people.*
- *That multi-agency services, working in partnership, promote the mental health of all children and young people, provide early intervention and also meet the needs of children and young people with established or complex problems.*
- *That all children, young people and their families have access to mental health care based upon the best available evidence and provided by staff with an appropriate range of skills and competencies.*

(DoH and DfES, 2004, n.p.)

As a vision statement, the above sets a comprehensive service approach and far-reaching goals. For your learning, we are focused on a smaller and more manageable objective which involves contributing to your growing awareness. Through reading this chapter, you will be able to consider several relevant themes affecting mental health in childhood and adolescence and will, hopefully, through reflection come to understand these in greater depth so that you will be able to incorporate this knowledge into your practice.

The prevalence of mental health need in young people

Mental health need in early life encompasses a range of difficulties. As with adults, children may experience problems in mood, have developmental difficulties, suffer from the effects of trauma and intrusion, and engage in behaviours that could harm themselves and affect their well-being. Also, similar to adults, there will be a range of severity in the difficulties they are experiencing and varying services to respond to the identified need or needs.

Service use data from the Department of Health (2006, n.p.) suggests that there was an 8 per cent increase in *cases handled by Children and Adolescent Mental Health Services* (CAMHS) in the year 2005. The same report also highlighted that *there are still considerable variations across England in the availability and length of wait for services*. This follows the NSF (DoH, 2004) noted above and its emphasis on improving the healthcare needs of children and young people, particularly on their mental, emotional and psychological health. Southall (2005, p1) notes that the NSF *has a focus on achieving common standards across the country and developing services through improvements, investment, expansion and reform over a ten-year period*. The earlier citation notes an increase in service delivery; however, there appear to be regional gaps and delays to access services, suggesting the continued need for investment and service expansion.

Data from the NSF (DoH, 2004) indicates that up to one million children have mental health problems; this means that 1 in 12 children – based on a census figure of 12 million children in England at the time of the report – has a mental health need. Such a finding seems significant. However, we need to understand this in terms of the context of childhood and adolescence in the twenty-first century. There is a growing understanding of the psychological pressures children face; studies inquire about the link between bullying and depression (West and Salmon, 2000) and media reports highlight the impact of bullying and exclusion for children in the contained but mandatory social setting of the school. A recent article reports that *conduct disorders are the largest single group of psychiatric disorders in children and adolescents, and they are the main reasons for referral to* CAMHS (Community Care, 2008, p24); yet there are no reported data to substantiate this. The effects of physical, sexual and emotional abuse as well as the impact of neglect have varying but documented effects both in the shorter and longer term on children's psychological development (Edgeworth and Carr, 2000). In addition, there seems to be an increase in violence and aggression which is acted out in age-similar peer groups, that there is greater substance use among young people and that it begins earlier; it also seems that there is an increasing incidence of self-harm, eating disorders and problems of attention and concentration which, in the latter, are frequently treated psychotropically, through the prescription of medication. Additional factors contributing to mental health distress in young people and children will stem from the effects of stress, genetic predisposition and the impact of environmental and systemic changes, such as loss, bereavement or disruption. Setting this context, we may be better able to understand the breadth, variety and varying severity of the emotional and psychological challenges present for young people, some of which will be highlighted in this chapter.

Understanding young people's mental health need

In their review of efficacious interventions for children who have experienced abuse, Edgeworth and Carr (2000, p17) define neglect as *the passive ignoring of the child's physical and psychological needs*. They go on to define needs as: *feeding, clothing and shelter; safety; nurturance; intellectual stimulation; social interaction and conversation; appropriate limit setting and discipline and age-appropriate opportunities for autonomy and independence.* They also describe what constitutes physical, sexual and emotional abuse, offering further specificity in relation to frequency, duration, intrusiveness and whether the perpetrator is a family member or not. Though the factor of abuse or neglect will fortunately not be the lived experience of all children with mental health needs, nor will those who have experienced this necessarily develop mental health difficulties, it does seem significant to me that the needs of children and adolescents in relation to their mental health and emotional development are for safety and security at a very basic level. From the earliest interaction between an infant and its primary caregiver, the contract that is in place or should be in place ensures a child's well-being. Thinking about care at such a fragile time in a human being's life course, in the earliest years, I recall the work of developmental theorists and practitioners who have contributed to our understanding of human emotional and psychological development. In working with young people, it seems essential to have a broad understanding of physical and emotional development and the capacity to apply and consider a range of concepts including attachment and psychodynamic theory, social learning, cognitive development, and systems theories. Fundamentally, it seems essential to highlight and consider the containing, didactic and facilitating nature of the child and caregiver bond as we use a variety of extracts to consider young people's mental health needs.

In the first extract, Kerfoot (2005) writes about mental health need in 'looked after' children and reviews studies documenting the prevalence of mental health need in this group. As this is a group of young people whose lived experience involves contact with social work practitioners over shorter- or longer-term periods, it will be necessary for you as students and practitioners to appreciate the implications of local authority care and the life circumstances that may contribute to this. Subsequently, Walker (2003) invites us to be cognisant of children's development in our assessment of young people and to embark on a multifaceted approach in our assessments, one that appreciates and incorporates the complexity and diversity in the systems in which children are living.

As attachment theory plays such a central role in understanding the development of children, it seemed useful to revisit this through an article by Wright, Briggs and Behringer (2005) in which they explore the idea of the impact of attachment experiences from early life on psychological difficulties in adolescents. They particularly consider a likely link between adolescents who report suicidal ideation or preoccupation with death and self-injury and earlier attachment inadequacies. By working with the narratives spoken directly by the adolescent participants in the study, the authors conceptualise a way of understanding adolescents' emotional lives in relation to the quality of their relationships to attachment figures. Building on this, Honig (2007) considers the importance of including the family in eating disorder treatment. The excerpt offers some context to understanding eating disorders, primarily anorexia nervosa, and its treatment through family interventions such as multi-family group therapy.

Mental health need in those 'looked after'

The phenomenon of being 'looked after' suggests the breakdown or problem in the care-giving process which may prompt children to be taken from parental care into care by others. Kerfoot (2005), prefacing the role of the state in the needs of children, writes *the Children Act 1989 was arguably the most comprehensive and far-reaching piece of legislation that Parliament had ever enacted in relation to children. Its effects on the future organisation, planning, provision, and delivery of services for children and their families was profound, as were its effects upon other agencies having responsibilities towards children* (p333). In the event that family caregiving may need to stop permanently or temporarily, the local authority social services department and, in direct and practical ways, the social workers employed by them must step in to assess, arrange and plan for the looking after of children in many cases by a governmental entity or its agents – foster carers and residential units. Similar to this and linked will be care in secure units where, in effect, parental authority is superseded by the institution.

As you will note in the following extract, there are a relatively small number of children who are in the care of local authorities when compared with the population of children on the whole. That is not to say, however, that the contributing factors that have brought this group of children into care will not have an impact – perhaps in less intensive ways – on other children and their mental health also.

EXTRACT ONE

Kerfoot, M (2005) Children 'looked after' by the state. Chapter 22 in Williams, R and Kerfoot, M (eds) (2005) Child and adolescent mental health services: Strategy, planning, delivery and evaluation. Oxford: Oxford University Press, pp333–4.

Epidemiology

In the year ending 31 March 2000, there were 58 100 children 'looked after' by local authorities in England (Department of Health 2001) and this represents around 0.5% of the total child population. The figure represents an increase of 5% on the previous year, and is an increase of 18% on figures published in 1994 (Wolkind and Rushton 1994). Around 65% of children looked after are placed with foster families and this proportion has changed little in recent years, while around 11% are in residential provision ...

Children who are looked after by local authorites have some of the highest rates of mental disorder when compared with young people in the general population. A study of children in care in Oxfordshire (McCann et al. 1996) gave a total prevalence of psychiatric disorder of 67% compared with 15% in a matched control sample derived from the same schools. Of those who scored for psychiatric disorder, 79% scored for major disorder. The study also showed that the distribution of disorders is different for those children placed in residential units (96%) and those placed in foster care (57%). The most common disorders were conduct disorder (28%), over-anxious disorder (26%), and depressive disorder (23%). A study from Glasgow of children entering the care system (Dimigen et al. 1990) also found that significant levels of mental disorder that was largely untreated, since many were not being referred for psychological interventions. The study highlighted a need for early-intervention policies to help these

---

EXTRACT ONE *continued*

vulnerable children and effective assessment through multidisciplinary discussion and strategic planning. The health needs and provision of healthcare to school age children in local authority care were compared, in a recent study, to those of children living at home (Williams et al. 2001). The study concluded that the overall healthcare of children who had been established in care for more than six months was significantly worse than for those living in their own homes, particularly with regard to emotional and behavioural health. The study highlighted the difficulty of gaining access to CAMHS once a problem had been identified, but also the high mobility in some social services that may mean a child is moved on while still waiting to be seen by CAMHS. It is an inevitable consequence, in some cases, that disturbed behaviour left untreated is very likely to contribute to placement breakdown and further disruption to the child.

A recent study undertaken in Leeds (Nicholas et al. 2003) explored the current and past contacts of children being looked after, with child and adolescent mental health services. Of the 177 children in the study, 64% had been in contact with these services during the past five years, and 27% had current contact with child mental health services. The authors concluded that the pattern of service delivery locally was changing from one of direct contract between users and services, to one of CAMHS consultation with, and training of, staff in residential children's homes.

POINTS TO CONSIDER

The following reflective task involves writing. This approach to reflection has been developed by Gillie Bolton (2005), author of Reflective practice: Writing and professional development, *and involves a period of free-flow writing and then a longer period of free-flow writing focused on a specific topic. I have adapted one of Bolton's exercises for your use here, but the process and approach are Bolton's.*

1. *To begin, I would ask you to write whatever comes to your mind for four minutes. Do not censor your thoughts or adhere to grammar or spelling rules; for this, you are free to write whatever you wish.*

2. *For the following writing exercise, I would ask you to take yourself back to your late childhood – to age nine or ten – and consider what would be the impact for you if you had to leave your family to be looked after by the local authority. What are your reactions? How might you feel? What will you be leaving? How would you imagine this would affect your life at that time?*

3. *As before, try not to censor yourself; simply allow yourself to write freely in response to the title below, allowing yourself to inhabit the experience of being looked after and capturing in words some of the ideas and emotions mobilised by the preceding questions in point 1. (Adapted from Bolton, 2005, pp147–8)*

Taking about eight to ten minutes, respond to the following in writing.

The time I was looked after

Comment

The data that Kerfoot (2005) presented in discussing the epidemiology of mental health difficulties in children within local authority care showed that 67 per cent of children in a study in Oxfordshire (McCann, et al., 1996) were described as having a psychiatric disorder; while, a more recent study (Nicholas, et al., 2003) which took place in Leeds indicated that 64 per cent of the children in the study had had contact with specialist child and adolescent mental health services. The Oxfordshire data offered a comparison sample – 67 per cent of looked after children possessed mental health difficulties versus 15 per cent in the general population, a rate that is over four times higher.

In the exercise that followed the extract, you were invited to place yourself – through your imagination – in the experience of a child who experiences local authority care. By engaging in this task, you also engage with the difficult and raw reality of family distress, the types of problems that may lead to the need for local authority care, and the varied reactions that children may have in relation to being removed from their family environment to live in an alternate setting. The following categories developed in the publication, *A handbook on child and adolescent mental health* (DoH and DE, 1995), suggest some of the life circumstances that may contribute to greater susceptibility to mental health need in children and their families:

- *young offenders and children from a criminal background;*
- *children who are being looked after by the local authority or who have recently ended a period of public care;*
- *children with learning difficulties;*
- *children with emotional and behavioural difficulties;*
- *children who have been sexually, physically or emotionally abused;*
- *children with chronic physical illness;*
- *children with a physical disability;*
- *children with sensory impairments;*
- *children of parents with mental illness;*
- *children of parents with a substance abuse problem;*
- *children who have experienced or witnessed sudden and extreme trauma;*
- *children who are refugees.*

Though this may be a useful listing, there is a risk with any list of categories that it may suggest that mental health difficulties and distress only arise for people in these situations. This would clearly be problematic as it would restrict our understanding of the breadth and complexity of mental health need among children. It may also divert our attention from other people who do not experience any of these circumstances but who may develop emotional or psychological distress due to other factors. In this listing for instance, some of the categories – though listed discretely – may in fact be correlated. Children who are refugees may of necessity be placed in local authority living arrangements, which may compound the emotional distress of forced removal. The multiple and interrelated effects of both the experience of fleeing a country experiencing war and/or political unrest and the experience of state-provided care may jointly contribute to mental health need. Respecting these caveats, though, the list does highlight issues of vulnerability and reinforces Kerfoot's (2005) report.

In addition, it seems important – particularly in writing this book and thinking from a strengths-based and inclusive perspective about those living with mental distress – to emphasise that children living in families where there is mental health need or substance use in parents will not necessarily be disadvantaged or experience deleterious effects. It may be more accurate to consider that the painful and troubling impact for both children and their parents would likely stem from excessive and intrusive substance misuse and untreated and debilitating mental health distress. This emphasises how important it is for professionals working with children and families to be able to gauge and understand factors that undermine parental caregiving and to forge collaborative partnerships with mental health and substance-misuse providers.

In thinking about parental mental health distress, it also seems relevant to consider the implications for the well-being and development of children and adolescents if they are engaged in caring for a parent; at times, young carers may have their ability to develop compromised if care demands are too great. Each of these influences will affect mental health need. Social work practitioners particularly should look for interventions to promote resilience in young people in these situations. Finally, as the numbers of young people in local authority care increases, our work as social work practitioners involves not only paying closer attention to their mental health needs but also we, along with staff in other areas of children's services, need to work with greater attentiveness to the provision of preventative and early intervention services.

Assessing mental health in young people

Understanding the impact of a mental health problem will be facilitated if you are able to really appreciate the experience of the child or young person and their family. If you think back to your ideas as you placed yourself in the context of being looked after, some of you may have determined that such an outcome was the most beneficial as you considered circumstances in your imagined life. For some children, placement may be a relief and the only option to secure safety and to develop greater potential. Using judgement to make the weighty decision to place a child into local authority care, or to identify and refer to supportive or therapeutic providers, stems entirely from the quality and comprehensiveness of your assessment and your grasp of the experience of the young person and their family or care context.

Walker (2003) in the following extract emphasises the importance of assessment, particularly in relation to children's mental health needs. He highlights the important themes that will be central in this work, such as understanding a child's developmental stage including needs and capabilities, recognising relevant cultural factors, and appreciating and inquiring about family and systemic variables. Walker (2003, 2004) also argues for a broad, multifaceted approach to assessment so that it is informed by the application of theory beyond that which is often used, such as attachment theory. Walker's recommendation is to engage in psychosocial work that appreciates the intrapsychic and emotional components of a child's development and is complemented by an awareness and understanding of the impact of sociocultural and sociopolitical variables, particularly those that are influencing the wider system in which the child lives in terms of community affiliation and familial cultural worldview.

Walker, S (2003) Assessing and understanding. Chapter 3 in **Social work and child and adolescent mental health.** *Lyme Regis: Russell House, pp36–7, 42–3 and 48–9.*

Principles underlying assessment

A development approach to assesment in child and adolescent mental health is a helpful base from which to build up a picture of the problem being presented and the prospects for appropriate intervention (Rutter et al., 1994). Children behave differently at different ages and some broad understanding of the range of expected behaviours expected at each age can assist in judging the nature of the problem. It is also useful to assess the severity of the problem by considering how far the course of psychological development has been interrupted …

Different phases of development are associated with different stresses and susceptibilities, which must be taken into account during assessment. For example very young children are prone to adverse reactions to hospital admission, or prolonged separation, while adolescents can be vulnerable to profound depressive mood swings. If social workers are to understand how problems have arisen they must clarify, or seek access to expertise that can help explain and distinguish what is normal from what is not. Normal in this sense means normal to that of a similar child, in that situation from that culture. Equally, it is important to disentangle direct and indirect effects and linking events, capacities and behaviours. Outcomes can be mediated or moderated by other concurrent factors.

It is not just individual children's capacities that are important but also the content of emotions and relationships. The timing of experiences influences their impact because of the stage of psychological capacity that are emerging and the relevance such as the response of others. There may be continuities and discontinuities in outward behaviour which need to be understood in the context of continuity and discontinuity in the environment. It is insufficient to know that major life events such as starting school, the birth of a sibling, or leaving home have occurred. It is crucial to understand individual differences in the meaning attached to such transitions (Cox, 1994).

The risk in relying on generalisations and assumptions about normality is that social workers will condense knowledge into pragmatic and quickly available guidelines to their practice. This can result in stereotyping, superficial assessment, and lead to inflexible, routinised practice. On the other hand trying to juggle all the infinite number of variables, nuances, distinctions, and disparate factors involved in a child or young person's experience is likely to lead to unhelpful paralysis. Accessing a diverse range of opinion, reviewing judgements, testing hypotheses, and bearing some uncertainty can help in this complex work. Each situation is unique and so is each individual social worker. Therefore the development of personal insight is crucial for the social worker involved …

EXTRACT TWO *continued*

Social workers need to embrace a more holistic approach seeking to identify and amplify strengths, coping strategies, alternative community resources, and user perceptions. It has been established that a confluence of several risk factors in childhood can create the conditions for later psycho-social difficulty, including socio-economic disadvantage, child abuse, and parental mental illness. However, there are protective mechanisms that can mitigate that chance of some children going on to develop anti-social behaviour or serious mental health problems.

A thorough assessment of risk and resilience factors is advocated (Rutter, 1985). These include the child's response to stress being determined by the capacity to appraise and attach meaning to their situation. Age-related susceptibilities that permit older children to use their greater understanding compared to younger children need to be understood. How a child deals with adversity either actively or reactively, and the ability to act positively, is a function of self-esteem and feelings or self-efficacy rather than indicating any inherent problem-solving skills. Features as varied as secure stable affectionate relationships, success, achievement, and temperamental attributes can foster such cognitive capacity.

These personal qualities seem to be operative as much in their effects on interactions with and responses from other people, as in their role in regulating individual responses to life events. Coping successfully with stressful situations can be a strengthening experience and promotes resilience, which can allow self-confidence to increase. Rutter (ibid) concludes that protection does not lie in the buffering effects of some supportive factor. Rather, all the evidence points towards the importance of developmental links. The quality of a child's resilience to developing mental health problems or emotional and behavioural difficulties is influenced by early life experiences but is not determinative of later outcomes.

This highlights the importance of assessment methods that take account of not just individual characteristics within the child but equally within the family and broader environment. In combination these protective factors may create a chain of indirect links that foster escape from adversity. Organising services across the spectrum of multi-agency provision in partnership between social work professionals and parents, offers the opportunity to bring out dormant protective factors to interrupt the causal chain of negative events (Little and Mount, 1999). A progressive, preventive environment that promotes children's emotional well-being is preferable to reacting to the consequences of neglect or abuse.

Individual factors regarded as promoting resilience include:

- *An even and adaptable temperament.*
- *A capacity for problem-solving.*
- *Physical attractiveness.*
- *A sense of humour.*

EXTRACT TWO *continued*

- *Good social skills and supportive peers.*

- *A sense of autonomy and purpose.*

- *Secure attachment to at least one parent.*

- *Links with the wider community …*

Multi-faceted assessment

The literature on assessment in child and adolescent mental health and current Department of Health guidance are nevertheless gradually improving to emphasise multi-faceted assessment. However, they are still influenced by Western psychiatric classifications located in a medico-biological model, and psychotherapeutic concepts narrowly focused on attachment theory (DoH, 1999; Baradon et al., 1999). There is less emphasis on psycho-social factors, including the effects of poverty, racism, unemployment and poor housing. There is evidence of some fresh thinking in this area where attempts to offer a more sopisticated model of assessment are being made stressing the interactive (quality of assessment variables and the need for enhanced interpretive) and planning skills (Middleton, 1997; Milner and O'Byrne, 1998).

The emphasis is on the need for analysing and weighing the information generated during the assessment process ensuring this is underpinned by partnership practice. A number of themes emerge from the research literature that helps to consider how to achieve this in the context of family and children's difficulties. These include the importance of multi-factorial causal explanations and the contribution of structural variables to childhood problems articulated by several authors (Sutton, 1999; Cole et al., 1995; Rutter et al., 1994). Understanding assessment as a process rather than a single event will help create the appropriate atmosphere with children and their carers, who require patience and a calm, measured stance from the assessing social worker.

POINTS TO CONSIDER

Previously, you imagined yourself as a recipient of local authority care. In the ensuing reflection, please consider how as a social work practitioner you would approach an assessment. The discussion offered by Walker (2003) in this latter extract signifies the importance of and important variables related to assessment.

- *How would you define multifaceted assessment? What would you incorporate in a multifaceted assessment when considering a child or adolescent's mental health needs?*

- *Do you have in mind any additional resilience factors to supplement the list offered by Walker?*

Comment

Your consideration of what constitutes a multifaceted assessment may be driven by your understanding of the Common Assessment Framework (CAF). You may have also drawn from Walker's (2003, p48) point that assessment may routinely be rooted *in a medico-biological model* influenced largely by *psychotherapeutic concepts … focused on attachment theory*. The idea of a multifaceted approach, which could also be termed holistic or multidimensional, suggests as Walker (2003, p48) does that there is a need to also assess *psychosocial factors, including the effects of poverty, racism, unemployment and poor housing.* With these variables, Walker (2002, 2003) is encouraging us to consider the impact of sociopolitical and structural effects on the mental health of young people as he clearly situates the experience of personal emotional distress or behavioural problems not only in the individual but also looks to understand the interwoven and contributory effects of family dynamics, the economic and political situation of the local community and society as well as cultural, ethnic and other social variables that influence and affect our lives. Walker (2002, p382) emphasises this when he writes that *institutionalized racism, failure of welfare services to listen and respond to the concerns of black communities, stereotypical beliefs about black families and barriers to access all inhibit equal opportunity for black children with mental health problems to receive help.* In this latter statement, we are asked to confront the presence of racism and oppressive, limiting beliefs and practices that occur within the institutions in which we work and affect the access to and delivery of services to varying groups and communities. As Walker (2003) emphasises that a child's behaviour and/or presentation and their family system will be affected by the assessment process, it also seems that we too will be able to effect change, hopefully, to promote more inclusive and culturally responsive ways of practising, engaging and intervening in young people's mental health.

Engaging with children

Additional facets of a child or young person's psychosocial functioning will include mental health aspects of difficulty that may be classified as medical, biological or psychiatric signs and symptoms that contribute to distress or impair a child's relationships or capacity to develop. Sharman (1997), whose background is in mental health nursing, offers a practical review of possible mental health problems in children and adolescents. Most helpfully, her work does not tie itself entirely to diagnostic categories, even though these are present, but offers chapters that consider children who may be *sad and self-harming* or those with *disturbed or unusual thinking*. In this way, she offers guidance about how to approach real difficulties in living for children and strategies to talk to children directly to understand what is happening for them. Sharman (1997, p18) advises that practitioners *should not push the child to reveal their innermost thoughts and feelings, but must go at the young person's pace.* Strategies to get to know children in the beginning of working with them are listed in the adjacent table (Figure 4.1); some of these approaches have been developed to facilitate therapeutic work and may be most clinically useful and therapeutically appropriate when approached by a practitioner with clinical training and experience in the type of expressive work. Nonetheless, some of the tasks may be useful not solely for their therapeutic exploration but to help practitioners engage with children respectfully and in age-appropriate ways.

Ways to get to know children	
Approaches	**Content and process of interaction**
• Play a non-threatening game	In playing a game, you are engaging with a child in a neutral, but still informative, way.
• Use fun questionnaires	By using ready-made or personally developed questionnaires, you are asking the child to respond to various areas: family composition, favourite toys, school, friendships, activities and household composition through drawing and with space to describe what these items mean.
• Play 'getting to know' games	Games have been developed to engage with similar material as noted above.
• Draw family tree or use a genogram	Through constructing a family tree, a child and practitioner are able to work to describe and get to know the different relationships and persons involved in a child's life.
• Make a 'button' picture of the family	Using an array of buttons, the child can select buttons to represent members of the family. Hearing from the child about their choices and reasons for making them will illuminate the child's perceptions of her family.
• Paint or draw a picture	Offering age-appropriate drawing materials, paints and papers frees up the child to develop an image fresh from their mind.
• Design a personal or family coat of arms	Using a clear objective, this task offers children an opportunity to design a symbol to represent their family or families.
• Use a doll's house	Again, working from a developmentally appropriate place, the use of a doll's house may reveal both real and imagined ideas about a child's family situation.
• Use a sand tray	Lowenfeld (1939, cited by Sharman, 1997) developed the use of a sand tray. Children work with the sand and objects to convey their thoughts from their inner world symbolically. Working to understand the meanings of their thoughts would require a practitioner versed in therapeutic interpretation.
• Work with puppets	A variety of puppet characters may allow children to express thoughts or feelings through an 'alternate' identity that may feel safer when slightly distanced from their 'real' self or voice.
• Learn about a child's 'special' object	Inquiring about a special or treasured possession may invite you into the world of what the child values.
• Inquire about what the 'special' object would say if able to talk	Related to the special object, this inquiry would invite the child to offer the perspective of the child's object if able to speak – again, it may be a way for a child to communicate about life circumstances from a safer, more distant place.
• Draw a road	Hane (1995, p22, cited by Sharman, 1997) suggests that inviting clients to draw a road – considering its shape, destination, size and condition – may *elicit spontaneous imagery that represents the origins, life history, past experiences and future expectations* of its creator.

(Adapted from Sharman, 1997, pp18–22)

Figure 4.1 *Sharman's (1997) recommended approaches to engaging with and getting to know children*

Through engaging with children, practitioners are assessing the nature and severity of the child's mental health distress and considering hypotheses about contributing factors. It may be necessary, for instance, to inquire about sad feelings, thoughts of death, fantasies or ideas of inflicting hurt on oneself or others, and direct questions about efforts to kill oneself (Pfeffer, 1986, cited in Sharman, 1997). When there are patterns of thinking that are unusual or do not seem based in reality, it would be necessary to work with specialists to rule out possible causes. Sharman (1997) notes that disordered thinking may be a feature in persons diagnosed with autistic spectrum disorders but emphasises that in these instances this is not considered to be psychotic thinking. However, there are times when children may present with disordered thinking that is psychotic, and it is essential to determine the most likely cause. Causes may stem from schizophrenia, brain disorders that cause neurological damage or dysfunction, the effects of drugs or other toxic substances, brain trauma from birth or other causes, cancerous masses or tumours affecting brain function, infection as well as social factors that intensify stress individually or within the family (Sharman, 1997). Through your awareness that there may be mood or psychotic problems in children and adolescents, you will be able to embark on assessments with greater skill – able to integrate an understanding of psychological and medical symptoms with social variables to develop a more holistic assessment.

The challenge of assessment

Working with mental health needs means that we and the clients with whom we work are influenced by society's perceptions of mental health problems and both the spoken and unspoken strictures about what is okay to talk about and what may be better left unspoken. In the following excerpt written by Jeanne Magagna (2007), a psychoanalytic consultant psychotherapist, we read firsthand about the powerful influences that often affect disclosure.

> *As I approach an assessment interview, I bear in mind three patients. One is an adolescent with AN (anorexia nervosa) who told me that she had never told the doctors who had treated her for several years prior to seeing me, or me in two years of therapy, about repeated experiences of sexual abuse in her early childhood. When asked why not she said,* No one has ever asked about sexual abuse. I felt awkward in bringing it up myself. *She said she feared both her parents and I would blame her for the abuse taking place. The second patient told me she had never told anyone about* her voices. When asked why this was, she said she was afraid people would think she was crazy and anyway she liked her voices because they kept her company. *She said she was* afraid of losing them. *The third patient, when asked about different suicidal impulses said she had none. However, when I asked her to describe a dream, it conveyed such a picture of hopelessness and despair that I pressed her further. She then did say that she had secretly recently taken an overdose but didn't want her mother to know.* (p265)

Magagna (2007) uses the term, 'patient', to signify the person with whom she is working, a term that is avoided in social work, but I would urge you to identify with her work as it suggests a respectful and engaged approach that through a safe container has allowed three children to express their innermost thoughts. This highlights the extreme sensitivity needed in working with and understanding a child's experience of surviving and recovering from sexual abuse, the experience of living with auditory hallucinations and the experience of living with despair to the point of attempting suicide. The multifaceted approach to assessment needed in working with children with mental health needs is a complex one.

Resilience

A further element in assessment is the appreciation of factors that are strengths within a family and child, factors that are protective and facilitate the promotion of resilience. Walker (2003) listed a number of them. In considering other aspects that promote resilience, were you able to identify additional protective factors? The following are additional ideas from both Walker (2003, p41) and Wallander and Varni (1998, cited in Shooter, 2005, p241) that appear to contribute to developing resilience: *self-esteem* and being *sociable*. In addition to the idea of a secure attachment with one parent, there are factors related to family dynamics such as the presence of *compassion* and *warmth* as well as an *absence of parental discord* or conflict. Children in families with access to financial and *practical resources* also benefit from this as a protective factor. Shooter (2005) investigates the presence of resilience and mental health need in children with chronic physical illness and their families. He writes that *the child with a severe handicap might survive psychologically, if blessed with intelligence and equable temperament, extended family support, good friends, a sympathetic school teacher, and the money to make major alterations to the house. A child with none of these advantages might succumb psychologically to a much more minor disability* (Shooter, 2005, p241).

As we reflect on that quote, we see the interplay – as emphasised by Walker (2003) – between the personal resources that a child may have in coping with mental health distress and variables in the larger system of a family, school and community which will in turn be affected by financial and social resources. It is essential, first, to assess each of these components and to appreciate their interactive influence and impact in understanding a child and their system of care and, second, to intervene to address any gaps in coping identified through your assessment.

Attachment and emotional state

As emphasised earlier, thoughts of death and suicide may be closely guarded by children and adolescents. We seem well-socialised to withhold certain material, realising that some subjects – such as suicide – are taboos and would be socially unacceptable to disclose. In the work that follows, Wright, Briggs and Behringer (2005) investigated the attachment experience of adolescents and linked this to their perceptions of their bodies and their suicidal risk. The study involved 35 adolescents aged between 15 and 20 years; the participants were divided into three groups. Twenty-five participants were receiving clinical services, either assessment or individual psychotherapy, and were divided into two groups based on suicide risk – high-suicidal risk (HSR) and low-suicidal risk (LSR) – established from screening results using the Pfeffer Child Suicide Scale (Pfeffer, 1986, cited in Wright, et al. 2005). The third group was a control *recruited from local schools and colleges* (Wright, et al., 2005, p480).

To access this extract fully, it may be helpful to review material on attachment theory (Bowlby, 1990) and the classification of attachment that was researched and implemented by Mary Ainsworth, et al. (1978) through her observational assessment, called the *strange situation,* as cited by Smith, et al. (2003). The categories of attachment were defined as *secure* and *insecure*, with a later category termed *disorganised*. Insecure attachments were further divided into *avoidant* and *ambivalent* types; these latter two types are prevalent in the extract as the authors report on adolescents' responses. Walker (2003) exhorted us in the previous extract from taking a narrow focus in assessment on the quality of attachment; yet this study, by exploring attachment types in relation to suicidality and adolescent psychopathology, is attempting to consider the potential link between attachment state and suicidal ideation and deliberate self-harm. The study analyses both quantitative data related to participants' suicide risk and qualitative data that includes participants' spoken-word narratives in response to the Adolescent Separation Anxiety Interview, which *is an adaptation of the Separation Anxiety Test (SAT), a semi-projective measure of attachment that assesses young people's responses to photographs depicting separation scenes* (Richard, et al., 1998, cited in Wright, et al., 2005, p480). The data from this and other measures used in the study were analysed by the researchers to consider how the quality of the participants' attachment in earlier relationships has an impact on current social links, suicidal preoccupations and self-perceptions.

EXTRACT THREE

Wright, J, Briggs, S and Behringer, J (2005) Attachment and the body in suicidal adolescents: A pilot study. Clinical Child Psychology and Psychiatry, 10 (4), pp478–80, 483, 485, 487 and 488.

A review of recent studies suggests that researchers are beginning to build up some details of adolescent attachment characteristics from different aspects of a biopsychosocial model of development … As opposed to 'classic' views of adolescent–parent struggles over independence, Bowlby (1973) argued for the importance of parent–adolescent attachment for the growth of the sense of self-reliance and social competence. Attachment to parents during adolescence thus differs from earlier ages because it emphasizes emotional autonomy while maximizing levels of support (Schneider & Younger, 1996). Research using different measures of attachment quality has supported this view (Batgos & Leadbeater, 1994; Resnick, 1991). Finally, biological maturation is also a hallmark of reorganizing adolescent attachments, adding reproduction and sexuality to the attachment equation. During adolescence the process of clarifying 'who am I in relation to you' is focused on how to combine sexual needs with safety needs, both within the individual and interpersonally (Crittenden, 1997; Kobak & Duemmler, 1994) …

Research into self-harm is directly relevant to suicide prevention, because the risk of suicide following self-harm is considerable. Hawton, Zahl, and Weatherall (2003) point out that 40–50% of people who die by suicide have a previous history of self-harm. Raising the profile of such issues has led to the realization that the relationship between incidence, risk factors and reasons for self-harm and suicide is extremely complex and varied (National Institute for Health and Clinical Excellence [NICE], 2004). It remains an extremely difficult task for the clinician, faced with a potentially self-harming or suicidal young person, to assess the presence and level of risks for the individual.[1]

---

[1] *It is estimated that there are currently 150,000–170,000 attendances at Accident and Emergency departments each year following self-harm. Self-harm resulted in 68,716 hospital admissions in 2001/2002 (NICE, 2004).*

Few studies have examined the potential links between self-harm, suicide and attachment status, although depression during adolescence has been linked to maternal attachment insecurity (Hofmann, 1997, cited in Allen & Land, 1999). Furthermore, Adam, Sheldon-Keller, and West (1996) found that adolescents who reported high levels of suicidality were significantly more likely to be preoccupied and unresolved in their attachment status. Taken together, these findings suggest a potentially important link between hopelessness in adolescence, specific attachment organizations and risk of suicide.

From a psychodynamic perspective it has been postulated that suicidal behaviour arises through a split between mind and body (Campbell & Hale, 1991). The body becomes the location of, or is identified with, aspects of internal relationships, and a life-or-death struggle can result. Aspects of the self (or other) identified with the body are attacked or felt to be dispensable (Laufer & Laufer, 1984; Perret-Catipovic & Ladame, 1998). Understanding body and sexual puberty transformations and their impact on perceptions of self and others may be a potentially useful link for under-standing the increase in self-harm and suicide during adolescence ...

In summary ... the current authors embarked on an exploration of the clinical utility of an attachment framework for understanding suicidal phenomena in adolescence with two broad aims. First, we examine the association between attachment styles and suicidality by comparing two groups of adolescent participants undergoing assessment for psychotherapy. Second, we explore the phenomenology of different presentations of suicidality in adolescence from a psychodynamically informed attachment theory perspective.

Results – Qualitative analysis

... The rich qualitative content of the interviews' thematically coded differences ... provides a rich source of material from which to develop attachment-based formulations and hence guide therapy. In the next section we hope to elucidate some of these aspects with quotes taken from a number of different participants' interviews ...

Story-stem content

Material from the story-stem photographs were characterized by bizarre features and themes that often lay at the extremes of, or were unclassifiable using, Resnick's coding system ...

Direct references to a suicide solution

Interviewer: *In this picture the father has been arrested...what might the young person do?*

Walk the streets ... become a druggy I don't know she could become anything she's got no parents and no-one else there to look after her...even go kill herself.

> **EXTRACT THREE** *continued*
>
> *In this example there is bleakness to the story including no sense of a reunion episode or available attachment figures, however, rather than a more typical insecure move into unrealistic self-reliance, there is escalating self-destructiveness as a consequence.*
>
> *Interviewer: [In the picture] Mum is going in to hospital, what do you think would happen in the end?*
>
> Don't know ... (Interviewer: any ideas?) No ... ideally mum would die, so I would have a perfect excuse to kill myself, and everybody would be happy ... including me.
>
> *In a variety of ways the HSR adolescents were characterized by experiences of their body as something out of control, that the attempt to exert control was overwhelming, and in the face of this difficulty submission and despair crept in ...*
>
> **Discussion**
>
> *The aims of this article were to report on a pilot exploratory study of adolescents' characteristic attachment styles and body narratives as potentially useful areas for understanding suicidality in this age group. We started with a speculative theoretical proposition derived from attachment and psychodynamic theories that the adolescent's potentially conflictual relationship with the body in the context of reorganizing affiliative attachment relationships and the transformations of puberty has a central role in suicidality.*
>
> *Results from the study suggest that suicidal adolescents are likely to be insecurely attached, in both dismissing and preoccupied ways ...*

Comment

The selected narratives of two participants evoke something of the extreme distress and disintegration that adolescents who are preoccupied with suicide experience in their ability to contain their developing bodies, their changing relationships with adults and their own psychological development. Wright, et al. (2005) suggest that further inquiry should occur to understand the attachment structures of young people, as they perceive this variable to be an insightful one which has a potentially predictive quality in understanding suicidality in young people. It is apparent in reading this extract that it will take significant resources as a practitioner to be able to allow a young person to be able to express such raw and distressing thoughts. It would be important for social work practitioners to prepare themselves to be able to engage and stay present with this material and to make links with expert practitioners.

A snapshot of mental health need: Eating disorders in young people

Distress becomes manifest in many ways. The chapter so far has considered a range of groups that may be at greater risk for mental health difficulties; this has been contrasted with potentially helpful and protective factors which may facilitate resilience in young people. An area that seems to be increasingly prominent as one requiring understanding and intervention is the assessment and treatment of eating disorders, which encompass a broad range of variation and severity. The authoritative text, *Eating disorders in childhood and adolescence*, provides the next extract. The book, now in its third edition, is comprehensive in that it offers an overview of types of eating disorders and incorporates pertinent chapters covering causes, medical intervention, nutritional perspectives, varying therapeutic treatments and the lived experiences of those coping with eating disorders as well as family members' voices. As social work practitioners, we consistently work with the interface between individuals and systems. It seems pertinent then to consider the intervention described in the next extract. Honig (2007) is a family therapist working in an adolescent eating disorders service and at the Tavistock Clinic.

EXTRACT FOUR

Honig, P (2007) Family approaches: Evidence-based and collaborative practice. In Lask, B and Bryant-Waugh, R (eds) Eating disorders in childhood and adolescence. 3rd edition. Abingdon: Routledge, pp215–16, 219–20 and 226.

Introduction

Family approaches to the treatment of childhood and adolescent onset eating disorders mean that parents, siblings and any significant others with whom the patient is closely connected may be included in the assessment and treatment process. This involvement is necessary both as a means of gathering information about the problem and in order to establish how family members might be able to support the young person by constructing a home environment in which eating, and subsequently retention of food can become an ordinary activity. Eating disorders, whether life threateningly severe anorexia nervosa in teenagers or food faddiness in younger children, have the capacity to create highly aroused emotions in families ...

The development of evidence

Researching the efficacy of family therapy for the treatment of anorexia nervosa began with the Philadelphia team (e.g. Minuchin, Rosman and Baker, 1978). It was continued by the Maudsley Hospital group in London through the 1980s and 1990s (e.g. Dare, Eisler, Colahan, Crowther, Senior, and Asen, 1995) culminating with the production of a treatment manual of this approach (Lock, LeGrange, Agras, and Dare, 2001). Latterly, the development of multifamily group therapy has proved of considerable interest (Schmidt and Asen, 2005).

In the UK a comprehensive anaylsis of research evidence has recently been completed by the National Institute for Health and Clinical Excellence (NICE, 2004). This body is responsible for producing guidelines for evidence-based treatments in the National Health Service. Based on this analysis the guidelines recommend, as a first line of treatment, that family interventions that directly address the eating disorder should be offered to children and adolscents with anorexia nervosa. This recommendation was based primarily on the finding from the first randomised control trial comparing family therapy with individual psychoanalytically oriented psychotherapy (Russell,

Szmulker, Dare, and Eisler, 1987). The study found that patients receiving family ther-apy performed better on a variety of outcome measures at follow-up. Other research trials have both supported and refined clinical understandings of the benefits of family therapy in the treatment of anorexia nervosa (Eisler, Dare, Hodes, Russell, Dodge, and Le Grange, 2000; Geist, Heinmaa, Stephens, Davis and Katzman, 2000). The relative benefits of conjoint (patients and parents seen together for therapy) and separated family therapy (patients seen on their own and parents seen without the patient – but with the same therapist) have been investigated by Robin, Siegel, Moye, Gilroy, Dennis and Sikand (1999) who found that both forms of family therapy have equal efficacy ...

Multifamily groups

Multifamily group therapy usually consists of between three and eight families meeting together with several therapists for a number of sessions (usually between eight and 12). During these sessions the families will discuss issues related to anorexia nervosa and participate in a meal together. Whilst evidence for the effec-tiveness of multifamily groups is awaited (there are currently a number of multicentre randomised control studies being conducted), there is a growing belief that bringing families together for treatment is popular with both families and clini-cians involved. There are currently multifamily groups in existence in a number of different settings (inpatient and outpatient) and reports of these (Honig, 2005: Schmidt and Asen, 2005) suggest a key factor of their success may be the collective sharing of experience and expertise, rather than the necessity for clinicians to follow a prescribed, manualised version of a specific model. The following comment by a parent who attended a multifamily group prior to and during her daughter's admis-sion is fairly typical:

> I know from the first group family therapy [that my daughter] felt enormous relief that she was not the only one who was going through this horrendous experience, and we as adults also got great comfort from the fact that other families were also suffering. Also, meeting other families who were similar to us and not dysfunc-tional as we had felt at times in the early days. Group family therapy was always a place where emotions ran high but a place where one could show emotions.

The format of these groups varies from place to place, but the common features are:

1. *An opportunity for patients and those close to them to meet others in similar situations – strength in collective experience.*

2. *Shared involvement in eating a meal.*

3. *Discussions proceeding to solutions about eating-related issues (e.g. how to encourage/support a reluctant child to eat a meal).*

4. *Explorations of potentially linked non-eating disorder themes (e.g. developmental issues and transitions in family life).*

5. *A resource-focused, non-pathologising approach to family involvement.*

EXTRACT FOUR continued

Some groups meet for intensive full days over a relatively short space of time (one week, followed by several follow-up days during the months ahead), while other groups meet on a weekly basis for several hours at a time. Some groups are closed to new members, others are open with families joining and leaving periodically. From this mix of formats it would seem that the key feature is the collective experience of learning together about anorexia nervosa and the ways in which it influences individual and family behaviours. Additionally, most of these groups will in some way utilise the 'expertise' of those families that have experience of the illness stretching back over time. In some groups experienced families are invited to share their knowledge of the multifamily group with new families and to discuss ways in which it was helpful to them. This may help to alleviate anxiety felt by new participants and acts as a bridge between clinicians and patients. In other groups more experienced families may be involved in the same therapy group as patients with a very recent diagnosis. This overlap offers opportunities for sharing expertise by integrating the perspective of experienced patients and families, so that it becomes an equally valid component of the therapeutic discourse ...

Conclusion

A family approach to the treatment of eating disorder in children and adolescents is now considered a central requirement. There is growing evidence that emphasises the likelihood of better outcome, at least in the treatment of anorexia nervosa, provided that this approach emphasises the importance of focusing therapy on eating disordered behaviours rather than on searching for underlying family pathology. Whilst similar claims cannot currently be made about the other eating disorders, there is a clinical consensus that supports family involvement on the grounds of developmental appropriateness and the need to ensure that families become contexts in which symptoms are not inadvertently maintained. The emphasis now needs to be on working collaboratively with families and placing parents in a position of partnership with those treating their child. The foremost principle of a collaborative approach is the development of communication mechanisms that operate in both directions: from clinician to patient/family and from patient/family to clinician. In this model there should always be opportunities for mutual influence in the creation and refinement of treatment programmes.

POINTS TO CONSIDER

1. *Honig (2007, p220) writes:* In some groups, experienced families are invited to share their knowledge of the multifamily group with new families and to discuss ways in which it was helpful to them.

   (a) *How might this approach be helpful to both the more experienced family members and the new members of the multifamily group?*

   (b) *What would be your concerns, if any, about this approach?*

2. *As a student on placement or a social work practitioner, you are working with a family in which its youngest son has been described as having anorexia nervosa. You have been asked by them for help to find suitable and helpful treatment.*

   (a) *Reviewing this extract, what evidence from research might you share with them to offer them information?*

   (b) *They have previously expressed some anxiety about sharing this 'problem'; what might you say to help educate them about available treatments, their efficacy and to help them make an informed decision about participating in treatment or not?*

Comment

Honig (2007) introduces information early in the extract about the evidence that is being developed in relation to therapeutic approaches offered to treat eating disorders and their effectiveness. Much of this, it should be noted, is generally linked with treatments related to anorexia nervosa rather than other eating disorders. However, it is helpful and hopeful to read that family interventions seem to demonstrate some effectiveness in promoting change and recovery from eating-disordered behaviour. As a practitioner, you will need to judge whether your clients find it helpful to be informed about research findings or when it will be most helpful to introduce this information. In the second point for reflection, you were asked to consider acting as a resource and agent for education for the family. In this, you also needed to work with the family's possible feeling of shame which may promote isolation and a reluctance to disclose their problem. Pertinently, Honig offered a parental perspective in the extract to highlight that through a group experience persons with eating disorders and their family members who had felt alone and isolated were able to find some solace in meeting others who were confronting similar problems.

In the first point, you were invited to consider how both experienced and newer group members may be helped through an interface. For the experienced members, it may be a mark of their change and development to be able to induct new members. It may also be a way of consolidating and reinforcing their knowledge both to shore up their progress and to reinforce their commitment to change and change strategies. Possible detractions may occur if families tend to focus their energy on helping others and lose sight of their own needs; and if the group's professional conductors or facilitators rely too heavily on experienced members to carry the culture and work of the group's facilitation. Overall though, this model with the valuable contributions of service users of help, support and information seems to offer a meaningful experience of the expert knowledge and power of service users.

Service user perspectives

In thinking about service user input – and input as power – the role of service users as contributors to training, service development, audit and consultation marks an empowering means of effecting change in the systems that serve those with mental health need. This is just as important in the field of child and adolescent mental health, as young people too can serve as resources. In Wedgbury, et al. (2005, p187), a number of service users contributed to a chapter in the text, *Consultation in child and adolescent mental health services*, which discussed advising services. In a focus group on service development, a young person stated: *It sounds selfish but if you are here to help us then for you to run smoothly you need to know what we want. There is no point in providing a service that no one has a need for; it's a waste of your time and a waste of our time.* In terms of how service users new to a service may benefit from hearing the perspectives of established service users, there were mixed opinions.

> *There was a feeling that other service users benefit from the hindsight of those who have experienced the process. However, there was also a view that it was concurrent involvement that was most helpful to individual young people themselves.* (Wedgbury et al., 2005, p188)

This latter finding supports the idea proffered by Honig (2007) in the previous extract in which, in some groups, experienced members of the group offer information to new members. To me, this suggests the power that service users may hold in helping others. This finding also highlights the relevance and necessity of securing evidence from service users as a means of service improvement.

Mental health promotion

This chapter has primarily focused on working with mental health need in children and adolescents once it has become manifest. Work in such a case means responding with an assessment, a treatment intervention and ongoing re-assessment to determine when, if ever, a difficulty has been resolved. In addition to the provision of services to respond to mental health need, there is also a mandate from central government to offer a preventative service in relation to children's mental health. Southall (2005, p1) writes that *children's mental health services are set up to facilitate all elements pertaining to emotional well-being and have a very significant preventative role.* She notes that *they are often unable to fulfil this role as demands for services have ... outstripped resources.* This will likely continue with the finding that service demand has increased (DoH, 2006). However, there is also a need to offer services that prevent the development of mental health need and offer early intervention. Efforts to address this through greater education to professionals and to young people may be found online and in developments attuned to the psycho-educational needs of young people, such as in the field of positive psychology.

C   H   A   P   T   E   R   S   U   M   M   A   R   Y

Considering the mental health needs of young people means needing to confront the often painful reality that a child's life is not going to plan; that learning, developing and growing are to some extent undermined through some disorder of emotions, thinking, behaviour, eating or relationships. In this chapter, we considered this perhaps most centrally by reflecting on the experience of looked after children. Mental health need was linked to certain risks or predisposing factors that encompassed both genetic and familial links but as strongly derived from socioeconomic, cultural and traumatic factors. The multiplicity of these factors both as contributors to mental distress and as areas for intervention and support were explored in light of the need for multifaceted assessment and an appreciation of both risks and resilience in young people and their families. It, too, seems essential to foster a culturally responsive approach to assessment, support and intervention.

Exploring more serious mental health distress involved considering the presence of suicidal risk, depressed mood, and disordered thinking and eating. Research provided an exploratory inquiry into understanding suicidality through an investigation of attachment patterns while additional research evidence suggested possible benefit from family interventions in the treatment of anorexia nervosa. In much of the material gathered for this chapter, there is a clear link to the possibility that family may offer a safe harbour for children and young people to develop and grow. When this dynamic is upset or caregivers are unable to facilitate care, it may be necessary for professional support to offer intervention. In order to do this, we need to maintain our own knowledge base about children's developmental changes within the ever-changing societal context of our work. Also, as we consider the complexity of working with children with mental health, emotional or behavioural distress or problems, we need to be mindful of how we feel about the children with whom we work and how we validate the experience of children's lived experiences so that there is a chance even in short-term professional relationships with children for them to have experiences of being known and understood.

FURTHER READING

Rutter, M, Bishop, D, Pine, D and Scott, S (2008) *Rutter's child and adolescent psychiatry*. 5th edition. Oxford: Wiley Blackwell.

The preceding text on child and adolescent psychiatry, referenced in Walker's (2003) extract, has been updated several times since its first publication. This is the most recent edition, with a slight change of name.

Chambers, H, Howell, S, Madge, N and Ollie, H. (2002) *Healthy care, Building an evidence base for promoting health and wellbeing of looked after children and young people*. London: National Children's Bureau. **www.ncb.org.uk**

This report adds to the knowledge base in relation to the health of children receiving local authority care.

WEBSITES

www.everychildmatters.co.uk/health/camhs/

www.everychildmatters.co.uk/socialcare/lookedafterchildren/

www.everychildmatters.co.uk/health/substancemisuse/

www.mentalhealth.org.uk/

www.youngminds.org.uk/

Chapter 5
Living with acute mental health need

This chapter will contribute to helping you to meet the following National Occupational Standards.

Key Role 1: Prepare for, and work with individuals, families, carers, groups and communities to assess their needs and circumstances.

- Work with individuals, families, carers, groups and communities to help them make informed decisions.
- Assess needs and options to recommend a course of action.

Key Role 2: Plan, carry out, review and evaluate social work practice, with individuals, families, carers, groups, communities and other professionals.

- Interact with individuals, families, carers, groups and communities to achieve change and development and to improve life opportunities.
- Address behaviour which presents a risk to individuals, families, carers, groups and communities.

Key Role 3: Support individuals to represent their needs, views and circumstances.

Key Role 4: Manage risk to individuals, families, carers, groups, communities, self and colleagues.

It will also introduce you to the following academic standards as set out in the social work subject benchmark statement.

Defining principles

4.6 Social work is a moral activity that requires practitioners to recognise the dignity of the individual, but also to make and implement difficult decisions (including restriction of liberty) in human situations that involve the potential for benefit or harm ... This means that honours undergraduates [and others studying social work] must learn to:

- Recognise and work with the powerful links between intrapersonal and interpersonal factors and the wider social, legal, economic, political and cultural context of people's lives.
- Practise in ways that maximise safety and effectiveness in situations of uncertainty and incomplete information.
- Work in partnership with service users and carers and other professionals to foster dignity, choice and independence, and effect change.

5.1.2 The service delivery context

- The changing demography and cultures of communities in which social workers will be practising ...
- The significance of interrelationships with other social services, especially education, housing, health, income maintenance and criminal justice ...

5.1.4 Social work theory

- Research-based concepts and critical explanations from social work theory and other disciplines that contribute to the knowledge base of social work, including their distinctive epistemological status and application to practice.
- The relevance of psychological, physical and physiological perspectives to understanding individual and social development and functioning.

5.1.5 The nature of social work practice

- The nature and characteristics of skills associated with effective practice, both direct and indirect, with a range of service users and in a variety of settings ...
- The processes that facilitate and support service user choice and independence...

Introduction

The duration of living with mental health need varies, as does its impact and the severity of its symptoms and the type of distress it brings. In this chapter, we think about the impact of acute or shorter-term mental health distress, and in the following chapter we consider the impact of living with chronic, or longer-lasting, symptoms and distress. In this way, we reflect on the impact of mental health need on individuals and their significant others.

Experiencing mental distress in an acute – shorter-term – period does not necessarily mean that the severity of the distress is lessened or less intense. In fact, through this chapter and Chapter 6, we will consider several variables in relation to mental health distress – such as duration, severity, symptom picture, diagnosis and treatment or intervention options – and how all of these most importantly affect people with mental health needs. To this end, we will look at the experience of postnatal depression in depth as a means of understanding acute mental health need.

Living with acute mental health distress

Mental health distress comes in many types. The health website of the British Broadcasting Corporation (BBC) lists certain mental health illnesses (BBC, 2008, n.p.) including anxiety disorders, bipolar disorder, Alzheimer's, depression and eating disorders under the heading, 'Disorders and conditions'. Separately, it lists stress, self-harming, suicidal feelings and phobias and panic attacks under 'Emotional health'. The website of the charity MIND, which focuses on mental health, includes both common terms such as depression and more detailed topics regarding medication and treatment approaches. In a search of MIND's online publications, the term 'depression' elicited further subcategories: advocating comprehensive assessment to differentiate depression, dementia and confusion; understanding depression; understanding postnatal depression; and understanding seasonal affective disorder (www.mind.org.uk, 2008). Additional related topics included an overview of anti-depressant medications, more specialised fact sheets on certain medications and counselling and psychotherapy services. What this very informal audit highlights is that for those with internet access information is available to provide a modicum of factual data regarding mental health need.

This and other information on mental health – which may be available through libraries, helplines, publications and other health resources – is meant to educate the public so that persons living with mental health symptoms or people close to them either personally or professionally will understand their symptoms and seek help. Living with mental health distress, however, may foster a reluctance to talk about and ask for help. In this chapter, we understand acute mental health need by focusing specifically on postnatal depression. Choosing postnatal depression (PND) as the focus of this chapter will hopefully educate you in relation to this serious mental health need. Additionally, knowing about PND may offer a foundation to help you understand and ultimately work with the broader range of problems that lead to acute presentations of mental health distress.

Mood disorders

In the list provided by the BBC, several of the conditions – anxiety disorders, bipolar disorder, and depression – fit into a category called mood disorders. In Chapter 2 we introduced the means by which different mental health symptoms are classified when we reviewed classification; this will be expanded further in this chapter.

In short, the term 'mood disorders' refers to an umbrella category or type of mental health difficulty that affects and upsets a person's emotional landscape. Someone experiencing persistent sad mood for several weeks, without relief, and who has also described thoughts of death or dying, felt hopeless and lethargic and found their sleep disturbed might be considered to have a mood disorder called depression. As with any terminology, there is a need for specificity and accuracy in making use of such terms as mood disorders or depression, for instance. Ultimately, understanding these terms and using them accurately should be a hallmark of being respectful about someone's emotional experience so that it helps the person living with mental health distress, their social network and you and your professional colleagues to speak clearly about a person's experience. One of the types of mood disorder which is commonly discussed is depression, and a subtype of this is postnatal depression.

Postnatal depression

The topic of postnatal depression is becoming more apparent in the media, with issues about treatment options courting controversy. Postnatal depression refers to a diagnosis of depressed mood in women in the period after giving birth, which is referred to as postpartum. In the types of mental health problems that present as acute, postnatal depression can be worrying and relatively quick to take hold.

In this chapter, I have chosen extracts that touch on the personal as well as the professional as we begin to understand acute mental health need. In the first extract, Stephanie Merritt, an author, writes about her personal experience of having postnatal depression and what led her to seek help. The extract gives us a glimpse of the difficulty that faces those who have depression. In the second extract, information about diagnosing depression is drawn from the *Diagnostic and statistical manual of mental disorders* (DSM-IV-TR) (APA, 2000). The detail in this provides an idea about what signs and symptoms medical professionals – physicians and psychiatrists in the UK – look for when making an official diagnosis of a mood disorder like depression. Because postnatal depression is a subtype of depression, additional specific detail is factored into making this diagnosis.

You will then have an opportunity to read excerpts from one of MIND's publications on understanding postnatal depression. Looking firsthand at a piece of public health information will give us an idea about how to convey the professional knowledge we have in accessible ways to inform, educate and empower people with knowledge and the potential for action. Finally, the Mental Health Foundation (MHF) has published a document about the need for talking therapies as part of the NHS's provision of mental health services. This extract offers a summary of the MHF's recommendations and demands and coincides with a very significant policy initiative which has funding to expand therapy services. The balance of these extracts is tipped firmly with non-statutory bodies and the voice of a service user; this seems appropriate as we work to understand the lived experience of people with mental health distress.

PND: Its incidence

Uncovering the incidence of postnatal depression has been helped through the use of an instrument called the Edinburgh Postnatal Depression Scale (EPDS) developed by Cox and his associates (Cox, Holden and Sagovsky, 1987, and Cox, Murray and Chapman, 1993) which is cited by Howard (2007). Howard (2007, n.p.) writes that *the symptoms* [of post-natal depression] *are similar to symptoms of depression at other times of life, but in addition to low mood, sleep disturbance, change in appetite, diurnal variation in mood, poor concentration, and irritability, women with PND also experience guilt about their inability to look after their new baby.* She further notes that *health visitors screen for PND using the EPDS.* Using this instrument is an effort in healthcare to uncover a health-related problem through screening and to intervene as necessary.

The extent of PND seems to vary internationally, with reports indicating that it may be more prevalent in developing countries (Patel, Rodrigues and DeSouza, 2002, and Cooper, et al., 1999, both cited by Howard, 2007). There seem to be similar rates of prevalence in depression between women generally and those following birth. However, it seems that in the month after childbirth the incidence of depression *is three times the average monthly incidence in non-childbearing women.* Additionally, *a meta-analysis of studies mainly based in the developed world found the incidence of PND to be 12–13%* (O'Hara and Swain, 1996, cited by Howard, 2007).

Living with PND

In the text preceding the following extract, Stephanie Merritt writes about her interaction with a health visitor and how she found the questionnaire, referring to the Edinburgh scale, *to be surprisingly easy to fake* (Merritt, 2008b, n.p.). She defends herself well from being detected as a woman with depression by circling all of the responses that position her in the 'non-depressed' category. Even though she dupes the health visitor, she acknowledges a pleading hope that the health visitor would have *read between the lines* and probed further into her situation. She notes that *she had a fleeting sense of having got away with something* (Merritt, 2008b, n.p.). The feelings of guilt and the closing in and constricted sense of depression are vivid in her writing.

EXTRACT ONE

Merritt, S (2008b) My private hell. The Observer, 6 April 2008 [online] http://books.guardian.co.uk.

Extract from Merritt, S (2008a) The Devil within: A memoir of depression. London: Vermillion.

If I had answered the questionnaire truthfully I would have come out with top marks, but I didn't need the Edinburgh Post-Natal Depression Scale to tell me that something was wrong. I understood this at the most basic level, because there had been a conspicuous absence of joy so far in this experience, and surely you were supposed to feel happy when you had a new baby, surely that was the natural way of things? No one looking on could have accused me of being a bad mother; I was not neglectful or short-tempered or unkind: to any impartial observer, I was doing a fine job. I was obsessively anxious about my son's wellbeing and attentive to his every need; I fretted over the correct number of blankets, the temperature of the house, whether I was bathing him too little or too often. I sat up all night in the armchair watching Open University programmes about integers and Wagner so that he could sleep face down on my front when that was the only position that soothed his colic; I submitted to the indignity and discomfort of breastfeeding, which I loathed both while I was doing it and when I was not, because I was told it was in his best interests; anyone watching might have said that, if anything, I needed to relax and take some time for myself, that I fussed too much over the baby.

Only I knew the dark motivations behind my earnest care; only I knew that I was over-compensating out of guilt, because in my heart I knew that I was a bad mother. I must be a bad mother because I didn't feel what I was meant to feel. In truth, I didn't feel anything at all. I was simply empty, scoured, a flimsy wicker framework built around a void. At my core, where a well of fierce maternal love was supposed to be, there was only absence, and to disguise this absence I put on a fervent show of motherhood ...

Recurring or obsessive thoughts of death, self-harm and suicide are on the basic checklist for any diagnosis of depression, and I had experienced all of these before at some level, but the incremental descent of my mind towards despair this time had passed the theoretical level; there was a strong current of will bearing these thoughts along. I became convinced of the world's indifference, its cruel emphasis on success and strength. If I lost my job, I would be replaced by someone better, stronger, some-one who did not fall apart, and if I could not make a living I would have to move back in with my parents and live like an invalid. I would lose all sense of identity and of my place in the world. I would be forgotten, replaced, cast aside, unwanted; if I could not achieve I was no one, I was not worth the space I took up in the world ...

Then, finally, I was returning home on the train later than usual and found myself alone in a compartment with a door you could open from the inside. Perhaps it was only the overwhelming despair of that daily journey, away from London and all its invigorating life, into the early dusk, back to the silence and the hours of dread that waited for me in the little house with the low ceilings; suddenly I felt I could not last another day. Standing there, minutes from falling, I had an image of my mother and my son, and myself as the line of continuity between them; I was struck, as if for the first time, by the understanding that I had once been a baby, that I had once been to my mother what my son now was to me. All those hours of patient, thankless care, the frustration and anxiety and tears, all that time and love invested: I had done it for a total of 13 months and already it had changed the texture and mean-ing of my life beyond measure, but she had done it for nearly 30 years – 30 years! – and for what? So that I could dash myself to pieces under the wheels of a Network South East commuter train? Would I make that the culmination of her work as a mother? And my son – would I leave him the legacy of believing that he was not reason enough for his mother to go on living?

This was the nearest I had come to ending my life, and though I stepped back at the last minute, I was profoundly frightened by the experience. Putting myself so close to self-destruction had not been cathartic; if anything, it had shown me that I might really be capable of the act. I did not feel a renewed connection with life, nor had the despair that had urged the gesture abated, yet the reasons for enduring would remain equally compelling and I was afraid that I would be caught permanently in this tension between the desire for oblivion and the need to carry on …

That same week, I went to the doctor to admit that I needed help. It was a conscious decision to turn and exist, to find some way to overcome this, and yet it felt like defeat. I had just turned 29 and it was the first time in my life that I had even contemplated consulting a medical doctor about my state of mind, which I still imagined to be wholly independent of somatic complaints and which therefore ought to have come under the jurisdiction of my will and was not the proper province of a GP. But I had passed a certain point: after that moment on the train I was quite certain that if someone did not help me, or at least give me some hope, I would not last very much longer …

Comment

The preceding paragraphs are poignant and frank. We not only gain an appreciation of the intense emptiness and despair that consumed Stephanie Merritt but we, objectively, are able to read into her words and find confirmation of postnatal depression. As Merritt writes, *only I knew that I was overcompensating out of guilt, because in my heart I knew that I was a bad mother*, we are able to see the link to Howard's (2007) writing that postnatal depression often is characterised by the mother's intense sense of what seems to be inappropriate and misplaced guilt. Consistent with a greater risk of developing PND, she also relates a previous history of depressed mood.

In the passages that have been excerpted here, we learn about her movement from obsessive thoughts of taking care of her son while on maternity leave to a fraught scene on a train when she is close to ending her life. Common to experiences of severe depression, she described frequent and intrusive thoughts of death and suicide. Thoughts of the impact of this eventually brought her to seek help; however, even in doing this there was a residue of defeat and failure that she could not manage on her own. In this account, we may find it important to question what impact societal or personal beliefs about being strong and stoic have on our ability as individuals and a society to acknowledge depression and mental health need and seek help.

1. In the statistics presented prior to the extract, there was a report that found a 12–13 per cent incidence of postnatal depression in developed countries (O'Hara and Swain, 1996, cited by Howard, 2007).

   (a) Identify the definition of the word, 'incidence'.

   (b) Using census information from the government's website **www.statistics.gov.uk** – (i) find statistics on the number of live births and (ii) based on this number, determine the likely incidence of PND.

2. Imagine that you are working with a new mother – how would you help make it safe to allow her to speak about her experiences? Generally, how might you inquire about depressed mood to help someone disclose something they may find difficult to accept or acknowledge? On separate paper, write some possible statements or questions.

Comment

In relation to point 2, a possible strategy may be to have a look at the questions on the EPDS to gain some insight into the themes or areas of inquiry included in it. I say this because it is likely that the EPDS has been validated as an accurate indicator of the presence of depressed mood post childbirth. As an aside, validity and reliability are research terms. As I inferred, a research instrument would be valid if it measures what it is supposed to measure – the EPDS is valid if it correctly shows the women who have symptoms of postnatal depression. An instrument is reliable when it can be used over and over to capture the same thing.

As we learned in Merritt's (2008b) extract, there may be a strong urge to deny or avoid detection of a problem for some people. What this shows is that even a valid and reliable instrument may be confounded or made invalid by a respondent eager to avoid detection. By following the questionnaire rigidly and without further probing or inquiry, it may not allow space for people to reveal their true feelings. Perhaps, when meeting with a new mother, it might be possible to use the content of the questionnaire as a starting point and to express how normal it might be to feel overwhelmed in the experience of being a new mother. It might also help to empathise with whatever emotion is expressed. Additionally, if it seems appropriate, it may be useful to relate that in some cases new mothers naturally feel stressed and may even feel guilty about what they are doing; further, it may be helpful to acknowledge that people do at times minimise or refuse to accept feeling intensely down. In any case, your efforts are to guide a client to state what they feel.

In relation to the incidence of PND, finding the number of live births, which is about 690,000, would roughly suggest that 83,000 women, or 12 per cent, may experience PND. This is not statistically accurate given that, for one thing, women may experience multiple births, so the number of women affected cannot be determined by number of live births. However, this is an effort to encourage you to begin considering how to extrapolate findings from data reports which could be applied in your communities or practice settings.

The diagnosis of depression

The previous extract ended when Stephanie Merritt sought help from her GP. As we will come to find out, there may be a range of responses and treatment interventions that may help persons experiencing depressed mood either generally or following childbirth, so prescribing medication is only one possible option. Decisions about which of a range of treatment responses to use will depend significantly on a variety of factors such as severity of symptoms, any prior history of mental health distress, any history of prior treatment and response and the two significant factors of service user choice and diagnostic accuracy.

In the following extract, you are invited to read about diagnostic criteria for depression from the DSM-IV-TR (APA, 2000), a publication used by physicians to make diagnoses in relation to mental health and behavioural distress. In this country, I appreciate that this is the domain of physicians; however, in some countries, such as the United States, social workers with specialist statutory licensing also engage in this process. The extract includes truncated passages from a section of the DSM-IV-TR covering 'Mood Disorders', of which 'major depressive episode' is one. The extract includes a narrative discussion of the different diagnostic criteria that physicians and other mental health professionals would look for in relation to someone's mood, symptoms and signs. It is worth saying that 'symptoms' generally refer to the statements and problems that service users report when they see a health professional; whereas 'signs' come from the health professional's observation of the service user. For instance, a service user saying, *I've been sleeping all night and day,* would be reporting a relevant symptom, and a service user who sits without showing any emotional change even after speaking about a very emotionally painful break-up may be showing a sign of flattened affect. Following the description of symptoms, there is a type of menu or checklist that guides physicians to check off what is happening for an individual and thereby determine a diagnosis or not. Finally, there is a further narrative about the onset of depression as it relates to the postpartum period. I appreciate that the inclusion of diagnosis even as concept may be contentious, so I would urge you to read this with a critical eye and a willingness to approach it reflectively.

EXTRACT TWO

American Psychiatric Association (2000) Mood disorders. In* Diagnostic and statistical manual of mental disorders. *4th edition, text revision. Washington, D.C.: APA. pp349–51, p356 and pp422–3.

Major depressive episode

Episode features

The essential feature of a Major Depressive Episode is a period of at least 2 weeks during which there is either depressed mood or the loss of interest or pleasure in nearly all activities. In children and adolescents, the mood may be irritable rather than sad. The individual must also experience at least four additional symptoms drawn from a list that includes changes in appetite or weight, sleep, and psychomotor activity; decreased energy; feelings of worthlessness or guilt; difficulty thinking, concentrating, or making decisions; or recurrent thoughts of death or suicidal

---

ideation, plans, or attempts. To count toward a Major Depressive Episode, a symptom must either be newly present or must have clearly worsened compared with the person's pre-episode status. The symptoms must persist for most of the day, nearly every day, for at least 2 consecutive weeks. The episode must be accompanied by clinically significant distress or impairment in social, occupational, or other important areas of functioning. For some individuals with milder episodes, functioning may appear to be normal but requires markedly increased effort.

The mood in a Major Depressive Episode is often described by the person as depressed, sad, hopeless, discouraged, or 'down in the dumps' (Criterion Al). In some cases, sadness may be denied at first, but may subsequently be elicited by interview (e.g., by pointing out that the individual looks as if he or she is about to cry). In some individuals who complain of feeling 'blah', having no feelings, or feeling anxious, the presence of a depressed mood can be inferred from the person's facial expression and demeanor. Some individuals emphasize somatic complaints (e.g., bodily aches and pains) rather than reporting feelings of sadness. Many individuals report or exhibit increased irritability (e.g., persistent anger, a tendency to respond to events with angry outbursts or blaming others, or an exaggerated sense of frustration over minor matters). In children and adolescents, an irritable or cranky mood may develop rather than a sad or dejected mood. This presentation should be differentiated from a 'spoiled child' pattern of irritability when frustrated.

Loss of interest or pleasure is nearly always present, at least to some degree. Individuals may report feeling less interested in hobbies, 'not caring anymore', or not feeling any enjoyment in activities that were previously considered pleasurable (Criterion A2). Family members often notice social withdrawal or neglect of pleasurable avocations (e.g., a formerly avid golfer no longer plays, a child who used to enjoy soccer finds excuses not to practice). In some individuals, there is a significant reduction from previous levels of sexual interest or desire.

Appetite is usually reduced, and many individuals feel that they have to force themselves to eat. Other individuals, particularly those encountered in ambulatory settings, may have increased appetite and may crave specific foods (e.g., sweets or other carbohydrates). When appetite changes are severe (in either direction), there may be a significant loss or gain in weight, or, in children, a failure to make expected weight gains may be noted (Criterion A3).

The most common sleep disturbance associated with a Major Depressive Episode is insomnia (Criterion A4). Individuals typically have middle insomnia (i.e., waking up during the night and having difficulty returning to sleep) or terminal insomnia (i.e., waking too early and being unable to return to sleep). Initial insomnia (i.e., difficulty falling asleep) may also occur. Less frequently, individuals present with over-sleeping (hypersomnia) in the form of prolonged sleep episodes at night or increased daytime sleep. Sometimes the reason that the individual seeks treatment is for the disturbed sleep.

EXTRACT TWO *continued*

Psychomotor changes include agitation (e.g., the inability to sit still, pacing, hand-wringing; or pulling or rubbing of the skin, clothing, or other objects) or retardation (e.g., slowed speech, thinking, and body movements; increased pauses before answering; speech that is decreased in volume, inflection, amount, or variety of content or muteness) (Criterion A5). The psychomotor agitation or retardation must be severe enough to be observable by others and not represent merely subjective feelings.

Decreased energy, tiredness, and fatigue are common (Criterion A6). A person may report sustained fatigue without physical exertion. Even the smallest tasks seem to require substantial effort. The efficiency with which tasks are accomplished may be reduced. For example, an individual may complain that washing and dressing in the morning are exhausting and take twice as long as usual.

The sense of worthlessness or guilt associated with a Major Depressive Episode may include unrealistic negative evaluations of one's worth or guilty preoccupations or ruminations over minor past failings (Criterion A7). Such individuals often misinterpret neutral or trivial day to day events as evidence of personal defects and have an exaggerated sense of responsibility for untoward events. For example, a realtor may become preoccupied with self blame for failing to make sales even when the market has collapsed generally and other realtors are equally unable to make sales. The sense of worthlessness or guilt may be of delusional proportions (e.g., an individual who is convinced that he or she is personally responsible for world poverty). Blaming oneself for being sick and for failing to meet occupational or interpersonal responsibilities as a result of the depression is very common and, unless delusional, is not considered sufficient to meet this criterion.

Many individuals report impaired ability to think, concentrate, or make decisions (Criterion A8). They may appear easily distracted or complain of memory difficulties. Those in intellectually demanding academic or occupational pursuits are often unable to function adequately even when they have mild concentration problems (e.g., a computer programmer who can no longer perform complicated but previously manageable tasks). In children, a precipitous drop in grades may reflect poor concentration. In elderly individuals with a Major Depressive Episode, memory difficulties may be the chief complaint and may be mistaken for early signs of a dementia ('pseudo-dementia'). When the Major Depressive Episode is successfully treated, the memory problems often fully abate. However, in some individuals, particularly elderly persons, a Major Depressive Episode may sometimes be the initial presentation of an irreversible dementia.

Frequently there may be thoughts of death, suicidal ideation, or suicide attempts (Criterion A9). These thoughts range from a belief that others would be better off if the person were dead, to transient but recurrent thoughts of committing suicide, to actual specific plans of how to commit suicide. The frequency, intensity, and lethality of these thoughts can be quite variable. Less severely suicidal individuals may report transient (1 to 2 minute), recurrent (once or twice a week) thoughts. More severely suicidal individuals may have acquired materials (e.g., a rope or a gun) to be used in the suicide attempt and may have established a location and time when they will be isolated from others so that they can accomplish the suicide. Although these behaviours are associated statistically with suicide attempts and may be helpful in identifying a high risk group, many studies have shown that it is not possible to predict accurately whether or when a particular individual with depression will attempt suicide. Motivations for suicide may include a desire to give up in the face of perceived insurmountable obstacles or an intense wish to end an excruciatingly painful emotional state that is perceived by the person to be without end ...

Criteria for major depressive episode

A. *Five (or more) of the following symptoms have been present during the same 2 week period and represent a change from previous functioning; at least one of the symptoms is either (1) depressed mood or (2) loss of interest or pleasure.*

   Note: *Do not include symptoms that are clearly due to a general medical condition, or mood incongruent delusions or hallucinations.*

   (1) *depressed mood most of the day, nearly every day, as indicated by either subjective report (e.g., feels sad or empty) or observation made by others (e.g., appears tearful).* **Note:** *In children and adolescents, can be irritable mood.*

   (2) *markedly diminished interest or pleasure in all, or almost all, activities most of the day, nearly every day (as indicated by either subjective account or observation made by others).*

   (3) *significant weight loss when not dieting or weight gain (e.g., a change of more than 5% of body weight in a month), or decrease or increase in appetite nearly every day.* **Note:** *In children, consider failure to make expected weight gains.*

   (4) *insomnia or hypersomnia nearly every day.*

   (5) *psychomotor agitation or retardation nearly every day (observable by others, not merely subjective feelings of restlessness or being slowed down).*

   (6) *fatigue or loss of energy nearly every day.*

   (7) *feelings of worthlessness or excessive or inappropriate guilt (which may be delusional) nearly every day (not merely self reproach or guilt about being sick).*

   (8) *diminished ability to think or concentrate, or indecisiveness, nearly every day (either by subjective account or as observed by others).*

   (9) *recurrent thoughts of death (not just fear of dying), recurrent suicidal ideation without a specific plan, or a suicide attempt or a specific plan for committing suicide.*

B. *The symptoms do not meet criteria for a Mixed Episode (see p. 365).*

C. The symptoms cause clinically significant distress or impairment in social, occupational, or other important areas of functioning.

D. The symptoms are not due to the direct physiological effects of a substance (e.g., a drug of abuse, a medication) or a general medical condition (e.g., hypothyroidism).

E. The symptoms are not better accounted for by Bereavement, i.e., after the loss of a loved one, the symptoms persist for longer than 2 months or are characterized by marked functional impairment, morbid preoccupation with worthlessness, suicidal ideation, psychotic symptoms, or psychomotor retardation.

Postpartum onset specifier

The specifier With Postpartum Onset can be applied to the current (or, if the full criteria are not currently met for a Major Depressive, Manic, or Mixed Episode, to the most recent) Major Depressive, Manic, or Mixed Episode of Major Depressive Disorder, Bipolar I Disorder, or Bipolar II Disorder or to Brief Psychotic Disorder (p329) if onset is within 4 weeks after childbirth. The symptoms of the postpartum-onset Major Depressive, Manic, or Mixed Episode do not differ from the symptoms in non-postpartum mood episodes. Symptoms that are common in postpartum-onset episodes, though not specific to postpartum onset, include fluctuations in mood, mood lability, and preoccupation with infant well being, the intensity of which may range from over concern to frank delusions. The presence of severe ruminations or delusional thoughts about the infant is associated with a significantly increased risk of harm to the infant.

Postpartum-onset mood episodes can present either with or without psychotic features. Infanticide is most often associated with postpartum psychotic episodes that are characterized by command hallucinations to kill the infant or delusions that the infant is possessed, but it can also occur in severe postpartum mood episodes without such specific delusions or hallucinations. Postpartum mood (Major Depressive, Manic, or Mixed) episodes with psychotic features appear to occur in from 1 in 500 to 1 in 1,000 deliveries and may be more common in primiparous women. The risk of postpartum episodes with psychotic features is particularly increased for women with prior postpartum mood episodes but is also elevated for those with a prior history of a Mood Disorder (especially Bipolar I Disorder). Once a woman has had a postpartum episode with psychotic features, the risk of recurrence with each subsequent delivery is between 30% and 50%. There is also some evidence of increased risk of postpartum psychotic mood episodes among women without a history of Mood Disorders with a family history of Bipolar Disorders. Postpartum episodes must be differentiated from delirium occurring in the postpartum period, which is distinguished by a decreased level of awareness or attention.

Women with postpartum Major Depressive Episodes often have severe anxiety and even Panic Attacks. Maternal attitudes toward the infant are highly variable but can include disinterest, fearfulness of being alone with the infant, or over intrusiveness that inhibits adequate infant rest. It is important to distinguish postpartum mood episodes from the 'baby blues', which affect up to 70% of women during the 10 days postpartum, are transient, and do not impair functioning. Prospective studies have demonstrated that mood and anxiety symptoms during pregnancy, as well as the 'baby blues', increase the risk for a postpartum Major Depressive Episode. A past personal history of non-postpartum Mood Disorder and a family history of Mood Disorders also increase the risk for the development of a postpartum Mood Disorder. The risk factors, recurrence rates, and symptoms of postpartum onset Mood Episodes are similar to those of non-postpartum Mood Episodes. However, the post-partum period is unique with respect to the degree of neuroendocrine alterations and psychosocial adjustments, the potential impact of breast feeding on treatment planning, and the long term implications of a history of postpartum Mood Disorder on subsequent family planning.

Comment

One thing that may have stood out in reading this extract was the effort taken to reduce the harrowing nature of someone's mental health distress to a representative description. The criteria for a major depressive episode attempt to define the number of symptoms and their duration as well as excluded factors to determine the accuracy of diagnosis. I should add that the diagnosis determined through these criteria only forms one part of the overall diagnostic decision. The DSM is based on a multi-axial or multidimensional set of factors (see Chapter 2). If a service user meets the criteria for a major depressive episode, this would only form one of the five axes or dimensions of the diagnosis. Additional axes address related mental health diagnoses if present, any relevant physical health factors, significant psychosocial stressors, and require the diagnostician to ascribe a score on a scale that describes different manifestations of social and emotional function-ing. Finally, this information is evaluated and the diagnostician – based on the criteria outlined in the extract – makes a decision whether the depression is classed as mild, mod-erate or severe. Hopefully the diagnosis should represent the true and valid nature of someone's mental health distress. The extract also included specific criteria for depression related to PND. In this, the passage emphasised that women may have 'baby blues', an experience of feeling low that would be less intense than mild depression.

- *What is your reaction to reading this extract?*
- *What if any advantages might there be to having a diagnosis? What disadvantages might there be?*

Comment

As you read this extract, you may appreciate the detail and effort it has taken to try to make sense of the often difficult-to-define aspects of mental health difficulties. You may have also questioned diagnosis as a tool and as an approach to labelling another person. One disadvantage of diagnosis includes the risk that both providers and others will treat people as if the diagnosis represents the totality of their being. Additionally, having a diagnosis may alter people's expectations of themselves and that others have of them. This is supported by Bjorklund (1996, cited by Hayne, 2003, p723) [who suggests that] ... *receiving a psychiatric diagnosis goes ... beyond acquiring knowledge about functioning in that the diagnostic label becomes a transforming influence to actually shape 'present and future life expectations'* (p1329).

Hayne (2003), who interviewed 14 service users to gain a phenomenological understanding of their experience of diagnosis, noted that participants reported that *diagnosis can introduce notions of enduring vulnerability ... [and] ... perpetuate resistance to [a] sustained sense of wellness in life, as captured in one person's account of forever 'feeling like a glass ball'* (p722). Hayne (2003, p723) also emphasises that *significant social powers issue from (diagnosis) at world and local levels* [such as] ... *power to institute policy, legitimate illness for access to care benefits, provide rationale in litigation, and so on.* As such, Hall (1996) points to the massive power of psychiatric diagnosis to devastate the identity of individuals designated ill and impose lifelong limitations through prophetic labelling. From this, we need to keep in mind whether for us diagnostic labels influence how we consider people's life expectations and if we hold limiting beliefs about people. We also need to recognise the power of this in the services where we work and in society.

Alongside that partial account of disadvantages, there may be advantages also. One of these may be in facilitating communication. This means using terms that are recognisable and understood by clinicians in different agencies, hospitals, mental health services and from country to country. In this way, a classification system of mental health difficulties may *give an idea of what sort of help to offer a person with this diagnosis* (Geraghty, 2002, p4). In addition, obtaining a formal diagnosis may support persons to make claims for entitlements such as disability benefits. This is complex as there may be both good and bad points to this. As Hayne (2003) suggested, diagnosis may mean individuals receive benefits which may be helpful financially but simultaneously provide concrete evidence of the debilitating nature of having an illness. In any event, the impact of mental health difficulties leading to disability would be more likely with more long-lasting conditions which will be covered in the following chapter. A further advantage may be in receiving a diagnosis which may confirm the distress that many people living with mental health needs may experience. In Hayne's study (2003, p726), a theme voiced by participants as *making the invisible visible* meant that receiving a *diagnosis ... made the illness evident and treatment possible.* One of the participants, Cheryl, noted that *with diagnosis she has been enabled to retrieve hope ...*

As we close this brief consideration of the benefits and problematic aspects of diagnosis, we should reiterate that diagnosis should be a means to an end – a means to identify a problem that is affecting someone's life and to provide guidance so that treatment or support might help resolve it.

- *Try to find out what happens if someone experiences puerperal or postpartum psychosis.*

- *The extract notes that postpartum psychosis can lead to a greater risk of infanticide. How would you need to intervene if you suspected that a new mother might be experiencing psychosis?*

Managing crisis and relieving suffering

In the preceding Points to consider, you are invited to think how you would approach and respond to a possible crisis, as the question implies that postpartum psychosis or the onset of psychotic symptoms in women who have given birth will be of great concern. The following statistics highlight the severity but rarity of this condition.

- *Postpartum psychosis is the most severe form of postpartum psychiatric illness.*

- *The condition is rare and occurs in approximately 1–2 per 1000 women after childbirth.*

- *At highest risk are women with a personal history of bipolar disorder or a previous episode of postpartum psychosis.*

- *Postpartum psychosis has a dramatic onset, emerging as early as the first 48–72 hours after delivery. In most women, symptoms develop within the first 2 postpartum weeks.*

(Nonacs, 2007, n.p.)

The data suggest a *dramatic onset* of symptoms which would require a rapid response by providers to reduce the risk and threats to both the mother's and child's health. The above figures offer some insight into the most critical periods for postpartum psychosis and the need to attend to these symptoms quickly, particularly in women with prior history of severe mental health need. In the following chapter, we will look more closely at the condition of bipolar disorder.

To understand mental health crisis and crisis stabilisation, it may help to revisit the general experience of living with mental health distress. Having an acute mental health problem could range in distress from a milder experience to a severe and immobilising one. How this will manifest will depend on multiple and contributing factors. An incidence of postpartum psychosis would be both acute and severe. Faced with this, you would need to realise that the situation requires emergency medical help and assessment. Depending on your role, you would likely need to liaise with family members, with current medical providers such as a GP and health visitor and, if part of the service user's system, members of a mental health team. If addressed successfully, the acute crisis may respond to the help and intervention offered and hopefully will be less likely to recur. For others, depending on the difficulty, mental health needs may recur and develop into a chronic condition requiring ongoing help.

Service user perspectives on being in crisis

In either case, the experience of a crisis prompts the need for or the seeking of help generally, and it may be helpful to think about the experience of someone in a mental health crisis. Depending on the symptoms, people may be cognisant of this or not – but there will be increased risk and need for relief. There is a growing body of research that documents service users' perspectives in relation to crisis. Golightley (1985), cited in *Social work and mental health* (2008), offers service user perspectives about what is needed during a crisis. He reports that service users need a *feeling of being in control* as well as *a choice of treatments*. He also emphasises the use of *crisis pre-planning*. In addition to receiving pertinent information, service users also *want to have someone to listen to them and to understand their explanation of what their crisis is about* (2008, p110). As Golightley (2008, p110/2005, p108) emphasises, *listening is an active process and ... one in which ... social workers need to be skilled*. The task of pre-planning can be likened to the use of advance directives which, produced by service users, outline service users' treatment requests if a crisis situation develops. Hopkins and Niemiec (2007) completed a study of service users to identify what was helpful and what did not help during a crisis. This was developed as part of a crisis assessment and treatment team's effort to evaluate its service using service user feedback.

The authors indicated that some of the feedback confirmed previous qualities related to crisis response; whereas novel findings also emerged that helped practitioners understand service users' perspectives more fully in relation to responding to mental health crisis. Several themes emerged from the data analysis. 'Accessibility' meant that services were considered helpful when they could be accessed at times of crisis as recounted by the following respondent.

> *The speed at which it happened was very important to me because I was in a state where I needed something urgently. That was important.* (Hopkins and Niemiec, 2007, p311)

Respondents emphasised the importance of good and clear communication between themselves and their service provider, between their partners or significant others and the crisis worker, within the mental health team and between the team and other services. Service users appreciated the availability of practitioners, particularly when service providers stayed to listen when needed, which concurs with Golightley (1985). In terms of choice and negotiation, Hopkins and Niemiec (2007, p315) reported that

> *(w)hile the person was in crisis, being able to make choices was not reported to be very important. Many of our participants said that they felt they were in no position, and had no wish, to make choices or to negotiate their options.*

> To me it wasn't important to negotiate. I just took what was offered to me at the time. I was in too much of an upset state to negotiate anything or to be bothered about things like that at that time ...

Respondents also appreciated being allowed to *feel normal*.

> *It seemed that 'being treated as normal' and being listened to respectfully were very important in helping the person in crisis to retain the capacity to establish their own solutions and thus retain the power in their lives (Barker, 2004).* (Hopkins and Niemiec, 2007, p314)

Hopkins and Niemiec (2007, p313) also indicated that *crisis theory suggests that when a person is in crisis … they face a situation which is not amenable to their usual coping strategies* [and] *they may become temporarily confused, anxious, depressed and tense and may become dependent upon negative coping strategies.*

These findings help to understand the crisis experience of those living with more severe mental health need. As Golightley (1985, 2008) and Hopkins and Niemiec (2007) relate, there is a need to respond quickly, to validate the person's crisis experience, to listen sensitively and to work collaboratively with the person in crisis and their system as well as with colleagues and other services to stabilise the difficulty and facilitate the service user's return to a more safe state of mind and a sense of physical safety.

Learning about mental health need: Information resources

In the prior extracts, we gained a sense of the personal experience of living with depression following childbirth. In reading about the definition of depression developed by the APA, you gained a sense of the medical approach to diagnosis. Above, we considered what might happen in a crisis given that the severe manifestation of postpartum psychiatric symptoms would likely lead to a crisis and need medical intervention. In an effort to increase information about and the understanding of mental health needs, MIND, a mental health charity, produces publications and offer training. The following extract describes treatment options and comes from one of the many publications produced by MIND in its efforts to educate the public, those living with mental health need and professionals.

EXTRACT THREE

Cloutte, P (2003) Understanding postnatal depression. *Revised edition.* London: MIND, pp9–11.

What sort of treatment is available?

PND is not only a distressing condition, it's a serious and disabling one, which can be nipped in the bud if it's spotted early. It can be hugely reassuring to both you and your partner to know what's wrong.

If PND isn't acknowledged and addressed, it's likely to last longer and be more severe than it need be, and this can affect the relationship between you and your baby. You need help, but you may need encouragement to seek it, and support in getting it. Feeling reluctant to ask for help is part of the problem.

Possible sources of help include your GP, midwife, health visitor, community psychiatric nurse, psychiatrist, psychotherapist or counsellor. Unfortunately, it's still true that some health professionals may not have received adequate training, or may simply be too hard-pressed to recognise the condition. There is now a questionnaire available to health visitors and GPs to help them distinguish the problem from the 'baby blues'.

Experts suggest that the best treatment for PND may be a combination of practical support and advice, counselling or psychotherapy, and if necessary, antidepressants.

Counselling and psychotherapy

Talking treatments, such as counselling and psychotherapy, offer you the opportunity to look at the underlying factors that have contributed to the PND, as well as helping you to change the way you feel. Many GPs now have a counsellor or psychotherapist attached to the practice.

They can also refer patients to a psychiatrist or psychologist on the NHS. Various organisations offer talking treatments, and some of them operate a low-fee scheme for those who can't afford to pay ... Cognitive behaviour therapy is increasingly popular as a short-term treatment, providing you with practical strategies for dealing with problems ...

Prescription medicine

A GP can prescribe various different kinds of medication to help, and it's important to discuss this fully, beforehand, and to keep monitoring progress. It may be necessary to try different medications, or to adjust the dosage, to achieve the best results. Any medication can enter the breast milk and this will be an important consideration.

Antidepressants are a possible answer, but you need to find one that suits you, and they take time to work. They can also have side effects. Most new antidepressants are not considered to be addictive, but you should be prepared to take them for at least six months. GPs sometimes prescribe a tranquilliser, such as Valium, to deal with severe anxiety and sleeplessness. These can be addictive and should only be used for a few weeks ... Treatments involving hormone supplements are still relatively untried, but, as yet, there is no strong evidence in support of them. Although oestrogen patches may benefit some women, this is not yet established.

How can family and friends help?

It may be both difficult and frustrating to live with someone who has PND. It may be helpful to think of the birth of the baby as a crisis that everyone has to adjust to, to avoid blaming any one family member for the distress ...

Try to find out as much as you can about postnatal depression, and, if necessary, be prepared to fight for more resources. Be prepared to talk about it, so that the problem does not remain invisible.

Comment

Hayne's (2003) writing about service users' perspectives of being diagnosed in the mental health system, discusses what it is like for a 'patient' to experience receiving a diagnosis from a medical provider. He notes that there is a power differential between the two parties, with the medical provider having expert knowledge that bestows a label and then prescribes treatment to the patient/recipient. Hayne (2003) referred to Bjorkland (1996) and others when highlighting the issue of power being held by providers – particularly the provider of the diagnosis, generally a physician. Though our healthcare system continues to operate with a medical model which relies on the doctor–patient dynamic, there has been a growing and vocal service user movement to try to temper what at times may be a power imbalance. Having access to understandable information about mental health may help to achieve greater parity for patients and doctors through public education, some of which may be written and disseminated by service users. The extract from Cloutte (2003) is an example of accessible information that may stimulate help-seeking.

POINTS TO CONSIDER

In Cloutte's (2003, pp9–10) extract, she writes that most new antidepressants are not considered to be addictive ... *and also notes that* talking treatments, such as counselling and psychotherapy, offer ... the opportunity to look at the underlying factors that have contributed to the PND, as well as helping you to change the way you feel.

Using the internet for research by accessing reputable media, health provider or health education websites, such as www.bbc.co.uk/health, www.rcpsych.ac.uk, *and* www.mentalhealthcare.org.uk:

* *identify what the new anti-depressants are and investigate if it is accurate to say that antidepressants are addictive; and*

* *look into different counselling or therapy approaches and determine which, if any, are recommended to offer help to people who report depressive symptoms.*

Comment

I urged you to investigate a few different sources in addressing the reflective tasks above because there may be widely divergent opinions – some of you may be in possession of strong feelings for or against anti-depressants, for instance – in relation to both anti-depressant medication and therapy. If you looked at the Royal College of Psychiatrists website, you would have found concise and understandable information. This body seems to take a balanced approach to the issue of addictiveness of anti-depressant medication and acknowledges their effects are not fully understood. Their position is that anti-depressants are not addictive, but that there may be withdrawal symptoms which might be more severe if the dose of the medicine is not tapered, or reduced over time. As for therapy, the obvious type is cognitive behavioural therapy, an approach that was developed to respond to depression because its founders, theorists such as Beck and Ellis, believed that negative thinking led to or worsened depressed mood. Prominent in the UK currently is the difficulty there seems to be in obtaining access to therapy in timely and responsive ways.

Therapeutic approaches to treating mental health need

Thinking about availability and access to therapy is the topic of the following extract. In it, a charity and policy-making organisation, the Mental Health Foundation, challenges the current mental health service delivery system and highlights the dearth of therapeutic approaches responding to mental health need. Related to this and perhaps borne out from this effort is the government's new initiative, *Improving access to psychological therapies*, a £200 million effort (Burne, 2008) to address the gaps in therapy provision which seem to be prompted by findings that link mental health need to under- or unemployment.

EXTRACT FOUR

Bird, A (2006) **We need to talk: The case for psychological therapy on the NHS.** *London: Mental Health Foundation, p2.*

1. SUMMARY

Psychological therapies are known to be effective for treating a wide range of mental health conditions. These include depression, anxiety and schizophrenia. The most widely accepted psychological treatment is cognitive behavioural therapy (CBT).

Availability of CBT and other evidence-based therapies on the NHS is extremely limited. Waiting times of more than a year are commonplace. This forces GPs to give, for example, antidepressant medications for depression when they think CBT would be preferable. While some people pay for private treatment, others cannot and go without.

This is a major inequality in health care. The NHS exists to offer effective and cost-effective treatments free at the point of delivery in a timely manner. A failure to offer evidence-based treatments for physical health problems like cancer would rightly lead to a national outcry. We believe the non-availability of psychological therapies is equally unacceptable.

The cost of not offering psychological therapy is considerable. The human cost of prolonged ill-health amounts to the equivalent of £41 billion a year. The economic cost of lost work is a further £23 billion. In addition, the NHS spends £338 million a year on antidepressant medication alone.

Offering timely access to evidence-based psychological therapies could help to reduce these costs. It can help young people achieve better educational outcomes. It can help people stay in work rather than go on benefits. It can prevent unnecessary suffering among people of all ages, cultural backgrounds, and with a range of mental and physical health conditions.

Better access to psychological therapies requires investment. We need resources to identify new and existing workers to provide therapies. We need a robust system of regulation and training to ensure high standards are met. And we need more investment in research to find out more about what therapies work in which cases ...

We recommend that:

1. *The NHS should implement NICE guidance as a matter of urgency.*

2. *The Government's 2007 Comprehensive Spending Review should provide for improved access to talking therapies.*

3. *The NHS should introduce waiting time measures for access to mental health treatments.*

4. *The Department of Health should make a realistic assessment of the workforce and training implications of delivering psychological therapies.*

5. *The Department of Health and regulatory bodies should ensure substantive measures for public protection from malpractice.*

6. *The Department of Health should investigate the current bias in research priorities and address it by supporting more research into psychological therapies.*

Comment

The Mental Health Foundation, in this extract, makes a case for offering psychological therapy more widely through the NHS. It links the availability of therapies as a means to address higher ancillary health costs. To take this beyond the individual realm, it also seems relevant to consider the policy implications of funding greater access to therapy. Bartlett and Sandland (2003), who contributed an extract to Chapter 3, astutely noted that power is not only manifested through what policy initiative is supported by government but is actually operationalised through funding. It is reasonable to ask with funding going toward one initiative, what other initiative is not supported? In the case of psychological therapies, the March 2008 (Burne, 2008) announcement to support greater access to psychological therapies with funding of £200 million is a significant manifestation of power.

C H A P T E R   S U M M A R Y

It seems hard to capture the breadth and diversity that living with mental health distress evokes for the people experiencing it. The perspective offered by Stephanie Merritt is one voice from the group of women who have experienced postnatal depression. More expansively, she is one of millions who have considered suicide as an option but have come back from this either to seek help or to simply carry on. In relating the story of those living with more acute mental health distress to the experience of postnatal depression, this chapter has made an effort to link mental health need to a very common experience which nearly all of us may be able to relate to in some way. Certainly it shows us that mental health need – along the continuum from 'baby blues' to the clinically diagnosable conditions of postnatal depression and postpartum psychosis – is prevalent and present to varying extent. The more specialised information relating to PND also holds the kernels of information related to the experience of depression and features of other mood disorders and, in terms of diagnosis, represents a similar framework that would be applied to other mental health need, such as anxiety disorders, substance misuse disorders, intellectual disability and adjustment disorders. By knowing something specifically about the diagnosis of PND as represented in the DSM-IV-TR, you will have the basic information to be able to learn in more detail about other mental health difficulties. And understanding this medical approach to diagnosis offered alongside the voice of someone living with depression and information prepared by a non-governmental body such as MIND, you start developing a linked and deeper awareness of the issues central to mental health social work. By being able to access a variety of perspectives – from medical and health sources, from reputable media like the BBC and from third-sector organisations like MIND, as well as service user forums, you draw from various sources of information to inform yourself about mental health subjects and to help you in your work with clients. This information also exists alongside the societal and policy-driven context of health and mental healthcare in the UK which was illustrated by policy initiatives to improve access to psychological therapies as a means of relieving mental health distress. By increasing our understanding of and sensitivity to the experience of living with mental health difficulties, we will hopefully offer more informed responses in practice.

FURTHER READING

Mustapha, A (ed.) (2003) *Depression during and after pregnancy*. London: Depression Alliance.

Depression Alliance, listed below as a useful website, also produces publications; this pamphlet is measured and informative.

National Institute for Mental Health in England (2006) National initiative will mean better access to talking therapies. In *NIMHE Update*, June. Leeds: NIMHE.

The government's update related to talking therapies.

WEBSITES

The MIND website has a rich source of fact sheets and publications available on a variety of topics in their Information section.

www.mind.org.uk

www.depressionalliance.org

The Institute of Psychiatry, part of King's College London, offers the following website as a source of information for providers and the general public.

www.mentalhealthcare.org.uk/

Information on the government's initiative related to psychological therapies is available below.

www.iapt.nhs.uk/

Chapter 6
Living with persistent mental health difficulties

This chapter will contribute to helping you to meet the following National Occupational Standards.

Key Role 1: Prepare for, and work with individuals, families, carers, groups and communities to assess their needs and circumstances.

- Work with individuals, families, carers, groups and communities to help them make informed decisions.
- Assess needs and options to recommend a course of action.

Key Role 2: Plan, carry out, review and evaluate social work practice, with individuals, families, carers, groups, communities and other professionals.

- Interact with individuals, families, carers, groups and communities to achieve change and development and to improve life opportunities.
- Address behaviour which presents a risk to individuals, families, carers, groups and communities.

Key Role 3: Support individuals to represent their needs, views and circumstances.

Key Role 4: Manage risk to individuals, families, carers, groups, communities, self and colleagues.

Key Role 5: Manage and be accountable, with supervision and support, for your own social work practice.

- Work within multidisciplinary and multi-organisational teams, networks and systems.

It will also introduce you to the following academic standards as set out in the social work subject benchmark statement.

Defining principles

4.6 Social work is a moral activity that requires practitioners to recognise the dignity of the individual, but also to make and implement difficult decisions (including restriction of liberty) in human situations that involve the potential for benefit or harm ... This means that honours undergraduates [and others studying social work] must learn to:

- Recognise and work with the powerful links between intrapersonal and interpersonal factors and the wider social, legal, economic, political and cultural context of people's lives.
- Practise in ways that maximise safety and effectiveness in situations of uncertainty and incomplete information.
- Work in partnership with service users and carers and other professionals to foster dignity, choice and independence, and effect change.

5.1.1 Social work services, service users and carers, which include:

- The social processes (associated with, for example, poverty, migration, unemployment, poor health, disablement, lack of education and other sources of disadvantage) that lead to marginalisation, isolation and exclusion, and their impact on the demand for social work services ...

5.1.2 The service delivery context

- The changing demography and cultures of communities in which social workers will be practising ...
- The significance of interrelationships with other social services, especially education, housing, health, income maintenance and criminal justice ...

5.1.4 Social work theory

- Research-based concepts and critical explanations from social work theory and other disciplines that contribute to the knowledge base of social work, including their distinctive epistemological status and application to practice.
- The relevance of psychological, physical and physiological perspectives to understanding individual and social development and functioning.

Introduction

In this and the preceding chapter we are working to capture the depth and breadth of mental health need. In an effort to do this, we are drawing distinctions between the former chapter's focus on more acute or shorter-term conditions and this chapter's focus on mental health needs that people experience for longer periods of time. Hopefully this division will accurately represent the wide range of mental health needs that affects adults. Henderson (2001), who contributes an extract in this chapter, writes that

> It is important that all people's needs should be recognised, whether they are 'carers' or users of mental health services, and that those services are responsive to the diversity of experience and need in mental health. (p151)

Appreciating the *diversity of experience and need in mental health* as stated by Henderson (2001, p151), I hope this book's discussion of mental health concepts and difficulties will serve as the starting point for further learning and inquiry.

This chapter will explore the experience of mental health that is more persistent in people's lives and look at conditions that, though responsive to treatment and at times lessened or absent, persist and mean that service users remain in ongoing contact with mental health services. For these service users, service delivery likely takes place in specialised settings such as community mental health teams (CMHTs) and, depending on crisis stablisation plans, may involve hospital stays if the more contained treatment of an inpatient hospital setting is needed. However, when people experience the beginnings of a mental health need that will persist, they may first go to a GP for help or be in touch with advice lines or other accessible services. For this reason, we use this chapter to think about what it may be like to make an effort to get help when suspecting a problem, what it might be like to be told of a diagnosis and also what kinds of treatment and support options there will be if needed both for users and people close to them.

Living with longer-term mental health need

In a similar way to Chapter 5, we use personal memoir as an entrée into understanding and framing the experience of mental health need. In this chapter, Kay Redfield Jamison (1995), a well known authority on mood disorders – particularly bipolar disorder – recounts her personal experience of living with manic depression, which is an earlier term synonymous with bipolar disorder and used to describe living with extremes of mood variance. The excerpt, which includes passages from her book, *An unquiet mind,* describes her early experience when she began to question her moods and when symptoms started affecting her, as well as her later perspective after some decades of treatment.

Henderson (2001), whose ideas introduced this chapter, contributes the second extract. She uses a qualitative methodological approach to explore the changing policy and personal perspectives of users of mental health services and carers by capturing their thoughts, feelings and opinions. The final extract, a second journal article, describes the impact of living with mental health needs on participants' social relationships. It also considers the consequences and impact that social relationships have on mental health needs. Throughout this chapter the narratives of service users will hopefully convey the diversity of the experience of living with mental health need.

A memoir of living with bipolar disorder

Kay Redfield Jamison is an academic, a psychologist, a successful author and a woman who has bipolar disorder. In her memoir, she offers an account of her early life, her achievements through secondary school – a period she describes as enjoyable and energetic – and the onset of mood changes that left her depressed, irritable and at times agitated. She chronicles moments of living which expand to include periods of deep depression interspersed with manic mood states and a psychotic episode. Throughout the book, she shares her thoughts and reactions on living with this. A significant part of Dr Jamison's (1995) story chronicles how she came to get help for her experience of manic depression. This is not fully recounted in the extract; however, if you have an opportunity to read her memoir, you will learn that she developed psychotic symptoms and the seriousness of this prompted her need for help.

EXTRACT ONE

Redfield Jamison, K (1995) An unquiet mind, A memoir of moods and madness. New York: Alfred A. Knopf, pp42, 44–5, 91 and 212–13.

College, for some people I know, was the best time of their lives. This is inconceivable to me. College was, for the most part, a terrible struggle, a recurring nightmare of violent and dreadful moods spelled only now and again by weeks, sometimes months, of great fun, passion high enthusiasms, and long runs of very hard but enjoyable work. This pattern of shifting moods and energies had a very seductive side to it, in large part because of fitful reinfusions of the intoxicating moods that I had enjoyed in high school. These were quite extraordinary, filling my brain with a cataract of ideas and more than enough energy to give me at least the illusion of carrying them out. My normal Brooks Brothers conservatism would go by the board; my hemlines would go up, my neckline down, and I would enjoy the sensuality of my youth. Almost everything was done to excess; instead of buying one Beethoven symphony, I would buy nine; instead of enrolling for five classes, I would enroll in seven; instead of buying two tickets for a concert I would buy eight or ten …

But then as night inevitably goes after the day, my mood would catch, and my mind again would grind to a halt. I lost all interest in my schoolwork, friends, reading, wandering, or daydreaming. I had no idea of what was happening to me, and I would wake up in the morning with a profound sense of dread that I was going to have to somehow make it through another entire day. I would sit for hour after hour in the undergraduate library, unable to muster up enough energy to go to class. I would stare out of the window, stare at my books, rearrange them, shuffle them around, leave them unopened, and think about dropping out of college. When I did go to class it was pointless. Pointless and painful. I understood very little of what was going on, and I felt as though only dying would release me from the overwhelming sense of inadequacy and blackness that surrounded me …

On occasion, these periods of total despair would be made even worse by terrible agitation. My mind would race from subject to subject, but instead of being filled with the exuberant and cosmic thoughts that had been associated with earlier periods of rapid thinking, it would be drenched in awful sounds and images of decay and dying: dead bodies on the beach, charred remains of animals, toe-tagged corpses in morgues. During these agitated periods I became exceedingly restless, angry, and irritable, and the only way I could dilute the agitation was to run along the beach or pace back and forth across my room like a polar bear at the zoo. I had no idea what was going on, and I felt totally unable to ask anyone for help. It never occurred to me that I was ill; my brain just didn't put it in those terms. Finally, how-ever, after hearing a lecture about depression in my abnormal psychology course, I went to the student health service with the intention of asking to see a psychiatrist. I got as far as the stairwell just outside the clinic but was only able to sit there, para-lyzed with fear and shame, unable to go in and unable to leave. I must have sat there, head in my hands, sobbing, for more than an hour. Then I left and never went back. Eventually, the depression went away of its own accord, but only long enough for it to regroup and mobilize for the next attack ...

[Kay Redfield Jamison graduated from university and went on pursue and complete her doctorate in psychology. She subsequently took up an academic post at an American university. Early in her appointment, she experienced psychotic symptoms and was diagnosed with manic depression or, as it is now known, bipolar disorder and prescribed lithium, a mood-stabilising medication.]

... Even though I was a clinician and a scientist, and even though I could read the research literature and see the inevitable, bleak consequences of not taking lithium, I for many years after my initial diagnosis was reluctant to take my medications as prescribed. Why was I so unwilling? Why did it take having to go through more episodes of mania, followed by long suicidal depressions, before I would take lithium in a medically sensible way?

Some of my reluctance, no doubt, stemmed from a fundamental denial that what I had was a real disease. This is a common reaction that follows, rather counterintuitively, in the wake of early episodes of manic-depressive illness. Moods are such as an essential part of the substance of life, of one's notion of oneself, that even psychotic extremes in mood and behaviour somehow can be seen as temporary, even understandable, reac-tions to what life has dealt. In my case, I had a horrible sense of loss for who I had been and where I had been. It was difficult to give up the high flights of mind and mood, even though the depressions that inevitably followed nearly cost me my life.

Although I am basically optimistic about remaining well, I know my illness from enough different vantage points to remain fatalistic about the future ... Many years of living with the cycle upheavals of manic-depressive illness has made me more philosophical, better armed, and more able to handle the inevitable swings of mood and energy ... Therefore, I now move more easily with the fluctuating tides of energy, ideas and enthusiasms that I remain so subject to.

Comment

This account relates just a snippet of the experiences that Kay Redfield Jamison has had over decades of living with a persistent mood disorder. As she writes, you get a sense of the challenge for anyone to fully accept and integrate the reality of living with a serious mental health need.

> *Moods are such an essential part of the substance of life ... that even psychotic extremes in mood and behaviour somehow can be seen as temporary, even under-standable, reactions to what life has dealt*. (Redfield Jamison, 1995, p91)

Bipolar disorder, like other mood disorders, may lead to psychotic symptoms when very severe. This corroborates with the discussion in Chapter 5 in relation to rare cases of severe PND. Subsequent to her first treatment for the psychotic symptoms of bipolar disorder, Dr Jamison gradually, over many years, worked to manage her mood instability through a strong relationship with a psychiatrist and therapist as well as support from work colleagues, family and friends.

Seeking treatment

You will note, however, that in this passage Dr Jamison recounts her effort to seek help by going to the university's student health service, but she writes that she sat ... *paralyzed with fear and shame, unable to go in and unable to leave* ... (Redfield Jamison, 1995, p45). Here, we might each of us be able to relate to the difficulty of talking about a problem that we fear disclosing and the resources of courage and willpower needed to attempt to address it. But as we have tried to convey, needing to speak about mental health difficulties is often hindered through feelings such as shame and fear. Such reactions may be more ardently present in a wide range of communities where talking about emotions or admitting to illness is less tolerated or accepted.

Types of bipolar disorder

As we have seen in Chapters 2 and 5, there are two main reference texts that help physicians and health professionals make decisions about mental health diagnoses. In the case of bipolar disorder, physicians would need to understand very clearly what a person's experiences are to diagnose the type of bipolar disorder. At present, there are two types of this disorder – Type I and Type II – that are distinguished by differences in symptoms and symptom length. For people living with bipolar disorder, the duration that symptoms are present and the more prominent level of intensity of symptoms are the two main items that separate Type I from Type II, with the former having a longer duration and more intensity of symptoms. Making sense of these distinctions and determining whether these distinctions are clinically helpful and relevant to service users' experiences and practitioners' work are part of ongoing critically reflective review. Relatively recently, there has been some question about whether these distinctions are adequate to describe the mood experiences of many people who do not fit these two diagnoses. As a result, there is a developing inquiry trying to describe the experiences of people who have a shift of mood but do not have discrete manic or depressed phases. At the moment, this is called bipolar spectrum disorder, and the themes that were discussed in relation to diagnosis in Chapter 5 would also fit nicely here.

Treatment approaches

Treating persistent mental health needs involves a range of approaches, but quite commonly this involves prescribing psychotropic medication, medication that is meant to have an effect on the symptom being described. In relation to treating bipolar disorder, medication would be prescribed to treat an acute manic episode, to prevent a recurrence of mania and to treat periods of depressed mood. Treatment is an individual choice, and clinical guidance developed by the National Institute of Health and Clinical Excellence (NICE) emphasises this. There may be gaps naturally between knowing intellectually that something may be helpful – such as a medication for a diagnosis that you find hard to accept – and truly choosing something with full commitment and acceptance. This is basic but important as we need to be able to appreciate the very human and very 'normal' difficulty of accepting having serious mental health difficulties. Dr Jamison (1995) writes about her *reluctance* to take ... *lithium in a medically sensible way* ... [linking this to] ... *a fundamental denial that what [she] had was a real disease* (p91). This tells us how an academic and specialist in treating mood disorders found it very hard to take a medication that has been shown to be effective in managing manic moods.

It helps to understand a bit about Dr Jamison's life to be able to think about what treatment approach was needed to help her. Her work, at the time she was describing, involved managing a research clinic into mood disorders, lecturing, research, clinical contact and supervising medical students. Her treatment involved lithium, a mood stabiliser, and therapeutic sessions. Having income and access to good-quality healthcare meant that she received a good standard of care. However, one of the major concerns she raises in her book is that she had a real worry that her statutory licence to practise psychology may have been at risk if the Board of Psychology in the state of California had determined she could not safely practise. Fortunately, she was able to document her adherence to medication and other treatment to demonstrate her safe level of practice. In fact, she has been very prolific and successful.

We should keep in mind, though, persons who, for reasons of other difficult life circumstances or purely due to the impact of mental health complications, experience problems of social disadvantage. It is possible that people living with bipolar disorder could experience work problems, disability, reduced income, difficult-to-resolve symptoms that do not respond to prescribed medication, and find it difficult to access adequate health and social care for any number of reasons. It is necessary to appreciate that there may be different responses to mental health need that may occur given different social circumstances. The table in Figure 6.1 offers a range of treatment options, many of which would be available contingent on adequate resources and service availability; as a result, it represents a rather ideal picture as offered by NICE from a series of clinical guidance publications.

Mental health condition	Treatment options		Other support
	Medication/Prescribed treatment	**Therapy and talking approaches**	
Bipolar disorder, Type I	• Medication to treat acute mania – such as lithium, valproate, or anti-psychotic medications • Prophylactic/preventative medication for long-term treatment (As above including anti-psychotic medicine like olanzapine) • Combinations of above medications, if needed • Anti-depressant medication during periods of depressed mood • Medication, such as anti-psychotics or tranquillisers, to manage agitated behaviour	• Various counselling approaches, such as cognitive therapy – recommended following acute phase • Family counselling sessions	• User support groups • Family and/or carer support groups • Advice on preparing advance directives • Discussion and preparation of crisis plans • Essential blood tests and/or health checks to monitor organ function, blood pressure, any development of adverse effects and levels of certain prescribed medication • Vocational support, if needed • Frequent medical monitoring during acute manic or severe depressive phases • Lifestyle support, such as promoting sleep hygiene • Psychosocial support offered by trained volunteers
Dementia – this may include Alzheimer's, vascular dementia or other types of dementia	• Cholinesterase inhibitors, such as donepezil, galantamine and rivastigmine (for moderate Alzheimer's only) • Anti-depressants if depressed mood is present • Medication to manage disruptive, aggressive or disinhibited behaviour (i.e. anti-psychotic or anti-manic medication)	• Structured cognitive stimulation programme • Supportive counselling • Reminiscence therapy • Music therapy	• Caregiver emotional support • Massage • Aromatherapy • Animal-assisted therapy (as a soothing treatment to manage, for instance, agitated behaviour) • Palliative care for advanced conditions
Major depression – this includes moderate depression in primary care or treatment in specialised mental health settings, such as CMHTs.	• Anti-depressant medication – treatment commonly begins with selective serotonin reuptake inhibitors (SSRIs) • Electroconvulsive treatment (considered while inpatient for entrenched and treatment-resistant depression)	Counselling and therapy approaches: cognitive behavioural therapy or interpersonal therapy	• Monitoring sessions with physican prescribing medication – frequency depends on risk for suicide and to check response to medication • Telephone support • Support groups • Support from trained volunteers • Crisis resolution treatment teams • Inpatient hospitalisation

Figure 6.1 *Treatment options in commonly experienced persistent mental health difficulties*

Mental health condition	Treatment options		
	Medication/Prescribed treatment	Therapy and talking approaches	Other support

Schizophrenia – treatment will vary depending on phase at : presentation first episode of schizophrenia, acute symptom period, promoting recovery	• Anti-psychotic medication
	   • Atypical oral medication – such as olanzapine, quetiapine, risperidone plus others
	   • Conventional/typical oral medication (i.e. haloperidol)
	   • By depot injection
	 • Medication to manage agitated or aggressive behaviour
		• Cognitive behavioural therapy (focusing on insight, understanding relapse and treatment adherence)
		 • Supportive counselling, if preferred
		 • Family therapy or family interventions
			• Supported housing
			 • Psychosocial programmes (i.e. clubhouse)
			 • Development of advance directives
			 • Crisis resolution and home treatment services
			 • Attention to service users' physical health, housing and social care needs
			 • Care and intervention in relation to substance misuse or learning difficulties, if present
			 • Supported employment
			 • Carer assessments
			 • Day programmes
			 • Inpatient hospital services

*Summary of points drawn from *Clinical guidelines* related to schizophrenia (NICE, 2002), bipolar disorder (NICE, 2006), depression (NICE, 2007) and dementia (NICE and SCIE, 2006) plus information at Medscape (2007). Consult guidance for comprehensive treatment recommendations.

Figure 6.1 *Treatment options in commonly experienced persistent mental health difficulties (continued)*

We should also note that information offered in Figure 6.1 is a brief summary of detailed guidance in relation to several persistent mental health conditions. The medication information is merely an overview of possible options. Treating the complex mental health symptoms that are present in major depression, dementia, bipolar disorder and schizophrenia with medication means that physicians need to follow clear guidance. Their professional responsibility will involve making medication recommendations in relation to a range of variables including but not limited to the following:

- severity of symptoms;

- previous medication treatment;

- current or previous treatment response;

- treatment for and/or the presence of other mental health conditions;

- treatment for and/or the presence of physical conditions;

- treatment for and/or the presence of substance misuse;

- age and sex of the clients.

The table, though, offers some idea of the range of options that should be available to respond to persistent mental health need. Many of the support options include areas for mental health social workers to make an impact on people's quality of life and their experience of living with mental health need. In addition, the guidance for certain conditions seems comprehensive in considering the needs of carers also.

CASE STUDY

Philip is a 57-year-old Irish man who was diagnosed with schizophrenia of the paranoid type 36 years ago. He lives in a bed-sit with a kitchenette and a separate bathroom; the property is managed by the local authority. He lives within walking distance of his CMHT, and he meets with his doctor once quarterly. A community mental health nurse (CMHN) visits him fortnightly to check on his symptoms and to give him an injection of haloperidol which he has been prescribed for 15 years; she notes the flat is not in very good order and remarks that Philip often appears dishevelled and without clean clothes. In his most recent CPA meeting, his sister – who attended – spoke about her concern for his health and hygiene. She noted that he smokes excessively and does not make much effort to clean his flat or discard rubbish that is piling up. She mentions that his diet consists of pies bought at the local bakery, save for a prepared meal she tries to bring every few weeks. She emphasises that he rarely sees people except for her, his nurse and the bakery staff. He used to enjoy music, both listening to it and making it, but he rarely does this anymore. When you have talked to him, he seems at times forgetful and sad when thinking about how long he has had to put up with schizophrenia.

1. *Highlight some of the concerns present in this case scenario.*

2. *Based on the concerns you identified and using the previous figure, identify two possible interventions to try to offer some relief or help to the situation.*

Comment

As you respond to this case, you would likely identify three themes in it: issues related to Philip, issues of his relationships and his living circumstances. In the first, he is being treated for schizophrenia and seems to be in the recovery phase as noted in the figure; he receives medication via injection, which may mean that he experiences both benefits and adverse effects of the medication. His mood is described as *sad*, and he seems *forgetful*. There seem to be health concerns, dietary concerns and a very limited social network. The latter also influences his relationships, which seem to be limited to his sister and professional carers – a psychiatrist and a CMHN. In addition, his sister has noted some issue related to housing.

Of the possible interventions, you may have made different choices based on what you assessed as priority areas. Determining if Philip is experiencing feelings of sadness or is experiencing a blunted, flattened affect which occurs with schizophrenia or has elements of both would be necessary before considering options to improve his mood. Possible interventions to help his mood may involve counselling or social support. Also, a detailed review of his medication and its continued effectiveness to address residual symptoms of schizophrenia may be indicated. In relation to his social isolation and his care of himself and his home, it may be useful to consider whether Philip would be open to relocating to supported housing and/or if he might be open to participating in a group or day programme to enhance his social network. His sister's concerns might be addressed through limited family meetings. You may have also noted a need to intervene in other areas, such as to facilitate his link to a physical health assessment or to offer support so that he might limit his smoking. These represent some of the ways mental health social work could offer a holistic approach to helping Philip.

'Carer' and 'user'?

The following extract from an article by Henderson (2001) generates a question about the concept of care and carers in mental health. We could easily find ourselves moving quickly beyond inquiry into care as a construct and concept to understanding it from the legal context as underpinned by the following statutes: Carers (Recognition and Services) Act 1995 (Great Britain, 1995); and the Carers (Equal Opportunities) Act 2004 (Great Britain, 2004). However, as part of critical understanding we will consider 'carer' as a concept affected by changes in society. The article – forcefully titled, 'He's not my carer, he's my husband' – interrogates and reviews the changing policy context related to the provision of informal care. Henderson (2001) considers what forces have influenced developments in this area and presents perspectives of people who are involved in informal care and their relationships with partners or family who are users of services. The change in roles and responsibilities forms the crux of this article as it underscores the variety of meanings attached to the concept of carer and its juxtaposition with the concept of service user.

Henderson, J (2001) *'He's not my carer, he's my husband': Personal and policy constructions of care in mental health.* **Journal of Social Work Practice,** *15 (2), 149–52 and 154–8.*

EXTRACT TWO

This paper argues that the development of informal care as a concept, and informal carer as an identity, have largely ignored the relationship in which the care is experienced. It further argues that mental distress poses a particular challenge to current models of care. In manic depression in particular, care involves a process of negotiation and re-negotiation between partners about the nature that care should take. Recognising the different individual needs of carers and cared for does not take account of their shared concerns or the experience, complexity and emotional content of care within relationships ...

Policy, discourse and care

In their analysis of the development of the concept of the informal carer, Bytheway and Johnson (1998) argue that 40 years ago the term 'carer' was barely in the English language. People who would now be identified as 'carers' would not have considered themselves in that way, or viewed themselves as belonging to a distinct group of people. In that way, Bytheway and Johnson suggest:

> We can think of the concept of 'carer' as a social construction, a category created by the interplay between individual experience and various interest groups – policy makers, researchers and pressure groups *(p. 241) ...*

However, neither Bytheway and Johnson nor Morris (1991, 1997) considered care within the context of mental health and distress. Definitions and discourses within mental health and illness are contested and changing. The dominance of mainstream psychiatry and medical explanations and treatments is being challenged and questioned by mental health system survivors. These challenges are taking place within the wider context of the government's 'safety first' approach with an emphasis on the importance of control. In this policy arena the carer role is assumed to have controlling, or at least monitoring, functions ...

It is important that all people's needs should be recognised, whether they are 'carers', or users of mental health services, and that those services are responsive to the diversity of experience and need in mental health. This, however, is where the problem with care intensifies, as assumptions are made about 'carers' and the role and place of care. Although there are several ways of conceptualising and describing care, it is treated as something separate from the regard and reciprocity that form the basis of many relationships. The emotional labour and relational dimensions of care within relationships are ignored apart from potential 'risks' to the carer's mental well-being that may stem from the burden of the care task.

Periods of distress may be experienced alongside periods of well-being. Care is part of a temporal process, or as Walmsley (1993) suggests, a continuum. Distress may be more painful at some times than others. Nor is experience of mental distress confined to one person in a couple. The identity of 'carer' and 'cared for' may be shared, with partners experiencing both identities at the same time. This dual identity may prove difficult for professionals to deal with, when expectations of the 'carer' role are at odds with those of the 'cared for' role. It is, perhaps, an example of the complexity of lived reality that is not matched by a similar complexity of policy response ...

Lived realities of care within relationships

Both people in a relationship may not always, or indeed ever, agree about the nature of care or the need for it. Is the identity of 'carer' inextricably linked with diagnosis? Does the diagnosis of one partner imply that the other is therefore a 'carer'? I would argue that just as some people will reject a diagnosis, so others will reject the 'carer' role. At times this will be complementary within a relationship – both partners accept or reject the ascribed identities. On the other hand, there may be disagreement within a relationship about diagnosis and therefore the need (or lack of it) for care ...

I can tell [doctors] at any given point this change has been going on, what my mood has been like. I've learned to look at it from a positive ten to a negative ten on a manic to depressive scale. I've learned with the help of some nurses how to quantify each and what does it exactly mean. So I keep good track of that as well. Ross has helped me with figuring out meds though. I don't know why that happened because I didn't need him to do that, but I think he needed to do something so he would put all the meds in the little pill boxes for me. I didn't need him to do it [laughter] [...] Well, I could do it myself but I thought he was just taking such an interest with something or maybe he felt helpless. I've never really asked him why he did it.

(Claire, user)

... The emotional component of the experience of care can be intense.

I sometimes think I'm exaggerating but other times, certainly at the time and looking back on it, I can see that it was worse than a bereavement. I'd lost the person during the depths of her illness, I had lost Teresa totally. In the early days I saw no reason to believe that she would recover, because nobody told me any different. I just thought this was a permanent deteriorating state that Teresa was in. I'd lost the person, I'd lost Teresa virtually totally, but I still had the body there which was haunting me. She was still wandering around, this body that was Teresa but now wasn't, was still wandering round haunting me. Taunting me when she was deluded and very sure that she was well herself really, I found that enormously difficult.

(Daniel, carer)

... Re-negotiating the terms of their relationship appears to be a major factor in determining the degree to which the changing relationship can be accepted by both parties ... Roles and responsibilities need to change or return to usual. Included in this process appears to be dealing with a (sometimes transient although intense) sense of loss ...

EXTRACT TWO *continued*

Conclusion

... The research is pointing to the centrality of relationship and the construction of care by both partners. Professionalisation, reciprocity and negotiation are key elements within relationships. Some professionals are moving towards an inclusive approach with carers as members of the care team, or at least integral members of aftercare discussions. Support systems for carers are being developed to provide them with information and education on various mental disorders. Initiatives like these, however, do not address the impact of 'care' on the relationship between two people. Individuals within relationships have their own concerns and needs. There is a need to consider the impact of these individual approaches on the shared and ongoing relationship. Professionals must take a step back and ground practice and services in people's own experiences and meanings.

Comment

One of the themes that Henderson (2001) highlights is the evolving social construction of care and the meaning of care as it is created and defined within the relationship(s) of user to carer. She also introduces the idea of fluidity of roles or identities. An overarching observation from her work reinforces the interplay between government provision of care, policy formulations that influence governmentally funded care and the input of service users to self-determination. Henderson (2001) gingerly introduces the potentially challenging aspect of caring in a mental health context which is borne out in the narrative examples used in the extract. In other work that looks at the support needs of family members of those with serious mental health needs, Pollio, et al. (2006) tried to respond to these needs by developing an intensive training that offered information and opportunities for psychological and emotional support. In the study, they investigate the helpfulness of psycho-educational workshops for family members of persons with severe mental illness in America. A factor that prompted this need was a trend toward and greater demand for family care.

Deinstitutionalization has shifted responsibility of care into community settings for even individuals with the most serious mental illnesses. Simultaneously, recent government policies have cut funding for intensive psychosocial stabilization services in the community. As a result of these changes, overburdened families are finding themselves increasingly responsible for care of a family member with a serious mental illness.

(Pollio, et al., 2006, p31)

Generalisation from an American system of care to the UK context is not entirely plausible; yet the same events have occurred and are occurring in the UK, suggesting some relevance of this statement to the UK experience.

Acknowledging loss in the experience of mental health need

The impact of serious mental health distress on family members is significant given the shifting focus of care from the state to the family. One of the participants in Henderson's (2001) research, Daniel, a carer, states:

> *... during the depths of (Teresa's) illness ... I'd lost the person, I'd lost Teresa virtually totally, but I still had the body there which was haunting me ...* (p156)

Such loss is not uncommon and, as Jones (2004) asserts, may need to be supportively accessed with the help of service providers so that carers or family members are able to acknowledge the difficult emotions associated with having a family member with mental health difficulties. Jones (2004), citing his earlier multicultural qualitative study about the impact of mental illness in families (Jones, 2002), delved into the emotional parameters of family members' reactions to mental health difficulties in a relative. In this, he explores what appear to be complex grief reactions in the family members in response to having a family member with serious mental health needs. Based on the participants' narrative data, he identified three strands of loss.

- Complicated bereavement due to the object of loss remaining present but altered (for example, a son still remains a son even if symptoms of mental illness irrevocably change personality characteristics).

- Feelings of anger – generally toward the person with mental health needs. For family members this anger feels 'wrong' creating a conflict and perhaps guilt, which further complicates the potential resolution of grief feelings.

- The stigma of mental illness may evoke a sense of shame, heightening isolation and insularity.

Jones (2004) also notes the tension for families of trying and needing to acknowledge these difficult emotions while simultaneously feeling a sense of commitment and love toward their relatives. He suggests that family members need sensitive intervention to help them to address their range of feelings – perhaps through group meetings. The model proposed by Pollio, et al. (2006) involves one-day intensive workshops with morning plenary sessions, such as 'What is mental illness?', lunchtime discussions based on themes identified by participants on the day, and afternoon breakout sessions focusing on local resources, more detailed but informal medical information and sessions showcasing incidents of success in how families live and work with mental health need in their family relationships. Overall, feedback from participants was positive, and quantitative analysis of a series of variables before and after the intensive sessions showed statistically significant change. I should note that the programme involves both family members living with mental health difficulties and relatives who choose to come. This active ownership and acknowledgement of the presence of mental illness in both users and carers through their participation may suggest an acceptance of these difficult issues that though not always achievable may be helpful. Hayne (2003, p723) writes that:

… Warner et al. (1989) revealed that 'label acceptors' manifested better overall functioning than 'label rejecters'. What was emphasized in the research of Vellenga and Christenson (1994) was the extent of … turmoil clients have in apprehending the… diagnosis and their need to cope with the deep losses evoked by it, in order to feel more reconciled with it.

Redfield Jamison (1995), herself, wrote … *I had a horrible sense of loss for who I had been* (p91). These powerful statements and the passages of people's lived experiences convey the challenge associated with this process. Through this, I hope you have gained some sense of the process of acceptance. Acknowledging painful and deep loss may be necessary to gain more reconciliation to the presence of serious mental health need. On top of this there also may be the need to accept the label of the diagnosis, as this may help with functioning.

The experience of stigma

Some of the reluctance that service users may feel in participating in mental healthcare may actually stem from the powerlessness of the 'patient' role and the associated stigma. Hayne (2003, p723) writes that:

… Raingruber (2002) reports stigma as [a] deterrent to seeking care and/or continuing in treatment. In all such cases, 'health' is compromised in the interests of evading stigma and retaining personal power.

Hayne (2003, p723) further cites the work of Keil (1992), who describes her reactions to *hearing the words of her diagnosis*:

Distorted and confused as my thoughts and feelings were when first diagnosed, the word 'schizophrenia' was momentous enough to account for the cataclysmic tremors I experienced inside. It rang in my ears, a death toll for the life I had once known. I sensed that then, but certainly could not have communicated it to anyone. The thoughts that emerged from my mouth were fragments, isolated snatches of what was going on in my mind. (p5)

With this, we gain a glimpse of Keil's (1992) reaction to being described as having schizophrenia. In it, she describes her diagnosis as a *death toll* (Keil, 1992, p5, cited by Hayne, 2003, p723). Redfield Jamison (1995) related her struggle to accept the diagnosis of bipolar disorder which she seems to have ultimately accepted. From Henderson (2001), both Daniel, a carer, and Claire, a user, shared their perspectives on the presence of mental health need in their lives. Woven into these narratives have been the theme of loss and at times feelings of anger, guilt and shame. Coping with difficult emotions is challenging. This is not to suggest that more positive emotions may not also accompany diagnosis. For some, diagnosis may be a sign of relief and a confirmation of the presence of difficulties; however, this conveys the importance for individuals and their close personal network of discussing and trying to make sense of the presence of mental health need in their lives.

Social connections and well-being

As the preceding narratives emphasise, the experience of living with mental health need challenges users and carers to attend to the intrapersonal and interpersonal dimensions of their lives. Section 4.6 of the social work benchmark statement expects us to work with service users' intra- and interpersonal experiences as well as the larger legislative and policy context. In practising mental health social work, we need to address multiple levels: by facilitating and making it possible for service users to relate their feelings and thoughts and their understanding of themselves; by understanding and responding to the context of their relationship; and by appreciating the broader social context and the policy and legislative decisions that influence society. Through the following extract, we may appreciate service users' perspectives regarding their social relationships. In the study, Green, et al. (2002) interviewed service users to find out about their social relationships and links, if any, to perceived well-being.

EXTRACT THREE

Green, G, Hayes, C, Dickinson, D, Whittaker, A and Gilheany, B (2002) The role and impact of social relationships upon well-being reported by mental health service users: A qualitative study. Journal of Mental Health, 11 (5), 567 and 570–7. [online] Available at http://dx.doi.org/10.1080/09638230020023912.

This study therefore, uses qualitative data based on the narratives of 27 mental health service users, to examine the relationship between social relationships and well-being from their perspective. Two specific issues are addressed. First, the extent to which social relationships are related to psychological well-being and social inclusion in the community, and secondly the impact that poor mental health may have upon the social relationships of service users. Greater understanding of these issues will assist interventions that aim to bolster weak support networks to prevent relapse and improve the quality of life of service users ...

The major themes identified are described below in three sections: close relationships; sociability and service related networks ...

Close relationships

... As well as offering good practical support, close family members often played a vital role by just 'being there'. This, however, was often accompanied by what respondents perceived to be a lack of emotional support and understanding. Said one woman, who has struggled with depression throughout her twenty years of marriage, I talk to my husband but I don't think he understands really what is going on (R1), a sentiment that was echoed by other respondents who reported that [there] was a tendency for their family to, as one woman said, brush it [their mental health problem] under the carpet. (R21).

Significant others were therefore seen to play an invaluable role by just being there but were often found wanting by respondents in terms of providing an appropriate response to mental illness ...

Sociability

'Friends drift away'

No respondent said that friends rejected them outright following their mental ill-ness, but there was a generalised perception that friends gradually drifted away. According to a young man with a long-standing personality disorder, I think they thought, 'He's gone downhill. I'm not going to bother with him no more *(R14). Another young man with depression commented ruefully:* Since my problems have been consistent, you know initially people might have thought it's a passing thing or whatever ... but a lot of friends have kind of drifted away *(R8).*

... A recurring theme in the interviews was the fear and damaging consequences of loneliness. Social isolation was perceived as having a direct and damaging effect on mental health. One man with a long-standing psychotic disorder said, All the anxiety and all the depression I have is because I'm lonely *(R10), and a woman recently discharged commented,* I'm not very good on my own, I get depressed *(R18). Loneliness was perceived as more damaging than most social contact, even social contact that was enforced and not particularly welcome ...*

Service-related networks

'You just get to know each other'

Contacts, lost during periods of illness, were sometimes replaced by people encountered during the course of treatment. Service users often perceived themselves as unfit to be a 'normal' friend, and distanced themselves from previous contacts, preferring to spend time with other service users. They reported feeling more 'normal' in the company of other service users, and in addition, the shared experience could foster a special bond ...

Therapeutic settings

Four respondents recruited from Mind centre were entirely negative about mental health services they had received and the staff they had been in contact with. In general though, relationships with individual care staff, either in a hospital or community setting or from voluntary or statutory agencies, were perceived to be beneficial. Individual care workers were singled out for praise and sometimes seen as friends in spite of the dependent provider/client nature that defined the relationship. Staff of non-statutory agencies, who do not have a custodial role, were more likely to be viewed as 'friends' ...

Unmet service support needs

Service users recognised that friends and family could not always provide appropriate support as they lacked the requisite professional skills. There was thus a stated need for more support from services at times of greatest vulnerability such as discharge from hospital.

Those who lived alone found the transition from a busy ward with many people around to a lonely flat with a weekly visit from a community mental health worker difficult to cope with and damaging to their mental health. There was also anger expressed that at discharge the mental health system relied so heavily on the good-will of family and friends, despite their lack of professional expertise. According to a man who had a very robust network of friends:

It was a shame, because I have so many friends. It was almost [assumed by my key-worker] that my friends would take over which I felt was, you know, that's not on. My friends are not nurses ... I am clinically depressed and ... I need professional care and [yet] they say 'Look we're discharging you now and your friends can take over'. (R17)

The impact of social relationships on well-being

... While respondents in general felt that they would be ill however supportive their social network was, the beneficial impact of supportive close relationships was clear and much valued particularly at times of greatest vulnerability, e.g. periods of acute illness and discharge from hospital. Many respondents were reliant on what they perceived as unconditional support (mainly from close kinship ties) and felt that they would have to spend more time in hospital or be more dependent on services without it. ...

In general though, the respondents recognized their need for interaction and a constant theme during the interviews was that any contact, even if it was neither volitional nor welcome, was better than none at all. This was even expressed by those who seemed natural loners and those who had always struggled to make and maintain social contact. All expressed a desire to spend less time on their own and generally tried to fill up their time with social activities, which were perceived as therapeutic.

Clinical implications

Clearly the main focus of mental health care is and should be the mental health of the client. However, the individual service user cannot be treated in a social vacuum. It is important that assessment for treatment takes account of the service user's social network. This raises the question of how to assess social networks. This study would suggest that quality rather than the quantity of social relationships is key, although clearly loneliness may be an issue for service users with very restricted social contact.

Having a large number of contacts may mask loneliness, and a close family member, however supportive, may have a negative impact on well-being. It cannot therefore be assumed that social ties are supportive. Clinicians need to seek ways to reduce overdependency on the family and to offer support to carers to enable them to care more effectively. Active family work such as a systemic therapy approach with the service user, and their family and friends, might help to decrease service users' dependence on their family.

It is also important to ensure that social ties are not used as a substitute for profes-sional care, as this can cause irreparable damage to the service user's social network.

Provision of 24-hour crisis support or at least a helpline, for all service users and their carers would greatly assist in this respect, in that it would reduce the burden on the social network during acute illness episodes. Likewise, at discharge professionals should not expect the social network to provide overtly therapeutic care. Rather, the professional should give guidance to the service user and their social contacts to help set boundaries about what support is appropriate. This would also assist the profes- sional to support the service user in their efforts to maintain their social network both during and after their illness and the service user is likely to benefit from support and encouragement to maintain contact with their friends and family.

Comment

In the preceding extract, service users comment on their social links and service networks, highlighting an experience of social disconnection and mixed reactions to professional helping networks. Since this is a smaller-scale qualitative study, it may not be representa- tive of mental health service users as a whole; yet it offers important insight into the theme of social relationship for service users. Green, et al. (2002) emphasise that profes- sionals should not rely on social networks to manage the mental health distress of friends or family. As we have seen in the earlier research of Pollio, et al. (2006), the reduction in the professional delivery system will of necessity make demands for informal carers to address the need. Hopkins and Niemiec (2007, p311), in their review of service users' and carers' perspectives regarding a crisis resolution home treatment team which focused on *crisis triage, assessment and resolution through home-based or community treatment*, indicated that *fundamental to the(ir) role [was] ... involvement with, and support of, carers of people in mental health crisis. A dedicated telephone line operate(d) to provide easy access to support from the team for users and carers.*

Evident from this approach and the latter two extracts, we as professionals need to work with service users' social networks. Mental health social workers need to respond to this very plainly and make social exclusion, social isolation problems in social relationships and key areas for assessment and intervention. This will allow social workers to address service users' social needs while appreciating the intrapersonal and larger systemic influences. The 'clubhouse' movement listed in the earlier table of treatment options (Figure 6.1) is a reha- bilitation approach grounded in relationship, work and psychosocial activity. In a recent conversation, Sue Bond (personal communication, 2008) of the Leatherhead Clubhouse commented on the declining number of clubhouses operating in the UK and indicated that commissioners who fund mental health services do not seem to be willing to fund user participation in traditional clubhouse activities. Her service has had to refine its serv- ice model to remain financially viable. The clubhouse movement promotes social relationships and activity to help facilitate change and recovery through a focus on voca- tional objectives and goals. Efforts to promote recovery need to be supported given its inclusion in the NICE guidelines on schizophrenia (NICE, 2002). Even with limited resources, it will be important in your work with other professionals in a mental health context to advocate for an appreciation and assessment of service users' social relation- ships and networks.

As we move into the final two chapters of the book, you will have a chance to think about working in partnership and working reflectively. The Care Programme Approach, one example of a meeting to facilitate joint working, operates in community mental health and involves users as agents of decision-making in their care. It is important that social needs be listed in the CPA document and the care plan interventions developed for users of mental health services. The following is a chance to think about a particular type of intervention.

POINTS TO CONSIDER

As a student on placement within a local CMHT, you and a fellow student – having paid close attention to the many discussions of clients' needs – have noticed a common thread, that service users seem isolated or lack consistent social networks. Drawing from information in the third extract and other ideas from this chapter, you decide that developing a group may be a good intervention as a group approach will automatically incorporate social interaction.

1. What would be your preliminary considerations in relation to setting up a group?

2. How would you recruit members to become participants in the group?

3. How would you structure the group? What would be its focus?

Comment

As you think about setting up a group, some preliminary considerations may relate to confirming that there will be a viable membership for the group by checking with colleagues and service users. You would then need to think about timing for the group, its location, the rooming for the group and options for your support and supervision. You may want to give thought to the group rules but ensure too that this is discussed among the group participants as a first order of group business. In recruiting, you would likely need to advertise, speak about it with colleagues, contact local non-statutory mental health and/or housing providers and be in touch with service user forums if present in your area. The structure for the group would entail whether it is a closed, time-limited group or an open-ended group that may function indefinitely. This may depend on the focus. A group that has a counselling focus with you as co-conductors may affect the structure, so that you interview prospective members to determine their interest in and capacity for the group and also offer the group enough time so that members feel safe expressing their feelings. Similarly but less formally, the group could offer a peer-support focus. Also, the group could have a psycho-educational focus with talks on specific topics and reflection by the members on how the topics relate to them. Another option may be a group devoted to social outings and social interaction. The focus and structure too would arise from what service need is apparent but may be a good means of improving social connections for service users.

C H A P T E R   S U M M A R Y

Thinking about the impact of more persistent or chronic mental health difficulties meant we needed to understand what the presence of mental health difficulties means for people throughout their life course. Kay Redfield Jamison – a successful author and academic – likely represents a success as a patient and survivor of living with intrusive mental health need and as a recipient of very good-quality mental health care. The implications of living with bipolar disorder may be less satisfactory across the spectrum of society, but her extract highlighted the challenge of taking steps to address mental health need and the difficult process of coming to accept persistent mental health need as a part of life. A link to how people grapple with living with mental health needs both as users and carers came alive in extracts from Henderson (2001) and Greene, et al. (2002), where qualitative research elicited pertinent themes. Central to this was relationship – between service user and carer – which as Henderson (2001) noted may involve interchangeable identities in flux as well as challenge. Greene, et al. (2002) emphasised how isolation is a prominent experience for those living with persistent mental health need. As a result this calls for greater resources to support service users in developing and maintaining social networks. Issues of loss and related emotions were evident and relevant as a means of understanding the lived and affective experience of those with persistent mental health difficulties and for their family and friends. Social work could serve an important function in this area of practice by working to improve and understand the family and social relationships that service users have and to strengthen these resources while also advocating for a robust statutory and non-statutory service sector to support both users and carers.

FURTHER READING

Jones, D (2002) *Myths, madness and the family: The impact of mental illness on families*. Basingstoke: Palgrave.

Jones, D (2004) Families and serious mental illness: Working with loss and ambivalence. *British Journal of Social Work*, 34, 961–79.

I would recommend reading both of Jones's works. The larger study Jones conducted is detailed in the book. The subsequent article offers a deep sensitivity and respect for the participants. By reading one or both you will familiarise yourself with research using qualitative methods and a humanistic or phenomenological perspective to understanding participants' narratives.

Lindsay, T and Orton, S (2008) *Groupwork practice in social work*. Exeter: Learning Matters.

Becoming familiar with and understanding group work is essential practice learning. This book offers a foundation to develop and conduct groups.

Sadock, B and Sadock, V (2004) *Kaplan and Sadock's concise textbook of clinical psychiatry*. 2nd edition. Philadelphia, PA: Lippincott, Williams & Wilkins.

A text that offers descriptions and details related to mental health diagnoses.

WEBSITES

Rethink is the website of a charity helping persons with more serious mental health difficulties recover; it includes a link to information about the media impact on mental health in the Muslim community.

www.rethink.org/

The following is a user-led web resource related to living with borderline personality disorder.

www.borderlineuk.co.uk/

An additional user group with a focus on bipolar disorder, the Manic Depression Fellowship may be accessed at the following link.

www.mdf.org.uk/

Chapter 7
Working in partnership and across services

ACHIEVING A SOCIAL WORK DEGREE

This chapter will contribute to helping you to meet the following National Occupational Standards.

Key Role 2: Plan, carry out, review and evaluate social work practice, with individuals, families, carers, groups, communities and other professionals.

- Prepare, produce, implement and evaluate plans with individuals, families, carers, groups, communities and professional colleagues.

Key Role 3: Support individuals to represent their needs, views and circumstances.

- Prepare for and participate in decision-making forums.

Key Role 5: Manage and be accountable, with supervision and support, for your own social work practice.

- Work within multidisciplinary and multi-organisational teams, networks and systems.

It will also introduce you to the following academic standards as set out in the social work subject benchmark statement.

Defining principles

3.7

- Contemporary social work increasingly takes place in an inter-agency context, and social workers work collaboratively with others towards interdisciplinary and cross-professional objectives ...

4.7 ... Learning to:

- Work in a transparent and responsible way, balancing autonomy with complex, multiple and sometimes contradictory accountabilities (for example, to different service users, employing agencies, professional bodies and the wider society).

5.1.1 Social work services, service users and carers, which include:

- The relationship between agency policies, legal requirements and professional boundaries in shaping the nature of services provided in interdisciplinary contexts and the issues associated with working across professional boundaries and within different disciplinary groups.

5.1.2 The service delivery context, which includes:

- The significance of interrelationships with other social services, especially education, housing, health, income maintenance and criminal justice ...

5.1.3 Values and ethics, which include:

- The conceptual links between codes defining ethical practice, the regulation of professional conduct and the management of potential conflicts generated by the codes held by different professional groups.

5.1.5 The nature of social work practice, which includes:

- The characteristics of practice in a range of community-based and organisational settings within statutory, voluntary and private sectors, and the factors influencing changes in practice within these contexts.
- The factors and processes that facilitate effective interdisciplinary, interprofessional and interagency collaboration and partnership.

Introduction

In responding to social need, social work practitioners in mental health work with a variety of individuals and agencies. This will include professionals from a mix of disciplines, service users and carers and agencies and organisations in the statutory, voluntary and private sectors. This is evident from the social work benchmarking statement which urges us to address the *factors and processes that facilitate effective interdisciplinary, interprofessional, and interagency collaboration and partnership* (QAA, 2008, p10). Similarly, one of the units in Key Role 5 of the NOS acknowledges that social workers should *work within multidisciplinary and multi-organisational teams, networks and systems* (Topss, 2004, p16). Both of these documents which influence social work education and practice highlight how essential working in partnership and across services is to effective service provision. In this chapter, our task is to understand what these statements mean generally and to begin to consider what *factors and processes* support *collaboration and partnership* in the practice of mental health social work. In thinking about partnership, we may also find it helpful to consider terms like *discipline* and *professional* as well the terms used to identify where we work such as *agency*, *network*, *organisation* and *system*, all of which are used in either the benchmark statement or the NOS. As most of these terms are now rooted in our culture generally and in the working culture of human services – health, social care, education and criminal justice – specifically it may be helpful to clarify and define current terminology.

In the preceding three chapters, we have focused on the lived experiences of persons with mental distress, attempting to understand the uncertainty and potential suffering that people may experience due to mental distress. We have also worked to understand the will to overcome this and the need, at times, to engage professional services in recovery or care. In this and the following chapter, we think and reflect on, primarily but not exclusively, the working culture and the support mechanisms of the providers of services. As part of this, you are invited to consider the work or learning contexts you have experienced that relate to working in partnership; these may have stemmed from work or voluntary activity prior to entering your training, from your learning and coursework experiences or from placement learning experiences. Through referring to your experiences, you may be able to contextualise the themes of professional identity and professional socialisation that follow as well as reference experiences of working with others in team or agency settings. Some of your reference points may highlight conflicting relationships or conversely incidences of successful collaboration within teams; either or an amalgam of the two is valid. Throughout, we will consider the factors that relate to working across disciplines, professions and agencies in mental health.

Partnership working in mental health

In writing this book, I have felt that the partnership that is so prominent in any social work interaction is the partnership between the practitioner and service user(s). This has hopefully come through in this book in the passages written by (or about) those who use services, such as Beresford (2005), Redfield Jamison (1995) and Southall's (2005) service user consultants, to name a sample. So, even though there is a focus on team and agency interactions in this chapter, it should not presuppose that this writing is not applicable to partnership working that incorporates service users and professionals in delivering or developing services.

In the extracts that follow, we review the changing aspects of working in mental health in relation to interdisciplinary teams and inter-agency work and through this highlight the changing membership of individuals involved in service provision and the concomitant change in terminology. Golightley (2008), whose text offers a foundation for this book, provides an introductory discussion about integrated working. Through an example of child and adolescent mental health services, he conveys the different professionals involved in mental health services and their working relationships as well as introduces relevant dilemmas to team working. Part of the change that has accompanied offering mental health services in more integrated ways over preceding decades has been in the language and terminology used in healthcare. In the second extract, Pollard, Sellman and Senior (2005) write about terminology that has developed to define and describe working collaboratively among disciplines and with multiple agencies. They offer a context to help us understand this change sociopolitically. Drawn from a recent text – perhaps the first on this subject – on integrated care pathways, the third extract by Wood and Green (2006) introduces inter-professional working as it relates to the use of the Care Programme Approach (CPA). The fourth extract develops this further. In it, Peck and Norman (1999) grapple with the impact of collaborative work specifically in the context of CMHTs by referencing the benefits as well as the demands on teams and those working in them.

Team approaches to delivering services

Depending on your work or learning experiences, you may not have been exposed so readily to the concepts of team working. Golightley (2008) introduces the distinctions between different approaches to joint working. He highlights some of the challenges that may arise in collaborative working and helpfully provides a schematic figure to demonstrate the different professionals that may be involved in CAMHS work.

EXTRACT ONE

Golightley, M (2008) Social work and mental health. *3rd edition. Exeter: Learning Matters, pp139–40.*

Working towards an integrated service

Integrated services are services that are joined together to provide one access route for service users. Such services imply common training to at least some extent and shared values. Multi-disciplinary approaches retain the professional and often organisational identity of the professional involved.

Multi-disciplinary teams

The multi-disciplinary team exists both as a community mental health team, and in a form that includes professionals who work in the team part-time and also work back in their own agencies. A child mental health team could comprise members as in Figure 7.1, although this will vary from agency to agency. The first point for involvement will usually be a referral from the family doctor to this team for assessment, and

---

if intervention is planned a care co-ordinator will be appointed who will carry the responsibility for the case. This can be the scene for some power struggles between the professions and also within the professions. General practitioners are often more comfortable dealing with another medical colleague than relating to a different professional. Consultants will point out that they have clinical responsibility for the individual and hence medical–legal responsibility. This has been further compounded with the emergence of nurse prescribers. These issues can be sorted out and it is important that the multi-disciplinary team establishes clear operating procedures.

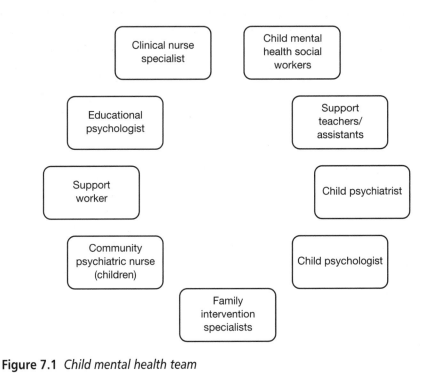

Figure 7.1 *Child mental health team*

POINTS TO CONSIDER

1. *Looking at the schema in Figure 7.1, identify the professions or educational backgrounds of the different members of the team.*

2. *Read through the following case study and respond to the subsequent learning points.*

   ● *Dennis is in his late adolescence – about 17 – and has been working with staff in the CAMHS programme for three years. He has just moved to live in a four-bedded residential group home. Like his housemates, Dennis has been in the Looked After service for several years. After some months of inquiry, the consultant psychiatrist at CAMHS has told Dennis that he believes that his symptoms are*

POINTS TO CONSIDER *continued*

down to having schizophrenia. Dennis had hoped to go to college, but he is now thinking of taking some short courses run through the local FE college and a day centre for people with mental health difficulties. One of the problems that has complicated his plans is that he was caught burgling a house; when the police spoke to him he was also found in possession of cannabis. It seems he has been steadily increasing his use of cannabis over the last year.

- *Based on the information in the case and the need to respond to each of these various issues, who do you think would need to be involved to help? To respond to this, make a circular diagram like Golightley's (2008, p140) Figure 7.1, identifying which professionals would be involved and their respective agencies.*

- *If you are not familiar with all of the possible agencies or educational backgrounds of differing professionals, feel free to identify them according to what help you think Dennis might need.*

Comment

Golightley's (2008) extract gives us an idea of possible professionals within a child mental health team. In response to my question, you may have identified that there were nursing professionals, psychology staff, a social worker, a doctor and staff with an educational background. In addition, support workers may be non-qualified, whereas family intervention specialists may have further therapeutic training or skill in targeted psycho-educational interventions. I wonder what you made of the case study – again, there would likely be nursing, psychology, medical and social work staff, but I also asked you think of other possible providers and services. To respond to Dennis's needs, other agencies may be a Youth Offending Team (YOT), a substance-misuse service, the college he hopes to attend as well as his housing provider. Depending on the criminal issue, he may be involved with the police and/or a solicitor.

What this case tries to highlight is that the clients with whom we work may be involved with different agencies or services and even with different professionals in the same service. Golightley (2008) introduced us to the multidisciplinary team. The multidisciplinary team as a concept means that staff from different professions come together to work and respond to a service need; in the CAMHS service, the staff would respond to mental health need in young people. There may also be – as it is in Dennis's case – multiple agencies involved to create an inter-agency system. In this example, Dennis would be involved with a system including CAMHS, Social Services Looked After Children team, his residential setting, his college, possibly a YOT service, a court, legal help and the police. This highlights the complexity involved when service users may be receiving a broad range of services. Ideally, there should be a clinical reason or clinical justification for the number of people and agencies involved in working with a service user. In Dennis's case, there appear to be needs for help in the following areas: mental health, substance misuse, housing, training and legal support.

Golightley (2008) also introduces the idea that at times there may be problems in communication between professionals and between agencies. It is also worth mentioning that there may be times that there are problems in communication with service users such as Dennis, who may find it helpful or overwhelming to have so many different agencies working with him. This means we need to think, too, about whether such inter-agency work leads to service integration or fragmentation. In the following Points to consider, please reflect on how you may have experienced working within a team or group as well as how members of teams work with each other and how teams interact across different services.

POINTS TO CONSIDER

Appreciating that you may have limited experience in formal work, consider any work experiences, placement experiences, group learning activities and/or voluntary experiences when considering the following questions.

- *What were or are your roles within the group or team you are considering?*

- *What are your relationships to the people to whom you reported?*

- *What are your relationships to your colleagues? Also consider your relationships to those who looked to you for guidance.*

- *What relationships, if any, did your system (your place of work or practice learning or where you volunteered) have with other groups or agencies?*

- *What, if any, significant changes happened that affected your work or the delivery of service?*

Describe the nature of both the interpersonal and inter-agency relationships at up to two places. In your descriptions, make note of the type of relationships and any emotions attached to the relationship such as whether it seemed easy-going or fraught.

We will call on your reflections throughout the work of this chapter.

Comment

In the initial questions above, I asked you to think about your role and your relationships to others in your workplace, your practice setting, university group learning or voluntary setting. I imagine that within this context, you positioned yourself in relationship to others so that either someone or several people would have presumably been in charge or taken charge; while others would have worked alongside you. Others may have worked in roles considered less significant or have contributed less. This suggests the levels and hierarchy that are present in work or practice settings. It also hopefully suggested the usefulness and possible conflicts that may emerge in working with others. Howard (2006) notes that issues of ownership, inter-professional rivalry and conflict, especially in relation to change, exist in health and social care arenas, and these may be present in our group and team work settings also.

Setting the context of modern team working

Changes that influence mental healthcare currently and historically have been stimulated by societal changes to human services delivery. Change has been influenced by policy, legislative parameters and funding as well as being stimulated by these factors. The shift from inpatient care to community-based care is a relatively recent development in the delivery of mental healthcare. Teams that incorporate different professions have been an extension into the community, at some level, of the professional groupings that deliver services in mental health inpatient contexts. Mental healthcare has also been affected by policy initiatives related to safety and risk (Bartlett and Sandland, 2003). Other influences that have affected mental healthcare are changes to the funding of services, the imposition or trial use of corporate or private business management styles in public organisations and the frequent interplay between these developments as governments have sought to contain their funding of social and public health services (Pollard, et al., 2005).

The concept of 'modern', and the 'modernising' of, healthcare services delivery may connote both service improvement as an impetus for change as well as an agenda that rejects the old or previous way of working as ineffective or inadequate, whether it is or not. Change may often represent a message that what has been is no longer good enough – an idea which suggests that the new is inherently better or improved. This assumption presents the risk that both the new and the old may be demeaned and diminished. It also suggests a rather relativistic interpretation of time. In mental healthcare, the new approach to care in the form of the Care Programme Approach (CPA) is actually 17 years old. However, it was new in that, on its arrival, it represented a shift to working more collaboratively with service users and was also supposed to highlight integrated working. As described in Chapter 3, truly new and very recent developments in law such as the 2007 amendment to the Mental Health Act and policy in mental health have recently been implemented. In fact, updated recommendations regarding the CPA are imminent.

Service user input to mental health services

Additionally Pollard, et al. (2005) note that *running parallel with these managerial and economic changes was the growing recognition that service users have rights to information and to involvement in the planning and prioritisation of services* (p9). They also offer a current context by noting that:

> *Whatever the gaps between rhetoric and reality, and whatever the differences between political parties and governments, the legacy of the changes in health and social care in the UK over the last two decades is an emphasis on cost-effective integrated services that meet the needs of, and actively involve, service users.*

> (Pollard, et al., 2005, p9)

The active involvement of service users emphasises the earlier point that for partnership working to have genuine meaning and substance partnership needs to take place between service users and practitioners. For me personally, in comparing my social work training with the current learning I facilitate, I see this borne out. My colleagues and I work jointly with members of the university's service users and carers steering group in a wide range of activities including: interviewing and making decisions about student selection, contributing to learning and assessing students' learning outcomes. This represents further development of the concept of working in partnership.

Clarifying terms and relationships

In the extract that follows, the authors seek to consider the current context of collaborative work following recent service changes. Their text offers an overview of inter-professional working while incorporating chapters about joint working within a variety of settings and from different disciplines perspectives.

EXTRACT TWO

Pollard, K, Sellman, D and Senior, B (2005) The need for interprofessional working. In Barrett, G, Sellman, D and Thomas, J (eds) (2005) Interprofessional working in health and social care, Professional perspectives. Basingstoke: Palgrave Macmillan, pp9–10.

What is inter-professional working?

Inter-professional working requires that personnel from different professions and agencies work together. There has been extended debate about terminology in this field. Readers will find, among others, the terms multi-professional, inter-professional, multidisciplinary, interdisciplinary, multiagency and interagency being used to describe what appear to be very similar activities. A broad rule of thumb is that the prefix multi *tends to indicate the involvement of personnel from different professions, disciplines or agencies, but does not necessarily imply collaboration. The prefix* inter *tends to imply collaboration, particularly in areas such as decision making (Øvretveit 1997, Payne 2000). One way of conceptualising inter-professional work is in terms of the effectiveness of coordination and communication. Social workers, for example, have traditionally emphasised the importance of coordination of services where more than one agency or worker is involved. This occurs in areas such as key aspects of mental health work, community care, and in child protection.*

Team is another term which is often used when describing working groups; however, what is meant (and understood) by this word can vary enormously. Teams may be tightly-knit units, composed of individuals who regularly work together; or they may be loosely-woven entities which emerge in an ad hoc *manner to meet specific demands. A team may just be a convenient way of describing a group of staff with a common manager, but with little else that brings them together. Teams may be formally constituted, with a specified structure and objective, or they may arise organically with no formal recognition. They may be consensual, democratic or hierarchical in nature, or all of these by turn, depending on circumstances. The members of a team may collaborate with one another in practice, or they may act alone on behalf of the team. Teams may draw their members from a single professional group, or from several. These are only some of the variations that can be found, in many different permutations, in team structure and process (Øvretveit 1997, Payne 2000).*

> **EXTRACT TWO** *continued*
>
> *In this book, we take inter-professional working to mean collaborative practice: that is, the process whereby members of different professions and/or agencies work together to provide integrated health and/or social care for the benefit of service users. This definition is consistent with that of Wood and Gray who write* Collaboration occurs when a group of autonomous stakeholders of a problem domain engage in an interactive process, using shared rules, norms, and structures, to act or decide on issues relating to that domain *(1991: 146). The structure and logistics of the systems through which professionals organise their collaborative efforts vary considerably, in part influenced by the history of each profession or service, but are often crucially dictated by government policy and directive. Collaborative practice might take place through a single team of mixed professionals or through different organisations cooperating in planning and providing services ...*

Comment

In this extract the authors clarify commonly used terms in the helping professions, terms that rely on the prefixes 'inter' and 'multi' to describe agencies, disciplines and professions. Such terms in common parlance may have come to seem synonymous. Perhaps the confusion about these terms or the assumption of sameness in relation to them offers an insight into how professionals and teams function. If interdisciplinary and multidisciplinary are the same, then there will be little need to reflect on whether the team's members work together in an interactive way or work as a group of individual differently trained professionals. The passage, though, acknowledges that social work is a profession with a focus on co-ordination and, at times, a statutory duty to consult and work with other professionals. As part of changing provider structures, integrating social work and mental health services has been achieved over the last decade through placing social services social work staff into NHS mental health trusts. The impact of integrating professionals in community mental health has been the source of research. Rees, et al. (2004) studied the reactions of a variety of staff – across discipline and across function – to joint working within several community mental health teams (CMHTs) in Scotland. In relation to the change process, they found the following:

> *Changing practice was identified as more difficult. As one team leader remarked:*
>
> Those of us who have to change from perhaps one way of working to another way of working, that's the bit that takes time. (TL)
>
> *Team members discussed the difficulties in changing the way they work, and the effort and time this requires:*
>
> I think the system is a good system, but they [management] want us to put it all together, you know, just like almost overnight. And we can't possibly do that. (CPN) (pp532–3)

The narrative reactions of two participants, one a team leader (TL) and one a direct practitioner working as a community psychiatric nurse (CPN), illustrate the need for time to implement changes to work expectations and the reality of the impact that change has for those delivering services. As the CPN emphasises, even a good change cannot just happen;

there is a need within an organisation to be able to manage change and appreciate the impact of changes on staff and service users.

Researchers have also explored what it means for different staff to work together and what factors seem to support integrated and inter-professional work. Findings indicate that characteristics of more 'joined-up' working seem to hinge on several factors: a shared value base (Carpenter, et al., 2003); a stronger identification with the team rather than identification with one's professional discipline (Carpenter, et al., 2003); and an induction and training process that orientates staff to an integrated way of working (DCSF, 2007). Findings from Carpenter, et al.'s (2003) study of the perceptions of staff in four CMHTs in Scotland showed that participants from all teams reported higher team identification than professional identification.

Pollard, Sellman and Senior (2005) also confirmed that government policy initiatives supporting an agenda of integrated working also influence team function. Consistent with this, the government initiative, *Every Child Matters* (ECM), has influenced the Children's Workforce Development Council (CWDC) to produce fact sheets which disseminate guidance about multi-agency and integrated working. In these and other publications, government initiatives and agencies are highlighting what they have found to be effective approaches to integrated working. The guidance and findings from the CWDC and the policy of the ECM strategy will influence mental health services offered to young people. According to the CWDC (2007), the following three structures exemplify interagency collaboration:

- A multi-agency panel *where practitioners remain employed by their home agency and participants meet as a panel ... on a regular basis to discuss children ... who would benefit from multi-agency input.*

- A multi-agency team *which includes practitioners who have been seconded or recruited into it and which works to a common purpose and common goals.*

- An integrated service *in which a range of separate services share a common location and work together.*

(Adapted from CWDC, 2007)

Facilitating team structures in adult mental health services

In adult mental health services, working collaboratively occurs via a structure called the Care Programme Approach (CPA) (Department of Health, 1990, 1999a). The CPA format of reviewing and documenting mental healthcare has been arranged and put forward by the government. It has undergone updates, and the outcome of a recent consultation is pending (Department of Health, 1999a, 2006). The CPA process operates structurally and clinically – as a network meeting to assess care needs and as a clinical vehicle to incorporate service users and care providers into a multidisciplinary review mechanism. It operates in specialised mental healthcare and is staffed by personnel representing several professional groups.

In the following extract, Wood and Green (2006) provide concise information about the CPA. As an interdisciplinary document, the CPA's plan of care is meant to be a collaborative document between service user and provider along with input from other providers, including non-mental health providers. To some extent, the CPA document suggests a formalised contract of service.

Wood, S and Green, B (2006) Integrated care pathways and integrated working. In Hall, J and Howard, D (eds) Integrated care pathways in mental health. *Edinburgh: Churchill Livingstone Elsevier, p57.*

A number of centrally generated frameworks have been developed for mental health (Jones et al 2000). These include the Care Programme Approach (Department of Health 1990), supervision registers, supervised discharge (Department of Health 1996), and more recently proposals for changes to mental health legislation (Department of Health 2004). Over the past two decades, legislation for mental health has moved from an institutional model towards community care, and from uni-professional to multi-professional recognition. Elements of government thinking have thus contained frameworks similar to some elements of an integrated care pathway (Aitken 2000, Jones et al 2000, Smith et al 2000). However, integrated working has been aimed towards, and perhaps described, but not necessarily achieved. More recently, emerging legislative change (Department of Health 2004) has recognised that some labels on former roles may be unhelpful and even an impediment: For example, the replacement of the term RMO (responsible medical officer) with a more realistic/plural descriptor – that of clinical supervisor. This reflects a more inter-professional/inter-agency scenario whereby multi agency working is both the norm and essential, particularly as the clinical load is able to be formally shared more widely. There is evidence from the user perspective that indicates increased satisfaction with the development of more specialist roles for nurses and other disciplines. For example, user satisfaction with nurse prescribing demonstrates the desire for more extended roles with respect to prescribing and medication management (Latter & Courtney 2003).

The Care Programme Approach (Department of Health 1990) is recognised as being an effective mechanism for integrating health and social service aspects of a care package in specialised mental health care (NHS Health Advisory Service 1996). In effect, the Care Programme Approach was a government-driven structure aimed at improving information sharing, recording and tracking. While falling short of being an actual pathway, it may perhaps be seen as prescribing elements of an integrated care pathway. It is disappointing though that it took a government to impose this and that the professions did not themselves combine to agree a common framework approach to describe what should already have been good practice. It remains the case, however, that the professions were handicapped by their separation. The integrated care pathway is thus a means of bridging this separation by converting the hierarchical content-driven approaches into a flatter process framework which not only binds professionals together but has some useful outcomes for the individuals using it.

Comment

Wood and Green (2006) are writing about the development of integrated care pathways (ICPs) which are relatively new to the UK. ICPs describe routes or maps of care to respond to specific illnesses or health problems. The pathway should take into account the specific services required by a service user while also emphasising their integration or, put more simply, that all services should work toward the same care plan. The newness of this – whether it is in fact a new approach or simply a new way of describing integrated working is a relevant question – represents the ongoing development of service provision in both health and mental health care to achieve integration between professionals and services. The extract raises the significant question about whether integrated working has, as yet, been achieved. More specifically to the CPA, the authors note CPA to be an *effective mechanism for integrating health and social services aspects of a care package* (Wood and Green, 2006, p57). They end with the hope that professionals will come to work more closely with reduced hierarchy.

> ### POINTS TO CONSIDER
>
> *Using the earlier case information related to Dennis, please review the case and determine who his providers of services are. Which of these providers would you invite to an upcoming CPA meeting? Justify who you are inviting to the CPA meeting based on Dennis's needs.*

The Care Programme Approach (CPA)

The government (Department of Health, 1990, 1999a) introduced the CPA structure to facilitate more collaborative work in mental healthcare. Additionally, a further goal involved improving service user input and participation in care planning so that service users were acknowledged both as care recipients and as agents who have the right to make choices about the service they receive and how it is delivered. With CPA, there was an expectation that professionals would work across agency and profession in offering services with a designated point of contact – a care co-ordinator – developing the CPA document and co-ordinating the related meetings. The CPA policy document (DOH, 1999a), which is under review, set out updated guidance about delivering the CPA. In the same document, the background for CPA was described:

> *The Care Programme Approach (CPA) was introduced in 1991 [HC(90)23/LASSL(90)11] to provide a framework for effective mental health care. Its four main elements are:*
>
> - *Systematic arrangements for assessing the health and social needs of people accepted into specialist mental health services.*
>
> - *The formation of a care plan which identifies the health and social care required from a variety of providers.*
>
> - *The appointment of a key worker to keep in close touch with the service user and to monitor and co-ordinate care.*
>
> - *Regular review and, where necessary, agreed changes to the care plan.* (DoH, 1999a, p2)

It emphasises that *(s)ervice users themselves provide the focal point for care planning and delivery.* (DoH, 1999a, p4).

Comment

Thinking for a moment about how CMHTs decide which staff work with certain service users as care co-ordinators, it may be helpful to return to Dennis and imagine what may be most helpful for him. To review, Dennis has been newly diagnosed with schizophrenia, has reported using cannabis, is in residential supported housing and is looked after by the state. Given the interface with housing and social services, there may be a preference in the team for the care co-ordinator allocated to be a member of the social work profession. Dennis is involved with a number of agencies, so it may be helpful for a social worker to draw on strengths of working in the system to advocate and support referrals with the local authority's social services and with its housing office's Supporting People service. However, as Dennis has a newly diagnosed mental health problem, a community mental health nurse may equally be suited to provide education about any medication, if prescribed, and its effects and perhaps to work with a model of early intervention if he is in the initial stages of experiencing psychotic symptoms. In a well-established interdisciplinary service, it may be most ideal if practitioners from both social work and nursing work together with one in the lead and one consulting on the case to support Dennis holistically.

Understanding the community mental health team

Service users receive specialised mental health services through CMHTs, an entity that is meant to be *one point of access for … coordinated health and social care* (DoH, 1999a, p10). In a CMHT, the team composition will include health staff such as psychiatry and medical personnel and nursing staff, additional allied health professionals, support workers, psychology staff and social work staff. The CMHT has been developed to organise its care around the needs of service users. The CPA care plan would respond to the service user's needs, address treatment issues, frame any pertinent data regarding history or current risk and capture and record the timeframes for service delivery. In effect the CPA meeting and its related document develops a contract for care between the service user and the CMHT – with the CMHT as noted above represented by an assigned care co-ordinator, additional CMHT personnel, and other providers in the service user's system.

Understanding and making sense of the professional functioning of the CMHT is the focus for the following article written by Norman and Peck (1999). In this and a related article, these authors uncovered relevant themes significant to a CMHT and the narratives and perspectives voiced by professionals involved with or working in CMHTs. The excerpt that follows draws from an article that captured the perspectives of strategic personnel involved in the delivery of adult mental healthcare. In this, they address issues of responsibility and accountability regarding the tasks and roles of staff. Please note that this article includes terminology – such as ASW and Responsible Medical Officer (RMO) – which is now supplanted by the terms AMHP and Responsible Clinician (RC) in line with the amended Mental Health Act 2007.

EXTRACT FOUR

Norman, I and Peck, E (1999) Working together in adult community mental health services: An inter-professional dialogue. Journal of Mental Health, 8 (3), 225–7.

Clarifying responsibility and accountability of CMHT staff

Onyett (1995) notes that the terms 'responsibility' and 'accountability' are used often interchangeably. He distinguishes between them as follows:

> Responsibility [refers to] a set of tasks that an employing authority, professional body or court of law can legitimately demand of a practitioner. Accountability describes the relationship between that practitioner and the authority. *(p281)*

Onyett points out that professional clinical staff within teams are accountable for different responsibilities to different authorities. Employee responsibilities are defined by a contract of employment and general management whereas professional responsibilities are defined by professional codes of conduct, a duty of care and state registration requirements. Professional responsibility can encompass legal responsibility to recognize and observe their training limitations and competence and be satisfied that those to whom they refer are also appropriately qualified and competent (Onyett, 1995). In the mental health context responsible medical officers and social workers have specific legal responsibilities under the Mental Health Act ...

Of course, the extent to which staff can be held responsible for their own work appears to differ between other mental health care professions. In social services departments Approved Social Workers (ASWs) have considerable professional protection through the supervisory responsibility of the employing organisation. NHS Trust personnel do not have this same level of professional protection. Most vulnerable are those staff who have no professional supervision or management. A good example is the professionally isolated occupational therapist who may be encouraged by their multi-disciplinary team colleagues to take on generic roles for which they feel untrained. Concern among the profession about moves to generic working emerged strongly from a recent survey of the Association of Occupational Therapists in Mental Health by Craik et al. (1998). Sixty-seven per cent (n=87) of the 129 respondents identified 104 examples of what they regarded as non-occupational therapy tasks. These included counselling and key working, but also tasks involved with medication, explaining blood results and testing urine.

Whether professional protection is afforded through clinical consultation, rather than professional supervision, is unclear and seems to require further exploration. For example, if a CPN receives clinical consultation from another team member from a different profession, how far is the 'consultant' liable for the actions (mistakes) of the CPN?

If mental health care professionals are responsible for their own work then the question arises as to the function of the CMHT in professional decision making. The National Reference Group concluded that while the team might assume collective responsibility, it has no legal responsibility. The team might be seen best as a resource for professional decision-making. The professional will consult the team but ultimately must make his/her own decision.

In sum, it is important to clarify exactly who is responsible for and accountable for what in adult community mental health services. It is our view that this is best done at the level of professional organisations rather than individual CMHTs. The literature and the work of the National Reference Group provides a good starting point for this task. Once clarified, responsibilities of professional staff should be incorporated within job descriptions that become part of the employment contract of team members across CMHTs nationally.

Furthermore, as part of this process of clarifying accountability and responsibility we need to confront the cultural myth, present still in some CMHTs, that team working necessarily involves all team members having an equal say on all decisions (Onyett, personal communication). Power is always going to be a major factor in inter-professional teams. Rather than hide behind the myth of democratic teamwork, the challenge is to establish a dialogue within teams to sort out those sources of power that are legitimate (e.g. based upon expertise) and need to be retained, and illegitimate (e.g. based on personality, race, charisma, etc.). An overvalued allegiance to democracy may mask an inability of the team to sort out clear roles of its members. It is to these roles that we now turn.

Clarifying roles of CMHT staff

Once responsibility and lines of accountability are established CMHTs are in a good position to clarify the roles of team members. Some CMHTs have sorted this out at a local level. For example, Budgen and Munday, CMHT managers in East Surrey (now the Surrey Oaklands NHS Trust), found that by identifying the role of the key-worker and common or core roles of team members, that specialist roles (taking account of legal and policy responsibilities) became clear. They propose (Budgen and Munday, personal communication) establishing a national 'blueprint' for roles in CMHTs with clear scope for local variation, but with some 'givens' which should be mandatory if equality of service is to be achieved. They argue that it is not good enough to leave this to local resolution, as experience with initiatives such as CPA, for instance, has shown that this does not occur. The National Reference Group endorsed this view. It suggested that roles of CMHT members, taking account of their responsibilities and lines of accountability, should be negotiated at the level of professional organisations and then adapted to local circumstances.

Comment

The authors introduce and consider the more diffuse issues that arise when a policy directive meets the real and practical considerations of everyday practice. The initial part of the extract confronted the differential issues that related to responsibility versus accountability, noting that different professional groups will demand that their members may have different accountabilities not only to differing bodies but in relation to the parameters and demands of their work. Though the CPA policy document (Department of Health, 1999a) recommends joint training and unified approaches to oversight, this article recognises the real dilemmas that organisations and their employees may face in working with a more integrated professional group. Two significant dilemmas relate to authority and decision-making and team dynamics, which refer to how professionals work together and manage their working relationships.

Power and authority in teams

The authors realistically confront how professional members of teams work in relation to their roles and clinical colleagues. The issue of roles and hierarchy conveys the impact of power in teams. As you may recall, we addressed the concept of power and authority in Chapter 1 – when it was raised in relationship to service users and service user choice and the impact of social work intervention. In that same discussion we highlighted how social workers may respond to perceptions of having power. I would urge you to review this.

Peck and Norman (1999) suggest that expertise is a reason for a team member to hold power legitimately; whereas sociocultural variables, such as race, ethnicity or others, would, depending on the wider society, instil power to certain groups illegitimately. They establish helpfully that power dynamics are a realistic variable that teams need to address and understand. In teams, as in any social structure, it is useful and politic to determine who holds power, who controls decision-making and who manages resources. Those who are nominally in charge may or may not actually be in charge. It is also essential to realise that groups – which teams are – often expect leadership. The dilemma may be that individuals as members of groups rely on leadership; whereas more optimal functioning of inter-professional groups may require a levelling of power. Barrett and Keeping (2005, p22), citing the work of Stapleton (1995) and Henneman, et al. (1995), note that *shared power based upon non-hierarchical relationships has been identified as central to effective interprofessional collaboration*. They also note that the shared distribution of power is harder to maintain as teams grow in number of personnel (Boulding, 1990, cited in Barrett and Keeping, 2005).

Team dynamics

It is also relevant to consider the relationships within teams among clinical staff, as well as between clinical and administrative staff, as the status of these relationships will highlight both team process and team function. Related to this are additional variables of difference, such as culture or management style, that may influence and affect team function, communication within the team and expectations related to the work itself and working relationships. Workplaces offer trainings that introduce the importance of diversity and cultural responsiveness to improve our work with service users; however, these variables of difference also influence our working relationships with team and agency colleagues. As a result and as members of teams, we contribute to a team's function through understanding our own values and biases and taking initiatives to increase our awareness of difference and capacity to work in culturally responsive ways.

Linked to this, Norman and Peck (1999) highlighted the utility of considering the impact of group dynamics on team relationships and team function as well as power differentials or other variables of difference. Group or team dynamics are hugely relevant. In addition to considering the impact that colleagues may have on each other in relation to work demands and expectations, there is the need to consider how our individual and unique characteristics may affect each other. There may be differences in assertion and communication styles, in learning styles, in how we adapt to work or personal stressors as well as potentially divisive or upsetting variables that may arise from direct practice with service users. A possible way of considering how we process our experience in teams is to consider how the impact of our earliest experiences of socialisation – that of our experience within our families of origin – may affect how we take up roles within teams in our workplaces. It is possible that any current roles we display may echo our earliest roles.

To respond to this latter dynamic and to improve team functioning, Norman and Peck (1999) identified a need for teams to confront and process the impact of the work. One way of doing this is through securing an external supervisor or conductor to facilitate a group for team members to discuss and reflect on its members' reactions to working with each other. By helping team members to reflect on the impact team members have on each other, the impact of the work on one's functioning and the impact of past and present material on each of these variables, there is an opportunity for team members to work more clearly with present material. This should also help teams to avoid becoming caught up in or repeating problematic interactions that may affect team working and individual members' morale and functioning.

However, evidence from a study conducted by Woodhouse and Pengelly (1991, pp185–186, cited by Warman and Jackson, 2007, p38) showed that *too often social workers do not receive this support and as a result they can develop a 'citadel' response, becoming defensive, sticking to procedures and sheltering behind 'the department'.* Warman and Jackson (2007, p38) go on to describe a model of supervision in which workers voluntarily participate in work discussion groups *in which staff are offered a unique and essential opportunity to share any concerns, difficulties or challenging issues preoccupying them in their work with clients: particularly those at risk.* An evaluation of workers' responses to this support was substantially positive and meant that team members came together to voice concerns and receive support.

Factors that support integrated working

The focus of this book is on the ability of social work staff to work skilfully with mental health material in support of service users. The following findings, though not specifically developed from a mental health perspective, are nonetheless helpful. They arise from a recent governmental audit which reviewed integrated working within children's services (DCSF, 2007). The advent and development of Children's Trusts mean that children's and young people's services are moving into a more integrated structure that *will bring together education, social work and health services for children ... (and allow) ... statutory agencies ... together with voluntary and private agencies ... (to) ... be part of local partnerships* (Taylor and Vatcher, 2005, p158). This will also include mental health, leisure and youth justice services.

The DCSF (2007, p7) audit found that *one of the most notable common features ... was that effective integrated working was primarily based on personal relationships, with integrated working apparently developing largely as a consequence of professionals from different sectors spending time in proximity with each other* ... Additional helpful factors included: team members working from a shared base; an emphasis on service users' needs; securing service users' consent for services; training staff to work in new ways; and maintaining contact with and providing feedback to referrers (DCSF, 2007).

In relation to adult mental health services, Onyett (2003, p49) summarises the findings from Norman and Peck's (1999) inquiry into what factors support collaboration in interdisciplinary mental health work. While reviewing the following factors, compare these and the DCSF (2007) findings above with your reflections about experiences of team participation.

- *Shared understanding of each other's cultures, roles and responsibilities, and methods of working.*

- *Direct and regular contact between those providing care. This was promoted by named care coordinators, contacts or link workers and clear systems for referral.*

- *Understanding the aims and methods of working of the organisations involved in collaboration.*

- *Good communication systems leading to trust between users, carers and health care workers.*

- *Access to practical local information about services and contracts.*

- *Individual commitment by all workers to a collaborative approach that is supported by management.*

- *Organisational structures that support inter-agency collaboration (for example, joint planning, commissioning and review committees) and, within this, individuals with the shared vision, inter-personal skills and knowledge required to make collaboration effective.*

- *Change champions and groups to push forward interdisciplinary/inter-agency initiatives.*

- *National policies that promote a coordinated approach supported by adequate resources.*

(Onyett, 2003, p49)

C H A P T E R   S U M M A R Y

The image of an interdisciplinary team working collaboratively with clarity in communication among its members and in its communications with other agencies and systems suggests a healthy approach to service delivery. Efforts to incorporate this approach have been ongoing in mental health practice over the last several decades, spurred on by the introduction of the Care Programme Approach. Refinements to this way of structuring care confirm that working in an integrated way is a strong initiative of the government and its policy in adult mental health services as well as in children's services. Though there is an emphasis on working in partnership, developing this service approach still needs the support and participation of professionals, team members and service users. Ensuring that this team approach to care is experienced as a supportive structure for team members and service users is an ongoing task.

In the hypothetical case of Dennis, we had the chance to reflect on the complexity and possible fragmentation that may occur in working to respond inter-professionally and across agencies. By thinking about the terms used to define mental healthcare currently and previously, we were able to consider the changing ethos from a uni-professional response to the multi-professional and multi-agency work of today. The CPA, with its emphasis on facilitating network dialogue and engaging service users in decision-making about their care, represents a high point in facilitating responsive care approaches. However, there is a reality to working collaboratively which means that teams will – just like employees at times — not perform satisfactorily. The challenge of working together in teams and across agencies was noted in terms of the dilemmas that present in these relatively new work structures – moving away from hierarchical settings in which physicians held power – to more shared thinking and consensus-driven approaches to care provision. Teams seem to function most effectively when established leadership offers oversight and guidance. Additionally, government policy has been a significant progenitor of inter-professional and inter-agency approaches to human services. This influence is not only present in direct practice but also in the training of professionals such as social work students, and incorporates group learning into the curriculum as a means of replicating and preparing qualifying practitioners for collaborative practice. Hopefully, this approach helps student learners to develop facility and confidence in consulting and seeking advice from other practitioners when faced with complex practice scenarios evident in today's human services work.

The chapter also acknowledged that team members are individuals who will need support to work collaboratively and to manage difference. Working as a part of teams and with members of other teams means being aware of and sensitive across profession and type of work – whether it is administrative, service-related or managerial. In the larger systems that are being developed to respond to mental health need and offer care, it is essential to remain mindful of the care needs of the individuals who are doing the work, specifically in their needs for training, discussion, clarity in communication and time to process changing tasks and systems.

FURTHER READING

Hafford-Letchfield, T (2006) *Management and organisations in social work*. Exeter: Learning Matters.

Quinney, A (2006) *Collaborative social work practice*. Exeter: Learning Matters.

These two books published by Learning Matters offer more detail related to the topics of joint working and organisational structure and dynamics.

Onyett, S (2003) *Teamworking in mental health*. Basingstoke: Palgrave Macmillan.

Onyett's book specifically addresses team work in mental health and covers various themes, such as policy, leadership, values and team performance, thoroughly.

Department for Children, Schools and Families (2007) *Effective integrated working: Findings of concept of operations study, Integrated working to improve outcomes for children and young people*. London: DCSF.

This report offers an overview of a qualitative inquiry into children's services settings that have embraced integrated working and offers insights from their experiences. Appendices include research materials and a series of case studies in which inter-professional and inter-agency approaches have had a useful impact.

Sainsbury Centre for Mental Health (2005) *Back on track*. London: SCMH. Available at: **www.scmh.org.uk**

This report developed by the Sainsbury Centre for Mental Health examined the effectiveness of the CPA for service users who had been subjected to conditions of the Mental Health Act.

The following website includes related documents and guidance about the CPA and will be the site to learn of findings from the recent public consultation.

www.nimhe.csip.org.uk/our-work/reviewing-the-care-programme-approach-cpa-.html

The Care Programme Approach Association (CPAA) supports the use of the the CPA as a significant component of the Department of Health's mental health strategy.

www.cpaa.org.uk/

The Sainsbury Centre for Mental Health (SCMH) offers a range of pertinent, third-sector perspectives on mental health services; it has produced surveys of service users' experiences of CPA.

www.scmh.org.uk

Chapter 8

Developing as a reflective practitioner

Introduction

Developing as a reflective practitioner suggests an ongoing process of growing and refinement. In the word, 'developing', we recognise a process of learning, improving and refining that may be bounded by your interests and needs and your commitment to learning. Reflective practice and its related concepts have become an integral part of social work education and practice in the UK. Developing your capacity to be reflective will be relevant to you in your studies generally and broadly applicable to practice in a variety of social work settings. Additionally, participating in practice reflection will be an essential component of continuing professional development once you are a qualified and registered member of the General Social Care Council (GSCC).

Yip (2006, p245) suggests that engaging in reflection helps social workers in mental health settings *to actualize social work values within medicalized and institutionalized mental-health services*. This is fundamental to offering social work services within mental health contexts, and it brings us to the beginning discussions in this book, particularly in Chapter 1, in relation to values and value-based practice in mental health. Yip (2006) emphasises that attitudes and values about mental health experiences as well as our feelings about and perceptions of mental health distress will affect our interventions with service users with mental health needs. As a first step in offering mental health social work, it will be important to reflect on personal attitudes, values and perceptions about mental health. Supplementing this more personal dimension to your reflection, you will also reflect on the knowledge you have about working in partnership; the legislative and policy dimensions of mental healthcare and mental health symptoms, treatment approaches and interventions. Hopefully this book has helped by covering the mental health aspects of these topics in the preceding chapters. Becoming more mindful and reflecting on the multiplicity of these factors is the focus of this chapter.

Reflective practice

Understanding how professionals continue to learn and develop their practice skills has been an area of increasing study by academics and writers. Schön (1983) contributed to this significantly, and the phrase, 'reflective practitioner', shows up as the title of one of his books. In it, he writes about the shifting conceptualisation of knowledge from a technological-rational one, which developed out of the industrial age of the nineteenth and earlier twentieth centuries, to a perspective of professional practice that recognises and appreciates learning that occurs when students or learners apply their didactic learning in practice situations. There is a trend in the study of professional fields, such as social work, to recognise the validity of practice knowledge, or rather how professionals think and interact in their practice moment by moment. In studying the process people go through to attain and develop practice knowledge, some relevant elements to appreciate include validating and respecting practitioners' intuitive reactions to practice, offering opportunities to reflect on practice experience and fostering a learning environment that allows student practitioners and practitioner teachers to be comfortable considering all elements of practice including aspects of practice and case work that is uncertain. Through practice learning and work experience as a practitioner, you may, as Schön expects, develop your practice skills over time until they are embedded and nearly autonomic, just like breathing. Schön's ideas exist alongside other theorists' writings about reflective knowledge and experiential learning, such as Kolb (1984) and Gibbs (1988), who were cited by Jasper (2003) and Mezirow (2001, cited by Newton, 2004).

These ideas have influenced teaching and learning in the professional fields of study and prompted further inquiry into and development of concepts, such as critical reflection and reflexivity, which capture the dynamic process that involves learning, practice and reflection. These concepts as relatively new knowledge formed in the last three decades or so, have been interpreted differently by various authors. As noted by D'Cruz, Gillingham and Melendez (2006, p74), these terms need clarity because ideas like reflective practice, critical reflection and others *are explicitly associated with approaches to improve professional practice, and are required as part of the accreditation of some social work programmes, for example, in Britain (Ixer, 1999; Deacon, 2000).* With reflective practice an important element in the accrediting of social work programmes in the UK, it is natural that reflective practice will influence your social work learning. As an example, the social work benchmark statement reads that *degree programmes in social work should be designed to help students learn to become accountable, reflective, critical and evaluative* (QAA, 2008, p7). To that end, you are probably involved in reflective writing or other reflective tasks in relation to your learning. Additionally, this book is an effort to invite you to read about and become increasingly reflective about mental health-related social work.

In this chapter's first extract, Brockbank and McGill (2007) expand on this book's overall approach and this chapter's explicit theme by offering a review of ideas about reflective practice developed by Schön. Their writing introduces and defines some of the central concepts in Schön's approach. In the reflective tasks related to this reading, you will have an opportunity to think about being engaged in mental health practice and to identify what types of reflective questions might arise.

The second extract includes a passage from a journal article authored by D'Cruz, Gillingham and Melendez (2006). The article involves a review of literature related to the varying terms used to refer to reflective practice. It aims to identify the most commonly used terms and to attempt to reach some clarity in their definitions and use. Given that social work practice in mental health relates frequently to understanding service users' emotional lives and experiences, the extract emphasises an approach to reflective practice which specifically attends to a practitioner's awareness of their emotional reactions through a process called reflexivity. Reflexivity seems to define the important capacity that seasoned and experienced practitioners have to be aware and mindful of their thoughts and feelings while remaining engaged in, focused on and attentive to practice tasks. In this chapter's third extract, the role and usefulness of supervision are highlighted. In this, several further concepts are introduced that offer a way of thinking about how our work with clients and service users may influence our relationships with colleagues. The extract includes an excerpt from practice and subsequent reflection by a practitioner and her supervisor.

Professional social work training: Comfort with uncertainty?

The development of social work as a profession on par with medicine, law and other allied health disciplines is an ongoing process. In the UK, elevating the minimum entry qualification into social work practice to a Bachelor level is a step along that path. Working to respond to difficulties and problems of living is worthwhile and in practice more than just helping – there is a skill set and growing knowledge base to support this work. In developing as a reflective practitioner, you will draw from that.

Spafford, et al. (2007) reviewed student narratives in relation to training and experiences of supervision, comparing student practitioners studying social work, optometry or medicine. Their research explored students' levels of willingness to accept uncertainty in relation to their work. The authors approached this inquiry by reviewing students' and supervisors' discussions. Students were considered willing to be uncertain when they were able to bring questions to their supervisors regarding case material. In comparing the three fields, they found that uncertainty and questioning were more prevalent and seemed more permissible in the context of social work training than in optometry or medicine. The findings, however, did not seem to suggest that social work practitioners or students were less interested in gaining clarity and knowledge in their work. In fact, the study seemed to suggest that the expectations of supervision and what material could be discussed differed among these professions. It seemed that there was a greater tendency for social work students and their supervisors to talk about uncertainty in relation to their case work. Working with uncertainty and being accepting of uncertainty rather than suggesting an indictment of social work as a field lacking technical knowledge suggests that social work practitioners work like the intuitive and reflective professionals described by Schön (1983).

Reflection as a component of professional practice

In the following extract, Brockbank and McGill (2007), who are involved in higher education and facilitating reflective learning in students and lecturers, offer a review of reflection, from its definition to some consideration of its components. They consider reflection to be a process, a means for *constant evaluation*. They assert that *(w)e need to be aware of our actions … in order that we may evaluate them* (Brockbank and McGill, 2007, p85). Their writing offers some context for the development of the ideas of reflective practice, and most helpfully they offer an overview of Schön's (1983) seminal ideas.

EXTRACT ONE

Brockbank, A and McGill, I (2007) Reflection and reflective practice. *Chapter 5* **in Facilitating reflective learning in higher education.** *2nd edition. Maidenhead: Open University Press. pp85–7.*

What does it mean to engage in reflection? What do we mean when we engage in reflective practice? When can we refer to ourselves as 'reflective practitioners'? …

Schön, in developing the notion of 'reflective practice', drew largely upon applied areas of university programmes where students were receiving an education designed to equip them directly into professional occupations such as architectural design, music and medicine. Schön set out the limitations of those teaching disciplines in universities that were in the business of creating and promulgating largely propositional knowledge (learning that, about things, concepts, ideas) in a technically rational value framework. Propositional knowledge is even more evident in courses where there is no vocational element where there is likely to be no action on which to apply the knowledge, for example philosophy.

Schön suggested that propositional knowledge, on its own, is of limited value for the emerging professional, for example lawyer, social worker, physician. Propositional knowledge is limited because it does not take into account the realities of professional life and practice.

EXTRACT ONE *continued*

Yet the emergent professional does go into practice and many of them are effective 'despite' their professional training. They develop practice experience and professional knowledge and excellence. This practice experience includes the propositional knowledge they acquired in order to qualify but is also more than that. So what is it that is more than propositional knowledge that nevertheless enables professionals to engage in their practice effectively? ...

Schön found the teachers and students engaged in reflection on emergent practice that was to underpin their learning and therefore enhance their practice. Putting it more simply, students learned by listening, watching, doing and by being coached in their doing. Not only did they, apply what they had heard and learned from lectures, books and demonstrations but when they did an action that was part of their future profession, for example using a scalpel, they also learned by reflecting themselves and with their tutors, how the action went. They reflected on their practice. In addition, they would 'take with them' that reflection on their previous action as a piece of 'knowledge' or learning when they went into the action the next time. Thus in the next action they would be bringing all their previously acquired understanding and practice and be able to reflect in the action as they did it, particularly if a new circumstance came up.

Thus for the moment we have built up a meaning for reflective practice as reflection-on-action and reflection-in-action. We also adopt Schön's use of the hyphen to suggest two things. One is to convey interaction between action, thinking and being. The second is to suggest an immediacy inherent in reflection and action. This is particularly apposite in relation to reflection-in-action where the professional may well be 'thinking on her feet' as we say.

Comment

Brockbank and McGill (2007) describe not only a significant shift in thinking in terms of the levels of learning for professionals but also highlight the validation of practice knowledge as a discrete kind of knowledge that arises from *learning on our feet*. The levels of learning entail both propositional knowledge – what Brockbank and McGill (2007, p89) call *textbook knowledge or 'knowing about'* – and practice knowledge that arises when learner practitioners are both engaged in practice and when they subsequently discuss and reflect on their practice. This means that for students engaged in practice professions like social work and medicine learning involves both learning in university through lectures, structured learning events and reading – what gives us propositional knowledge – and the practice experiences that occur during placements. In studying social work, this highlights the importance of your days in placement as part of your development as a social work practitioner and hopefully their role in supporting you to apply your learning when delivering social work.

The steps in Schön's reflective practice

The layers of Schön's reflective process involve knowing-in-action, knowledge-in-action, reflection-in-action and reflection-on-action. The hyphens between words in each of these layers suggest that there is a relation between the two – that knowing is happening during the action of practice. Schön (1987, p28, cited by Brockbank and McGill, 2007, p89) states that *knowing-in-action is tacit.* Through action or doing, a person is displaying their *knowing.* When you are interviewing someone and decide to shift from using closed-ended questions to using open-ended questions to facilitate obtaining more and more detailed information, you are displaying knowing-in-action. This knowing transforms into knowledge-in-action when we discuss and describe it to colleagues, supervisors and our tutors. As an example, describing the distinction between closed-ended and open-ended questions and your application of the latter during an interview to improve the assessment content means that you have transformed your knowing/doing into knowledge. You now have knowledge about interviewing that will likely inform your subsequent interviews. As you develop as a practitioner, you will find, too, that you may be able to evaluate your practice in the moment – that you will reflect-in-action. When you discuss your practice in supervision or with colleagues, you will engage in reflection-on-action. This reflective process is highlighted in Figure 8.1.

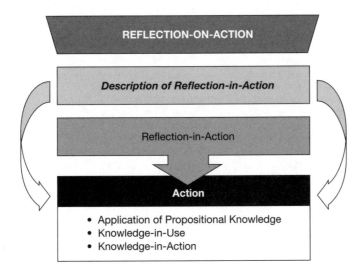

Figure 8.1 *A schematic of Schön's concepts of reflection-in-action and reflection-on-action Adapted from Brockbank and McGill (2007, pp92–3), after Schön (1983).*

If we use the earlier example of changing the types of question used in an interview as an example of action, then we can see that it contains propositional knowledge, such as types of questions, interviewing skills and how questions are framed. With this, we have evidence that your knowledge is now being used in practice. Reflection-in-action, though schematically resting on top of action, is meant through the arrow to signify that reflection is occurring immediately within and during a practice activity. Schön (1987) describes this process as a *rethinking of some part of our knowing-in-action (which) leads to on-the-spot experimentation and further thinking that affects what we do* (p29, cited in Brockbank and McGill, 2007, p89).

Schön (1987) also conceives of reflection-in-action not only as a means of checking progress and revising practice but also as a route to developing insight into *strategies of action … phenomena or ways of framing problems* (p28, cited in Brockbank and McGill, 2007, p89). Though this sounds lofty, seasoned practitioners probably do this routinely. In Figure 8.2 there is an effort to convey how this might occur during an interview when talking with a service user about potentially distressing information related to mental health history. In this example, it is natural that someone may feel uncomfortable needing to talk about a difficult time in their life. The larger box shows the practitioner describing their reflection in-action.

Yip (2006, p250), in learning sessions with students, encourages *them to disclose their own experiences in stress and coping, mental health, mental illness, interventions and services in dealing with …* those with mental health difficulties. By working to help students share *their own perceptions, experiences and beliefs about mental health and mental illness*, Yip (2006, p249) engages students in reflection-in-action. He identifies three components to reflection: the feeling, thinking and doing aspects. In the example of the interview with A in Figure 8.2, the interviewer seems to respond to each of these. In reflecting on the feeling aspect, the interviewer acknowledges the uncomfortable quality

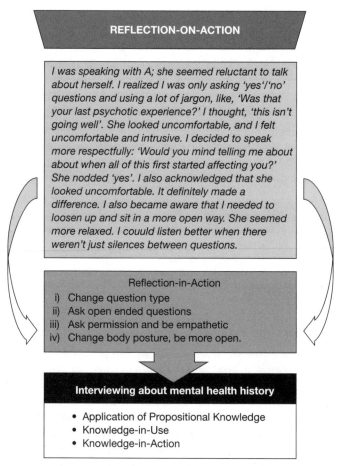

REFLECTION-ON-ACTION

I was speaking with A; she seemed reluctant to talk about herself. I realized I was only asking 'yes'/'no' questions and using a lot of jargon, like, 'Was that your last psychotic experience?' I thought, 'this isn't going well'. She looked uncomfortable, and I felt uncomfortable and intrusive. I decided to speak more respectfully: 'Would you mind telling me about about when all of this first started affecting you?' She nodded 'yes'. I also acknowledged that she looked uncomfortable. It definitely made a difference. I also became aware that I needed to loosen up and sit in a more open way. She seemed more relaxed. I couuld listen better when there weren't just silences between questions.

Reflection-in-Action
i) Change question type
ii) Ask open ended questions
iii) Ask permission and be empathetic
iv) Change body posture, be more open.

Interviewing about mental health history

- Application of Propositional Knowledge
- Knowledge-in-Use
- Knowledge-in-Action

Figure 8.2 *Applying Schön's concept of reflection-in-action and reflection-on-action in a hypothetical interview. Adapted from Brockbank and McGill (2007, pp92-3), after Schön (1983).*

of the interview and becomes more empathic to help A feel more comfortable. The interviewer, realising that using jargon is not an effective way to engage with A, changes the use of language and interview approach. In addition, the interviewer also changes what is being done, or the task of the interview, by gaining permission from A to ask about A's history and through this becomes more relaxed.

Reflection-on-action

Once you have engaged in the simultaneous process of an interview or other practice action and reflection-in-action, you describe what you were doing and what reflections were occurring during the action. Through discussing what happened or describing your reflection-in-action, you distance yourself from the action and attempt to provide an objective overview of the practice encounter. Once you reach this level, you are engaging in reflection-on-action. Discussing practice encounters or visits with service users or groups after they happen will often involve this reflection when you find yourself speaking to peers, colleagues or a supervisor.

As you will know, it is not always easy or possible to recall fully the material that takes place during practice encounters. What you feel and think will change in the course of a practice encounter and will hinge on what happened. Trying to retrieve these changing states may seem very difficult initially. Through repetition of this approach, you should be able to recover more and more of this material. All of this talking and reflecting is work. So the work of describing what took place – the action – and your recollection of your reflections during this – the reflections-in-action – also provide a means through which you may recover more of what happened during the practice encounter. Once you have this material, you are then able to engage in reflection-on-action, when it will be possible to consider the personal and wider systemic influences that may have affected the practice encounter. Through reflection on these influences you may develop insights that help you to understand the interactional dynamic of the practice encounter. Such reflection will also be helpful as you face value conflicts or need to increase self-awareness or develop awareness of value conflicts. You may be able to draw from interactions with service users to gain greater appreciation of the difficulties facing them. In addition, you may have practice realisations or insights that help you understand how to respond to a case dilemma.

POINTS TO CONSIDER

Imagine that you are working as a social worker within a mental health team. Today, you are contributing to the duty service and have just begun meeting with a female client who has come into the office. She seems distressed, and you ask what is troubling her.

The top half of my head feels quite light but the thread that runs down from my head to my stomach is soaked in deep despair. Maggots in my belly multiply. Rotting flesh. Want to drink bleach to cleanse them or a sharp knife to cut them out. They told me I needed a psychiatrist and not a medical surgeon back in September. They said Graham (the psychiatrist) *would get rid of the maggots but he hasn't.* (Hart, 1995, p19, cited by Bartlett and Sandland, 2003, p5)

POINTS TO CONSIDER continued

In this practice scenario, your action is listening to a female client describe her current experience.

To respond to the preceding scenario, what are your reflections-in-action? To get started, consider the following questions, taken from Brockbank and McGill (2007, p29).

- Is what I am doing appropriate at this moment?

- Do I need to alter, amend, change what I am doing and being in order to adjust to changing circumstance, to get back into balance, to attend accurately, etc?...

- If I am not on the right track, is there a better way?

Feel free to ask yourself any other questions that come to mind.

Comment

Linda Hart's writing about her experiences offers an insight into the distress of a person living with schizophrenia. In relation to Brockbank and McGill's (2007) possible questions, you may reflect by asking: Is listening appropriate at this moment? If the answer is no, you may wonder if you should try to do something immediately. You might ask, do I need to change what I am doing? You may wonder, what do I need to do? Is she safe? As part of your duty practice, you will be involved in assessing what a person is reporting, gaining more detail, and offering an immediate and likely longer-term response to stabilise the situation and respond to the individual's distress. On a feeling level, your reflection of your emotional response to this material may be one of upset, anxiety or some other reaction. On a thinking level, drawing on information on mental health diagnoses, symptoms and treatments, you would likely be hearing information that seems to relate to a kinaesthetic hallucination, that is, a physical feeling or sensory experience of discomfort that does not seem based in reality. However, as part of your effort to reflect and practise holistically, you may ask about physical problems, wondering if Linda has seen her GP or presented to the A & E. You would likely need to know about the length of the problem, any previous help for mental health problems and any history of taking medication. As for medication, you would likely need to know what tablets someone currently takes and what they used to take, what type of tablets have been taken and if these offered any relief or caused problems. Another part of your work – the knowledge and skills that may have come through your university studies and your practice knowledge – would involve listening to the client's story. She speaks about *rotting flesh*, *despair* and *maggots* (Hart, 1995, p19, cited by Bartlett and Sandland, 2003, p5). You may be able to use skills of empathy to acknowledge Linda's distress, her sense of being unclean and if there are any other factors that contribute to her despair. With reflection, you have the opportunity to engage in some depth with the complexity of a service user's situation. Just through using this short passage as an example, you have been invited to think about psychiatric diagnosis, symptomatology, symptom duration, treatment options, emotional content and issues of risk. To delve further into risk factors, it would be essential to inquire about thoughts of self-injury – self-inflicted surgery to remove the *maggots* or a plan to ingest bleach. By asking about distress, you may validate her experience of constant intrusion. In addition, you may be able to think with her or colleagues about how to secure a safer way of offering help and providing relief. You may also reflect – as highlighted in the previous chapter – that it would be necessary to consult with team members, such as a psychiatrist or a psychiatric nurse, to assess and plan how to be helpful to Linda. In the Figure 8.3, possible questions that a practitioner might reflect in action are listed with a description of what took place from the practitioner's point of view as part of describing reflection-in-action.

REFLECTION-ON-ACTION

I was speaking with L. It was a painful conversation. L came in while I was on duty. She was describing really intense hallucinations, it seems. She didn't think the prescribed medicine was helping and was thinking about how to treat herself – but this was dangerous – taking bleach or cutting. I actually felt pretty anxious when she first mentioned this. We took a short break and fortunately I was able to talk to Graham. He and I decided that though the medicine didn't seem to be helping, we should try to continue it but see if L would be open to going into the crisis house for a week. I spoke with L who definitely wasn't interested in the hospital but preferred going to the crisis house rather than being on her own. I'm going to follow up tomorrow with her at the crisis house.

i)   I feel worried about her. Is Linda safe? Might she actually take bleach or try to cut herself to release the maggots?
ii) The symptoms she is describing seem to suggest a thought disorder; I wonder what medicine Linda is taking? Does it offer any relief?
III) Who else in addition to Graham is working with her?
iv) How does Linda manage? Is she living on her own?
v)   I wonder if she feels frightened? Might I need to speak with colleagues about getting immediate help to help her feel safer? I think I'll check with Graham.

Interviewing about mental health history

- Application of Propositional Knowledge
- Knowledge-in-Use
- Knowledge-in-Action

Figure 8.3 *Schön's concepts of reflection-in-action and reflection-on-action as applied to a mental health interview. Adapted from Brockbank and McGill (2007, pp92–3), after Schön (1983).*

In the figure, the reflection-in-action comprises a series of questions that may help the practitioner remain focused during the interview as well as realisations about personal feelings and decisions about what to do. The description which comes after the interview and reflection-in-interviewing offers a chance for a practitioner to reflect on the interview and whatever intervention occurred and to gain perspective and become evaluative of their practice and the service offered to the service user.

Reflective practice in mental health social work

Practising social work within a mental health context means that we need to consider the knowledge and skills specific to working with service users who are experiencing mental health distress. For instance, more specific mental health knowledge would include types of mental health distress, approaches to offering help or treatment, the roles and strengths of different professionals and legislation and policy in this field. In relation to skills, mental health social workers would need the foundation of social work skills of interviewing, observation, decision-making and linkage along with abilities to diffuse crises, to work across professions, and to manage potentially volatile emotional presentations in their work. Yip (2006, p249) introduces possible dilemmas that may arise for social workers practising in mental health. These include:

1. Social control as opposed to humanistic orientation in treatment and rehabilitation.

2. Medical treatment as opposed to psychosocial intervention for clients with mental illness.

3. The role dilemmas of social workers in multidisciplinary settings.

These dilemmas will provide opportunities for reflection to appreciate differences in treatment approach and in understanding service user needs. As the preceding hypothetical interview based on Linda Hart's experience attempted to show, there will be dilemmas about safety and risk and decisions to be made about which help to offer. The intervention involved a balance with medicine being continued but with crisis support being offered through a crisis house that offered some containment but was not a hospital.

Reflexivity and critical reflection

In the area of social work scholarship and inquiry, there is an ongoing discussion about concepts of reflection. As noted earlier, reflective practice has been incorporated into social work training and in the assessment of your practice learning. Reflecting on your practice and then thinking about reflecting itself involves metacognition, or thinking about thinking. Compared with the busy, active and often pressured environment of social work practice, it may seem alien to talk about having time to stop and think. However, with reflection highlighted in your study and training, it seems essential to grapple with this, as being able to reflect on your emotions and thoughts may help your practice.

A number of terms are used to describe the process of thinking about practice beyond the concepts developed by Schön. Two of these are 'reflexivity' and 'critical reflection'. By discussing and clarifying terms and concepts that attempt to shed light on, define and describe social work practice, the academic inquiry into reflexivity and critical reflection provides a vocabulary to describe the processes of social work practice. To this end, D'Cruz, Gillingham and Melendez (2006) have reviewed literature to identify some commonalities and propose some consistency in relation to these terms. As you read the following extract, which is taken from a journal article, you will note that it includes a general overview of reflexivity and critical reflection plus a more in-depth discussion of the role that emotions play in social work practice. In working in mental health, practitioners are working squarely with the emotional and psychological well-being or, more accurately, distress of individuals. As a result, it is important for reflective practitioners in mental health services to be able to manage and use their emotional experience.

EXTRACT TWO

D'Cruz, H, Gillingham, P and Melendez, S (2006) Reflexivity, its meanings and relevance for social work: A critical review of the literature. British Journal of Social Work, 37 (1), pp74-5, 80-1 and 83.

This article aims to answer the following questions: What is 'reflexivity'? How is 'reflexivity' defined as a concept and described as a practice? What is the relevance of 'reflexivity' for social work? And how does 'reflexivity' fit alongside concepts like 'critical reflection'? ...

Different meanings of 'reflexivity'

In presenting different meanings of the concept of reflexivity in the following discussion, we have separated them into three categories that we have described as variations. Within the three variations, there are subtleties and nuances of meaning which we explore through the differences and the articulations between them.

The first variation regards reflexivity as an individual's considered response to an immediate context and making choices for further direction. This variation is concerned with the ability of individuals to process information and create knowledge to guide life choices, and has implications for both the role of social workers and the relationships between social workers and clients. The second variation defines reflexivity as an individual's self-critical approach that questions how knowledge is generated and, further, how relations of power operate in this process. The third variation is concerned with the part that emotion plays in social work practice ...

Defining 'reflexivity': the third variation

... Historically, emotional responses of practitioners to the situations they face have been cast as problematic and requiring control: workers have been exhorted to manage anxiety *and* gain a sense of ego mastery and control by *the acquisition of theory to enhance skill-based practice expertise (Miehls and Moffat, 2000, abstract). The emphasis has been on empathy rather than sympathy and on controlled emotional involvement and a non-judgemental attitude (Biestek, 1961). Early practice literature encouraged practitioners to be aware of how their life experiences influenced their responses to clients (Kondrat, 1999), expressed as the part that the 'self' played in a session with a client (Hook, 2000). Practitioners were encouraged to develop 'objectivity' in relation to their own values, needs and biases and be able to distance themselves from the experience of dealing with clients (Kondrat, 1999).*

EXTRACT TWO *continued*

Objectivity was to be enhanced by the use of peer and expert supervision and, more recently, by the monitoring of practice through technical measures, known as the 'technocratization' of practice (Dominelli and Hoogveldt, 1996). Practice approaches that promote forms of reflexivity (as defined in the third variation) on the part of the practitioner, however, take a different stance in relation to the place of emotion in practice, as being inherent to professional knowledge and professional power and to be recognized rather than avoided or repressed ...

We have included in the third variation of meanings of reflexivity approaches to social work practice that acknowledge the part that emotions, particularly anxiety, play in social work practice. In summary, these approaches propose that the acknowledgement of emotional responses by the practitioner can be used to promote deeper understanding between practitioner and client and ultimately enhance practice. The implication of this approach is that it is acceptable, even desirable, for practitioners to have emotional responses to their work. It is also necessary that practitioners develop their awareness of their emotional responses rather than repressing them. As suggested by Ruch (2002), this represents a considerable shift from current practice approaches and may have beneficial consequences for dealing with what Thompson (2000) describes as the very real dangers of stress and burnout in social work practitioners. The inclusion of emotion as an important factor in social work practice is inconsistent with current practices such as versions of 'evidence-based practice' (Webb, 2001) which exhort practitioners to be objective in their decision making by the application of 'evidence' derived from research (as a set of neutral techniques for achieving an objective truth) (D'Cruz and Jones, 2004).

'Reflection' and 'critical reflection'

... In our understanding, an important difference between 'critical reflection' and 'reflexivity' as defined in the three variations concerns timing. In critical reflection, the use of a critical incident as the basis for knowledge generation can be considered as 'reflection-on-action' rather than 'reflection-in-action' (Schön, 1983). The critical incident is firmly in the past, and is represented as a learning opportunity for the future from this selected incident. Reflexivity, in contrast (in its various conceptualizations), can be described as a critical approach to the generation of knowledge that operates 'in the moment' (Sheppard et al., 2000); the reflexive practitioner or researcher is constantly engaged in the process of questioning (self-monitoring) their own knowledge claims and those of others as he/she engages in social interaction and the micro-practices of knowledge/power. This has also been referred to as 'practical consciousness' (Young, 1990) or as 'reflection-in-action' (Schön, 1983). Hence, the learning is potentially both momentary and transferable, as the participants review and adapt to the relationships in context (time and place).

Comment

The material offered by D'Cruz, et al. (2006) introduced the meanings of reflexivity and critical reflection. The former was noted, in the authors' estimation, to represent three variations. In the passage extracted, the third variation comprised a perspective that being aware of, acknowledging, validating and using emotional reactions represented a reflexive social work practice. Further, D'Cruz, et al. (2006) offered this as a valid form of practice knowledge that may enhance practice. In the previous point to consider, you imagined yourself interacting with a woman describing sensations of despair and seemingly intrusive sensory hallucinations. It is likely that upon hearing this material you may have naturally felt anxious or upset or may have become detached. It is possible that you may have been able to acknowledge feeling repulsed by the images. Also you may have felt overwhelmed when faced with seemingly difficult-to-resolve distress. By asserting any or all of these emotional experiences as a valid part of interacting with clients, this article frees you and other practitioners to consider what you feel as part of your reflection-in-action. This means working with your feelings to understand and reflect on case material. With this, you may build on the subjective and objective information that you have gathered to ensure that you respond professionally, taking into account and working within the parameters of professional conduct and values. Additionally, through this you may be able to feel more emotionally connected to your work and in mind of your needs for further development.

D'Cruz, Gillingham and Melendez (2006) also described their perspective on the difference between reflexivity and critical reflection. Bolton (2005, p7) in her work on how writing may facilitate reflective practice, offers the following:

Being reflexive *is focusing close attention upon one's own actions, thoughts and feelings and their effects …*

Being reflective *is looking at the whole scenario: other people, the situation and place, and so on.*

Bolton's (2005) interpretation of reflection differs slightly from the extract's; yet there is similarity in regards to the concept of being reflexive. In the second extract, the authors state that critical reflection takes place after the event; whereas Bolton's (2005) ideas on being reflective seem to echo Fook (2002), who suggests that being critically reflective involves paying attention to larger systemic influences and their impact during one's reflection. Yip (2006, p246), citing Habermas (1973) and others (Clift, et al., 1990; Habermas, 1973; Mezirow, 1981; Ruch, 2000), writes that *critical reflection is based on Habermas's (1973) critical and emancipatory sources of knowledge. It transforms practice by challenging the existing social, political and cultural conditions and structural forces that distort or constrain professional practice.* This would involve reflecting on the interaction that took place; the outcome of the practice encounter; and what influenced this in relation to understood social variables like class, ethnicity, power and social status and the dynamics of the interaction. As you will note, the process of reflection requires a mindfulness and appreciation of the variables relevant both to the interaction between the service user and provider as well as the interaction between the larger macrosystem and the practitioner/service user dyad. In mental health practice, being critically reflective may involve questioning the funding of medical treatments at the exclusion of providing funding for residential services that promote social inclusion or questioning the seemingly excessive use of anti-psychotic medication in men of colour.

Becoming culturally responsive through reflection

As the last point indicates, a significant area of reflection in both practice and coursework relates to our thoughts and perspectives in relation to becoming culturally aware and responsive in our work. In their study of how field educators and student social workers address issues of oppression in field placements, Maidment and Cooper (2002) recommend Gould and Taylor (1996) as a text promoting critical reflection in social work. They noted that *critical reflection is only possible if the educator is able to identify oppressive structures in order to address these in supervision* (p401). This illustrates that the process of critical reflection should not solely be the task of students but will naturally be facilitated by supervisors and practice teachers who have developed their capacities for critical reflection. Linking Maidment and Cooper's (2002) quote to the work of mental health social work, it would be relevant to reflect on and consider the oppressive structures that may exist in mental health practice. The research by Maidment and Cooper (2002) encourages us to think about how to address issues of oppression reflectively and helpfully draws us to the topic of supervision.

Supervision

One of the means by which learner practitioners and qualified practitioners of social work come to appreciate the systemic impact on their work and also think about their practice is through supervision. Supervision may vary and could involve tracking progress on a case as well as considering more clinical aspects of practice. In the following quote, supervision involves reflection.

> Supervision is a working alliance between a supervisor and a worker or workers in which the worker can reflect on herself in her working situation by giving an account of her work and receiving feedback and where appropriate guidance and appraisal. The object of this alliance is to maximise the competence of the worker in providing a helping service. (Inskipp and Proctor, 1988, p4, cited by Scaife, 2001, p2)

This definition sits nicely with the social work benchmark statement in its expectation that social workers need to engage in evaluative, critical and reflective approaches to their learning and practice.

Inskipp and Proctor (1988, n.p., cited by Scaife, 2001, pp7–8) also identified a number of responsibilities of supervisees when participating in supervision sessions.

- *Considering how to share your current understanding of your strengths and points for development with the supervisor.*

- *Taking a position of openness to learning which includes communicating your thoughts and feelings in supervision.*

- *Noticing what you find threatening in supervision.*

- *Noticing how you typically show defensiveness.*

- *Identifying your own ideas about boundaries in supervision and working out how to let your supervisor know should they begin to stray beyond them.*

- *Being prepared for and having the skills to negotiate disagreement.*

- *Identifying your expectations about the focus of supervisor.*

- *Working out how to stay in control of feedback that might be given by the supervisor.*

- *Examining your views about having your work observed either directly or indirectly.*

- *Working out how to show your supervisor your fears and anxieties without undue apprehension in anticipation of negative evaluation.*

- *Letting the supervisor know what is proving helpful and unhelpful to your learning and development.*

- *Acknowledging errors with a view to learning from them.*

This list would certainly not be exhaustive in terms of how supervisees approach supervisory contact; however, it may help to prompt some thinking about your relationship with supervision and with supervisors.

POINTS TO CONSIDER

One of the recommendations for supervisees is to ... show ... your fears and anxieties without undue apprehension ... (Inskipp and Proctor, 1988, n.p, cited by Scaife, 2001, pp7–8). Please give some thought to this. If you imagine yourself taking up a placement in a mental health team, what kind of emotional response might you have? It might be natural to have some anxiety in relation to this – even if it was just hoping to do well; if so, how would you discuss this with your work-based supervisor and/or practice teacher? What help might support you to express your feelings and/or develop greater confidence?

Reflecting amidst the challenges of social work

In the above Points to consider, you had the opportunity to think about how you might discuss any fears or anxieties you may have when engaged in practice. Hopefully, you were willing to go beyond a perfunctory *I won't feel anxious*. As previously highlighted, the capacity to be reflexive about emotional reactions may be an advantage in practice that could illuminate your case work and facilitate your own personal awareness. At a more developed level, becoming aware of feelings and thoughts during practice encounters may also highlight relevant elements in what may be happening for service users and is in line with the concept of emotional reflexivity discussed earlier.

Hughes and Pengelly (1997), in a passage from their book, *Staff supervision in a turbulent environment*, highlight some of the emotional impact of working in a mental health setting. The authors capture the pressure of social work as they write about supervision with a focus on the difficult and often complex work settings in which social workers practice. The extract includes case material and how – through reflection – it may be possible to speculate about the impact of clients' experiences on the work we do. You may have come across some of the terms used in the book, such as 'transference' and 'countertransference', which have come into human services work from psychodynamic thought and practice. Those terms at a very basic level refer to feelings or thoughts that, in the former, a service user may have in relation to a practitioner and in the latter describes reactions that a practitioner may have in relation to service users. The premise is that these reactions have their roots in our earlier relationships with family members, but reactions may relate to other experiences and relationships also. In the extract that follows, there is a description of a phenomenon described as 'mirroring' which has links to the process of countertransference. Included in this is an excerpt about a case in which the social worker and the supervisor seemed to behave in a way that mirrors the case material discussed. This relates to how emotions and patterns of relationships from earlier experiences may have a dynamic impact on more current experiences.

It is fair to say that there are contentious aspects to the use or application of psychodynamic theory. In light of that, I think it is important to consider this extract as a positive example of the helpfulness and utility of having time to reflect and think about the work we do. By having time to reflect, the supervisor and supervisee are able to come together and think about both the service user and her mother and their working relationship. Please do not let any concerns or criticisms about psychodynamic theory dissuade you from the possible benefit in reviewing the extract as a helpful example of supportive supervision.

EXTRACT THREE

Hughes, L and Pengelly, P (1997)* Staff supervision in a turbulent environment: Managing process and task in front-line services. *London: Jessica Kingsley, pp83–5.

Mirroring

Mirroring, *also known as* reflection process *(Mattinson 1975)* or paralleling *(Wilmot and Shohet 1985), is one aspect of counter transference that merits discussion in its own right …*

Mattinson, adapting Searles (1955), establishes the thesis that in social work supervision 'the processes at work currently in the relationship between *client and worker are often reflected in the* relationship between *worker and supervisor'. The core idea is that dynamic interactions that belong and originate in one area of relationship are acted out in an adjacent area as though they belong there, being carried from one area to the other by a 'player' common to both … These dynamic issues, usually seen as originating in the service-user and projected (by transference) into the relationship between the service-user and worker, may then in turn be imported into the supervision session where they are unwittingly replayed by the worker and, sometimes, the supervisor. Mirroring is thus a secondary effect of countertransference that is not fully known about, but enacted; the practitioner, like the service user, is compelled to act rather than feel or think, and may then (by a further projective identification) draw the supervisor into joining the enactment in supervision. The next example shows both worker and supervisor caught up in a mirroring interaction.*

EXTRACT THREE continued

EXAMPLE S.d

A social worker and supervisor, based in a child and adolescent psychiatry setting, discussed in supervision a case that had been preoccupying them for some months. It involved Nadia, a girl of thirteen, who had been admitted in crisis to a young people's psychiatric unit. On admission she had been in a serious physical state, having refused for some time to eat or drink. She was assessed as being severely depressed. Nadia lived alone with her mother (Mrs D), a refugee from persecution in her country of origin, who was viewed by her compatriots in the local community as a strange woman with whom it was impossible to communicate. Mrs D led an isolated life, focused on her one child, whom she treated physically and emotionally as an infant and whom she had protected from the 'dangerous' outside world by often locking her in the house alone. After admission to the psychiatric unit (following her mother's sudden panic at her physical state), Nadia had blossomed dramatically, gaining inches in a few weeks and for the first time enjoying being playfully naughty. Her mother, visiting regularly, had great difficulty in coping with the changes in her and in her relationships with others, and had quickly made a range of complaints to various bodies about staff mistreatment of Nadia and herself, so that a series of investigations was under way The (experienced and gifted) social worker, alongside colleagues of other disciplines, had worked sensitively with Nadia and her mother together and separately, highly mindful of the pain of both, and had taken steps to involve a psychiatrist who spoke Mrs D's language and members of Mrs D's church community to act as advocates for her.

The supervision session in question had focused on the impending care proceedings. Immediately after the session the supervisor was taken aback to realise that she had quite inappropriately volunteered to draft the court report for the social worker, and the social worker had raised no question about this unusual offer. The ostensible reason the supervisor had given that the social worker was very busy providing the extra reports required for the investigations into Mrs D's complaints about the case made no real sense. The supervisor was even more puzzled as writing court reports was something she particularly disliked. Clearly some interaction that was hard to understand had taken place in the session.

Gradually the supervisor came to the view that she and the social worker might be blindly enacting the key dynamics of the case, an understanding confirmed and developed in her next discussion with the social worker. They saw they had been caught up in an interaction between regression (the social worker) and overprotection as the only means of helping (the supervisor), an interaction that mirrored the relationship between the daughter and her mother. Though the social worker and supervisor had previously been thoughtfully aware of the importance of this core dynamic in the case, their experience of its so 'getting under their skin' gave them a new conviction of its power and control, especially the pressure to regress that would continue to undermine Nadia's progress.

> ### EXTRACT THREE *continued*
>
> *Mirroring may also take place in a less noticeable way around the fringes of supervision, or in behaviour connected with it. For example, a supervisee might 'forget' (or find plausible reasons to postpone) a supervision session where a particularly elusive or resistant service user was due to be discussed or might omit to present such a case for discussion at all (Vincent 1995).*

Comment

Supervision may be a strategy to facilitate and guide you in improving your practice, as the definition used to open this section highlighted. In addition to serving that function, in the hands and minds of skilled and thoughtful colleagues, supervision may also be a means to provide understanding about ourselves, our working relationships and provide insight about our work with service users. In the preceding extract, you were introduced to the concept of mirroring, a term used to describe when professional relationships – such as that between a supervisee and supervisor – mirror something of the service user's system. In the example of the two practitioners working with Nadia, it transpired that the supervisor was able to reflect following supervision and wonder about how her behaviour towards her supervisee seemed to replicate or mirror the overprotective stance of Mrs D toward her daughter Nadia. Even if the psychodynamic concepts of transference, countertransference, projection or mirroring do not fit comfortably with your theories about practice, it seems meaningful that the supervisor and supervisee were able to consider how their work affects them. Being able to think about work's effects on us – particularly in mental health social work – may help us to remain engaged in difficult and complex practice situations.

Highlighting the important role of supervision in facilitating development of learner practitioners and qualified practitioners may suggest that this is the primary role for supervision. However, as McCafferty (2004, 2005) notes in developing a model of group supervision for social work students, there is also a substantial aspect of supervision focused on ensuring that social work tasks adhere to agency and government policies and procedures and relate to expected service delivery targets. He draws from a range of authors to identify *five main functions of supervision [as ...] administration, teaching, helping (Pettes, 1967), mediation (Richards et al., 1991; Morrison, 1990), and assessment (Evans, 1990; Sawdon and Sawdon, 1995) ... with the latter seemingly referring to assessment of performance* (McCafferty, 2005, p30). Clearly, supervision has a role in assessment and administration, but it would be unfortunate to diminish its teaching and helping functions with its aims to facilitate awareness, learning and growth also.

C H A P T E R   S U M M A R Y

As we have introduced in this chapter, reflective practice has become central to the social work curriculum and the assessment of qualifying and post-qualifying social work students. The GSCC has emphasised this through the accreditation of social work courses and in the renewal of registration of qualified social workers. Being able to identify your learning needs, participate in pertinent learning and subsequently highlight your reflection about your learning's application to your practice are required elements for social work registration.

Social work practice across varied settings involves responding to turbulent and challenging material; this will particularly be the case in mental health service contexts. Having the space to think and reflect is vital to personal and professional development and the offering of responsive services. Through reading, engaging in *points for consideration* and becoming aware of your thoughts and affective responses to the material included in this book and its prompts to reflect on your life and practice experiences, you have actively participated in your practice of reflection. The models of consideration – particularly that of Schön – as well as the concepts of reflexivity and critical reflection offer a structure for reflecting and ways to describe and map your reflective process. Reflexivity identifies and confirms the work you engage in when you develop a mindful, conscientious attention to your practice in the moment. In addition to reflexivity, critical reflection gives you a further approach to use in taking stock of your practice. Both concepts validate the ongoing, daily work you do to attend to your practice. They also highlight the ongoing development of terms and concepts that respond to the need to understand and define social work practice.

Supervision will also be used to facilitate insightful understanding of complex cases and their impact and should provide a means to reflect on both the clinical and administrative aspects of social work. The tension among the differing functions of supervision illustrate

> that supervision is both central and marginal to social work. It is central because the most vital social work resources are the personal resources of the workers (Payne and Scott, 1982). It is marginal because in practice its efficacy is undermined by lack of commitment. A result of this is that supervision in terms of regularity, content and outcome is patchy and variable in quality (Pritchard, 1995). (McCafferty, 2005, p30)

The introduction of the idea of marginality brings me back to the central tenet of this book and the importance of social work practice in the area of mental health. Social work has a role in mental health practice in helping to ensure that the whole reality of a service user's experience is addressed in responding to mental health need and its related effects. Social work and the other helping professions also have a role in supporting those living with mental distress to have a place in their communities and in society without stigma and without being marginalised. To remain engaged and robust in the sometimes challenging but often meaningful practice of social work in mental health, it will be necessary to reflect by taking time to take stock by engaging in an inventory of your social work knowledge from both your foundation studies and your practice experiences. In the area of mental health social work, developing as a reflective practitioner means reflecting on your knowledge about mental health, processing your emotional reactions and perceptions to mental health distress, intervening so that the values and holistic nature of social work practice are offered to service users, and critically considering the impact of systemic forces like oppression, government policy and legislation. Through practice and reflection on your practice, you will be able to develop further as a social work mental health practitioner remaining mindful that the mental health needs of service users will be relevant in a variety of social work settings.

FURTHER READING

Bolton, G (2005) *Reflective practice: Writing and professional development*. 2nd edition. London: Sage. Bolton has facilitated reflective practice seminars with a variety of allied health professionals; this book is accessible and inviting as she facilitates readers to access thoughts and feelings through writing as a means of enhancing practice. An updated third edition is to be published in 2010.

Knott, C and Scragg, T (2007) *Reflective practice in social work*. Exeter: Learning Matters.

Parker, J (2004) *Effective practice learning in social work*. Exeter: Learning Matters.

Yelloly, M and Henkel, M (eds) (1994) *Learning and teaching in social work: Towards reflective practice*. London: Jessica Kingsley.
Several texts that address reflective practice and social work practice.

The General Social Care Council. The website of the council overseeing social work education and registration.

www.gscc.org.uk

References

Ainsworth, M, Blehar, M, Waters, E and Wall, S (1978) *Patterns of attachment: A psychological study of the strange situation*. Hillsdale, NJ: Lawrence Erlbaum.

Allott, P (2004) What is mental health, illness and recovery? In Ryan, T and Pritchard, J (eds) *Good practice in adult mental health*. London: Jessica Kingsley.

American Psychiatric Association (2000) *Diagnostic and statistical manual of mental disorders*. 4th edition, text revision. Washington, D.C.: APA.

Barrett, G and Keeping, C (2005) The processes required for effective interprofessional working. In Barrett, G, Sellman, D and Thomas, J (eds) (2005) *Interprofessional working in health and social care, Professional perspectives*. Basingstoke: Palgrave Macmillan.

Barron, A (2001) *Literature review: Good practice research: Effective multi-agency working between schools and child and adolescent mental health services (CAMHS)*. London: Mental Health Foundation.

Bartlett, P and Sandland, R (2003) *Mental health law, Policy and practice.* 2nd edition. Oxford: Oxford University Press.

Beckett, C and Maynard, A (2005) *Values and ethics in social work: An introduction*. London: Sage.

Beresford, P (2005) Social approaches to madness and distress: User perspectives and user knowledges. In Tew, J (ed.) *Social perspectives in mental health: Developing social models to understand and work with mental distress*. London: Jessica Kingsley.

Bird, A (2006) *We need to talk: The case for psychological therapy on the NHS*. London: Mental Health Foundation.

Bolton, G (2005) *Reflective practice: Writing and professional development.* 2nd edition. London: Sage.

Bond, S (2008) Conversation with John Archambeault, 29 May.

Bowlby, J (1990) *A secure base: Parent–child attachment and healthy human development*. New York: Basic Books.

Bowles, M, Collingridge, M, Curry, S and Valentine, B (2006) *Ethical practice in social work: An applied approach*. Maidenhead: Open University Press.

British Association of Social Workers (BASW) (2002) *Code of Ethics for Social Work*. Birmingham: BASW. **www.basw.co.uk**

British Broadcasting Corporation (2008) *Mental health*. [online] Available at **www.bbc.co.uk/health/conditions/mental_health/**

Brockbank, A and McGill, I (2007) *Facilitating reflective learning in higher education*. 2nd edition. Maidenhead: Open University Press.

Burne, J (2008) Can you really beat depression talking to a computer? *The Daily Mail* [online] Available at **www.dailymail.co.uk/health/article-537589/Can-REALLY-beat-depression-talking-computer.html**

Campbell, J, Brophy, L, Healy, B and O'Brien, A (2006) International perspectives on the use of community treatment orders: Implications for mental health social workers. *British Journal of Social Work*, 36, 1101–18.

Carpenter, J, Schneider, J, Brandon, T and Wooff, D (2003) Working in multidisciplinary community mental health teams: The impact on social workers and health professionals of integrated mental health care. *British Journal of Social Work*, 33 (8), 1081–103.

Chenoweth, L and McAuliffe, D (2005) *The road to social work and human service practice: An introductory text*. Victoria: Thompson.

Children's Workforce Development Council (2007) *Multi agency working, Fact sheet*. London: CWDC.

Clark, C (2000) *Social work ethics: Politics, principles and practice*. Basingstoke: Macmillan.

Cloutte, P (2003) *Understanding postnatal depression*. Revised edition. London: MIND.

Colman, A (2006) *Dictionary of psychology*. Oxford: Oxford University Press. [online] Available at **www.oxfordreference.com/views/GLOBAL.html**

Community Care (2008) Conduct disorder programmes. *Community Care*, 10 May, p24.

Crawford, K (2006) *Reflective reader: Social work and human development*. Exeter: Learning Matters.

D'Cruz, H, Gillingham, P and Melendez, S (2006) Reflexivity, its meanings and relevance for social work: A critical review of the literature. *British Journal of Social Work*, 37 (1), 73–90.

Department for Children, Schools and Families (2005) *Aims and outcomes*. London: DCSF. [online] Available at **www.everychildmatters.gov.uk/aims/ www.dfes.gov.uk**

Department for Children, Schools and Families (2007) *Effective integrated working: Findings of concept of operations study, Integrated working to improve outcomes for children and young people*. London: DCSF. [online] Available at **www.ecm.gov.uk/integratedworking**

Department of Health (1990) *The Care Programme Approach for people with a mental illness referred to the specialist psychiatric services. HC(90)23/LASSL(90)11*. London: DoH. **www.doh.gov.uk**

Department of Health (1999a) *Effective care co-ordination in mental health services, Modernising the care programme approach, A policy booklet*. [online] Available at **www.doh.gov/pub/**

Department of Health (1999b) *Working together to safeguard children*. London: HMSO.

Department of Health (2001) *Statistical press notice – children looked after*. [online] Available at **www.doh.gov.uk/**

Department of Health (2003) *Inside outside: Improving mental health services for black and minority ethnic communities in England*. Leeds: National Institute for Mental Health in England. **www.nimhe.org.uk**

Department of Health (2004) *Advice on the decision of the European Court of Human Rights in the case of HL v UK (the 'Bournewood' Case)*. [Gateway Reference 4269] London: The Stationery Office.

Department of Health (2005a) *Delivering race equality in mental health care*. London: The Stationery Office.

Department of Health (2005b) *Psychiatric morbidity among adults living in private households*. [online] Available at **www.dh.gov.uk/PublicationsAndStatistics/Publications/PublicationsStatistics/PublicationsStatisticsArticle/fs/en?**

Department of Health (2006) *Reviewing the Care Programme Approach 2006*. [Gateway reference: 7274] London: DoH.

Department of Health (2007) *Reforming the Mental Health Act 1988*. [online] Available at **www.dh.gov.uk/en/Healthcare/NationalServiceFrameworks/Mentalhealth/DH_077352**

Department of Health and Department for Education (1995) *A handbook on child and adolescent mental health*. Manchester: HMSO.

Department of Health and Department for Education and Skills (2004) *National Service Framework for children, young people and maternity services*. London: DoH. [online] Available at **www.dh.gov.uk/en/Publicationsandstatistics/Publications/PublicationsPolicyAnd Guidance/Browsable/DH_4868696**.

Edgeworth, J and Carr, A (2000) Child abuse. In Carr, A (ed.) *What works with children and adolescents? A critical review of psychological interventions with children, adolescents and their families*. Abingdon: Routledge.

Fakhoury, W and Wright, D (2004) A national survey of Approved Social Workers in the UK: Information, communication and training needs. *British Journal of Social Work*, 34 (5), 663–75.

Fernando, S (1995) Social realities and mental health. In Fernando, S (ed.) *Mental health in a multi-ethnic society*. Abingdon: Routledge.

Fook, J (2002) *Social work critical theory and practice*. London: Sage.

Freud, S (1946/1967) *The ego and the mechanisms of defence*. Revised edition. New York: International Universities Press.

General Social Care Council (2007) *The social care register*. London: GSCC. [online] Available at **www.gscc.org.uk/The+Social+Care+Register/The+Social+Care+Register+explained/**

Geraghty, R (2002) *The Dialogue guide to personality disorder: A guide for anyone who wants to know more about personality disorder*. Sutton: Henderson Hospital.

Glover-Thomas, N (2007) A new 'new' Mental Health Act? Reflections on the proposed amendments to the Mental Health Act 1983. *Clinical Ethics*, 2 (1), 28–31.

Golightley, M (2008) *Social work and mental health*. 3rd edition. Exeter: Learning Matters.

Grant, V (2007) Conversation with John Archambeault and Juliette Flynn, 22 May.

Great Britain. *Carers (Recognition and Services) Act 1995: Elizabeth II. Chapter 12*. (1995) London: The Stationery Office.

Great Britain. *The Mental Capacity Act 2005: Elizabeth II. Chapter 9*. (2005) London: The Stationery Office.

Green, G, Hayes, C, Dickinson, D, Whittaker, A and Gilheany, B (2002) The role and impact of social relationships upon well-being reported by mental health service users: A qualitative study. *Journal of Mental Health*, 11 (5), 565–79. [online] Available at: **http://dx.doi.org/10.1080/09638230020023912**.

Gross, R (2001) *Psychology: The science of mind and behaviour*. 4th edition. London: Hodder and Arnold.

Haigh, R (2006) People's experiences of having a diagnosis of personality disorder. In Sampson, M, McCubbin, R and Tyrer, P (eds) (2006) *Personality disorder and community mental health teams: A practitioner's guide*. Chichester: John Wiley & Sons.

Hayne, Y (2003) Experiencing psychiatric diagnosis: Client perspectives on being named mentally ill. *Journal of Psychiatric and Mental Health Nursing*, 10, 722–9.

Henderson, J (2001) 'He's not my carer – he's my husband': Personal and policy constructions of care in mental health. *Journal of Social Work Practice*, 15 (2), 149–59.

Honig, P (2007) Family approaches: Evidence-based and collaborative practice. In Lask, B and Bryant-Waugh, R (eds) *Eating disorders in childhood and adolescence*. 3rd edition. Abingdon: Routledge.

Hopkins, C and Niemiec, S (2007) Mental health crisis at home: Service user perspectives on what helps and what hinders. *Journal of Psychiatric and Mental Health Nursing*, 14, 310–18.

Hotopf, M (2005) The assessment of capacity. *Clinical Medicine*, 5 (6), 580–4.

Howard, D (2006) Integrated care pathways and the mental health modernisation agenda. In Hall, J and Howard, D (eds) *Integrated care pathways in mental health*. Edinburgh: Churchill Livingstone Elsevier.

Howard, L (2007) Postnatal depression. *BMJ Clinical Evidence*. [online] Available at **clinical evidence.bmj.com/ceweb/conditions/pac/1407/1407_background.jsp**

Hughes, L and Pengelly, P (1997) *Staff supervision in a turbulent environment, Managing process and task in front-line services*. London: Jessica Kingsley.

Hutchison, E, Matto, H, Harrigan, M, Charlesworth, L and Viggiani, P (2007) *Challenges of living: A multidimensional working model for social workers*. London: Sage.

International Association of Schools of Social Work and International Federation of Social Work (2002) *International Definition of Social Work*. Geneva: IFSW. [online] **Available at http://www.ifsw.org/en/ p38000208.html**

Jasper, M (2003) *Beginning reflective practice*. Cheltenham: Nelson Thornes.

Jones, D (2004) Families and serious mental illness: Working with loss and ambivalence. *British Journal of Social Work*, 34, 961–79.

Kerfoot, M (2005) Children 'looked after' by the state. In Williams, R and Kerfoot, M (eds) *Child and adolescent mental health services, Strategy, planning, delivery and evaluation*. Oxford: Oxford University Press.

London Health Observatory [n.d.] *Disease groups: Mental health prevalence*. [online] Available at **www.lho.org.uk/viewResource.aspx?id=9532**

Magagna, J (2007) Individual psychotherapy. In Lask, B and Bryant-Waugh, R (eds) *Eating disorders in childhood and adolescence*. 3rd edition. Abingdon: Routledge.

Maidment, J and Cooper, L. (2002) Acknowledgement of client diversity and oppression in social work student supervision. *Social Work Education*, 21 (4), 399–407.

Marsella, AJ and Yamada, AM (2000) Culture and mental health: An introduction and overview of foundations, concepts and issues. In Cuellar, I and Paniagua, F (eds) *The handbook of multicultural mental health: Assessment and treatment of diverse populations*, 3–24, New York: Academic Press.

Martin, E and Law, J (2006) *Oxford dictionary of law*. Oxford: Oxford University Press. [online] Available at **www.oxfordreference.com/views/BOOK_SEARCH.html?book=t49**

McCafferty, P (2004) Group supervision for social work students on placement: An international comparison. *Journal of Practice Teaching*, 5 (3), 55–72.

McCafferty, P (2005) Developing a model for supervising social work students in groups. *Journal of Practice Teaching*, 6 (2), 24–42.

McDaniel, S (1999) Psychiatric and neurologic conditions. In Acuff, C, Archambeault, J, et al. *Mental health care for people living with or affected by HIV/AIDS: A practical guide.* Bethesda, MD.: U.S. Department of Health and Human Services.

Mencap (2004) News, in *Viewpoint.* Nov/Dec. [online] Available at
www.mencap.org.uk/download/viewpoint_nov_dec_04.pdf p4 www.mencap.org.uk

Merritt, S (2008a) *The devil within: A memoir of depression.* London: Vermillion.

Merritt, S (2008b) My private hell. *The Observer,* 6 April 2008. [online] Available at
books.guardian.co.uk/extracts/story/0,,2270668,00.html

MIND (2008) *Information.* [online] Available at www.mind.org.uk/Information/ **www.mind.org.uk**

National Institute for Health and Clinical Excellence (2002) *Schizophrenia: Core interventions in the treatment and management of schizophrenia in primary and secondary care, Clinical guideline 1.* London: NICE.

National Institute for Health and Clinical Excellence (2004) *Self harm: The short-term physical and psychological management and secondary prevention of self harm in primary and secondary care.* London: NICE. Available at
www.nice.org.uk/page.aspx?o=213665.

National Institute for Health and Clinical Excellence (2006) *Quick reference guide, Bipolar disorder: The management of bipolar disorder in adults, children and adolescents, in primary and secondary care.* London: NICE.

National Institute for Health and Clinical Excellence (2007) *Quick reference guide (amended), Depression: Management of depression in primary and secondary care.* London: NICE.

National Institute for Health and Clinical Excellence and Social Care Institute for Excellence (2006) *Quick reference guide, Dementia: Supporting people with dementia and their carers in health and social care.* London: NICE and SCIE.

National Institute for Mental Health in England (2003) *Personality disorder: No longer a diagnosis of exclusion.* Leeds: NIMHE. **www.nimhe.org.uk**.

National Institute for Mental Health in England (2004) *NIMHE emerging national framework of values for mental health.* [online] Available at **213.121.207.229/upload/NIMHEValuesFramework-Workbook.doc**

Newton, J (2004) Learning to reflect: A journey. *Reflective Practice,* 5 (2), 155–66.

Nonacs, R (2007) *Postpartum depression.* emedicine.com [online] Available at
www.emedicine.com/med/topic3408.htm www.emedicine.com

Norman, I and Peck, E (1999) Working together in adult community mental health services: An inter-professional dialogue. *Journal of Mental Health,* 8 (3), 217–30. Available at **http://dx.doi.org/10.1080/09638239917382**

Onyett, S (2003) *Teamworking in mental health.* Basingstoke: Palgrave Macmillan.

Payne, M (2005) *Modern social work theory.* 3rd edition. Basingstoke: Palgrave Macmillan.

Peck, E and Norman, I (1999) Working together in adult community mental health services: Exploring inter-professional role relations. *Journal of Mental Health,* 8 (3), 231–43. Available at **http://dx.doi.org/10.1080/09638239917391**

Pollard, K, Sellman, D and Senior, B (2005) The need for interprofessional working. In Barrett, G, Sellman, D and Thomas, J (eds) (2005) *Interprofessional working in health and social care, Professional perspectives.* Basingstoke: Palgrave Macmillan.

Pollio, D, North, C, Reid, D, Miletic, M and McClendon, J (2006) Living with severe mental illness – What families and friends must know: Evaluation of a one-day psychoeducation workshop. *Social Work,* 51 (1), 31–8.

Prilleltensky, I (2001a) Cultural assumptions, social justice and mental health. In Shumaker, J and Ward, T (eds) *Cultural cognition and psychopathology.* Westport, CO: Praeger.

Prior, L (1993) *The social organization of mental illness.* London: Sage.

Quality Assurance Agency for Higher Education (2008) *Honours degree benchmark statement: Social work.* Gloucester: QAA. Available at
www.qaa.ac.uk/academicinfrastructure/benchmark/statements/socialwork08.pdf

Reamer, F (1995) *Social work values and ethics.* New York: Columbia University Press.

Redfield Jamison, K (1995) *An unquiet mind: A memoir of moods and madness.* New York: Alfred A. Knopf, Inc.

Rees, G, Huby, G, McDade, L and McKechnie, L (2004) Joint working in community mental health teams: implementation of an integrated care pathway. *Health and Social Care in the Community,* 12 (6), 527–36.

Scaife, J (2001) *Supervision in the mental health professions, A practitioner's guide*. Abingdon: Brunner-Routledge.

Schön, D (1983) *The reflective practitioner: How professionals think in action*. New York: Basic Books. Reprint, Aldershot: Ashgate Publishing, Ltd., 1995.

Secker, J and Hill, K (2002) Mental health training and development needs of community agency staff. *Health and Social Care in the Community*, 10 (5), 323–30.

Sharman, W (1997) *Children and adolescents with mental health problems*. London: Baillière Tindall.

Shooter, M (2005) Children and adolescents who have chronic physical illness. In Williams, R and Kerfoot, M (eds) *Child and adolescent mental health services, Strategy, planning, delivery and evaluation*. Oxford: Oxford University Press.

Smith, E, Nolen-Hoeksema, S, Fredrickson, B, Loftus, G, Bem, D and Maren, S (2003) *Atkinson and Hilgard's Introduction to psychology*. Belmont, CA: Wadsworth/Thomson Learning.

Southall, A (2005) *Consultation in child and adolescent mental health services*. Oxford: Radcliffe Publishing.

Spafford, M, Schryer, C, Campbell, S and Lingard, L (2007) Towards embracing clinical uncertainty: Lessons from social work, optometry and medicine. *Journal of Social Work*, 7 (2), 155–78. [online] Available at **jsw.sagepub.com/cgi/content/abstract/7/2/155**.

Taylor, P and Vatcher, A (2005) Social work. In Barrett, G, Sellman, D and Thomas, J (eds) *Interprofessional working in health and social care, Professional perspectives*. Basingstoke: Palgrave Macmillan.

Tew, J (ed.) (2005) *Social perspectives in mental health: Developing social models to understand and work with mental distress*. London: Jessica Kingsley.

Tilbury, D (2002) *Working with mental illness: A community-based approach*. 2nd edition. Basingstoke: Palgrave.

Topss (2004) *The national occupational standards for social work*. Leeds: Skills for Care.

Walker, S (2002) Culturally competent protection of children's mental health. *Child Abuse Review*, 11, 380–93.

Walker, S (2003) *Social work and child and adolescent mental health*. Lyme Regis: Russell House.

Walker, S (2004) Community work and psychosocial practice – Chalk and cheese or birds of a feather? *Journal of Social Work Practice*, 18 (2), 161–75. [online] Available at **http://dx.doi.org/10.1080/0265053042000230981**.

Warman, A and Jackson, E (2007) Recruiting and retaining children and families' social workers: The potential of work discussion groups. *Journal of Social Work Practice*, 21 (1), 35–48. [online] Available at **http://dx.doi.org/10.1080/02650530601173599**. (Accessed 23 February 2008)

Wedgbury, D, Denny, M, Stokes, K, Barlow, T, Staples, C, and Probert, E with Southall, A (2005) The last word…Consultation with service users. In Southall, A (ed.) *Consultation in child and adolescent mental health services*. Oxford: Radcliffe Publishing.

West, A and Salmon, G (2000) Bullying and depression: A case report. *International Journal of Psychiatry in Clinical Practice*, (4) 1, 73–5.

White, P and Clare, A (2002) Psychological medicine. In Kumar, P and Clark, M (eds) (2002) *Clinical medicine*. 5th edition. Edinburgh: W.B. Saunders.

Williamson, T (2007) Capacity to protect – the Mental Capacity Act explained. *Journal of Adult Protection*, 9 (1), 25–32.

Wood, S and Green, B (2006) Integrated care pathways and integrated working. In Hall, J and Howard, D (eds) *Integrated care pathways in mental health*. Edinburgh: Churchill Livingstone Elsevier.

World Health Organisation (1992) *The ICD-10 classification of mental and behavioural disorders: Clinical descriptions and diagnostic guidelines*. Geneva: WHO.

Wright, J, Briggs, S and Behringer, J (2005) Attachment and the body in suicidal adolescents: A pilot study. *Clinical Child Psychology and Psychiatry*, 10 (4), 477–91.

Yip, K (2006) Reflectivity in social work practice with clients with mental-health illness: Promise and challenge in education. *International Social Work*, 49, 245–55. Available at **http://isw.sagepub.com/cgi/content/abstract/49/2/245**

Glossary

Adjustment disorders A diagnostic category which describes shorter-term emotional or behavioural reactions to significant psychosocial stressors, such as unemployment or relationship breakdown.

Approved mental health professional (AMHP) The term refers to mental health professionals who assess persons for compulsory admission to hospital in line with the Mental Health Act 2007. AMHPs function on behalf of the local social services authority to reduce conflicts of interest and promote objectivity in decision-making.

Autism spectrum disorders A category of disorders in which persons display a range of difficulties in understanding and processing social norms and social interactions and display impaired communication. Asperger's syndrome is a more mild type in this category; while autistic disorder is more severe, with prominent difficulties in social development, language and play before age 3.

Bolam test The principle that a health professional, such as a social worker, is not negligent if acting in accordance with practice accepted at the time as proper by a responsible body of medical opinion or a professional body, such as the GSCC.

British National Formulary (BNF) The BNF is a reference text published twice yearly jointly by the British Medical Association and the Royal Pharmaceutical Society of Great Britain. It lists available medications and treatments which can be prescribed to treat medical conditions; this includes the range of medicines used for mental health symptoms. A separate formulary covers prescribed medicine for children. **www.bnf.org/bnf/**

Bournewood gap A term describing the gap in law relating to a human rights failing in relation to the earlier Mental Capacity Act (MCA) and the deprivation of liberty of persons without the ability to communicate consent to treatment. This has been addressed in the revised MCA 2005.

Care Programme Approach (CPA) A service delivery approach in adult mental health services based in policy which involves the joint meeting of service users and professionals to determine care planning and treatment approaches.

Child and adolescent mental health services (CAMHS) The specialist agency that offers mental health services to young people; this service may involve outpatient appointments as well as more intensive residential services.

Cognitive therapy A form of psychotherapy aimed at modifying people's beliefs, expectancies and styles of thinking, based on the assumption that psychological problems often stem from problematic patterns of thinking and distorted perceptions of reality.

Community mental health nurse (CMHN) Nurses with specialised training and education to work in mental health settings. Also known as community psychiatric nurse (CPN).

Community mental health team (CMHT) A CMHT is a specialist mental health provider that responds to those with more serious mental health needs than can be managed within a general practice. It involves a multidisciplinary team of practitioners including psychiatrists, nurses, social workers, psychologists and occupational therapists among other disciplines.

Community Treatment Orders See supervised community treatment (SCT).

Consultation Offering specialist advice in relation to a case or a service to improve service response.

Counselling The practice of applying psychological perspectives through talking and thinking with clients about their life circumstances, goals and emotional experiences. Counselling sessions may take place with individual clients or with couples, families or groups. Counsellors train in and practice using a variety of theoretical approaches.

Court of Protection A court that administers the property and affairs of persons of unsound mind.

Delusions False beliefs which are not based in reality and which may be contradicted by other evidence. Delusional beliefs may have an overarching quality such that false beliefs of a suspicious nature would be described as paranoid. Describing something as delusional would not apply to strongly held cultural or religious beliefs.

Dementia An organic brain syndrome in which a range of cognitive functions decline, including memory, language, judgement and thinking such as problem-solving, planning and attention and concentration. Types of dementia include Alzheimer's and multi-infarct dementia, also known as vascular dementia; the latter develops as a result of infarcts or dead tissue in the brain from a lack of blood supply due to cerebrovascular disease.

Diagnosis The process of gathering data about a person's signs and symptoms to make a decision based on agreed criteria. It is also the term referring to the medical condition. In psychiatry, the two common diagnostic references are: the *Diagnostic and Statistical Manual of Mental Disorders* (DSM) and the *International Classification of Disorders* (ICD).

Eating disorders A range of diagnoses that relate to impairment of eating or feeding. Commonly known eating disorders include anorexia and bulimia; there are also disorders of eating in infancy and early childhood.

Epidemiology The statistical tracking of disease or illness to include incidence, prevalence, control and distribution.

Experts by experience A phrase describing current or historic users of mental health services who by virtue of experiencing services and mental health needs offer training or consultation. This may also include family, friends and carers.

Forensic mental health Services that respond to mental health need in relation to legal matters.

Government policy protocols Green Papers and White Papers are both types of Command paper and may be the subject of statements or debates in the House of Commons.

Green Papers A Green Paper is a consultation document issued by the government which contains policy proposals for debate and discussion before a final decision is taken on the best policy option. A Green Paper will often contain several alternative policy options. See also **White Paper**.

Hallucinations A term describing sensory phenomena not based in reality and not due to stimulation of a sense organ. Hallucinations may occur in relation to any sense. They may stem from psychosis but may also be a result of substance misuse or a feature of withdrawal from substances.

Independent mental capacity advocate (IMCA) A relatively new role which supports those determined to lack mental capacity by advocating for their views and wishes, securing their rights, exploring options, safeguarding their interests and accessing treatment and services.

171

Mental capacity This term describes the capacity of individuals to understand information regarding decision-making, to retain relevant information, to analyse and apply the information in relation to a decision and to communicate that decision to other parties. It is relevant in relation to medical, financial and psychiatric decisions. Lacking capacity would mean that someone is unable to engage in the above process due to an impairment of or a disturbance of functioning of the mind.

Mental Capacity Act (MCA) Legislation updated in 2005 to govern issues of mental capacity.

Mental Health Act (MHA) Legislation, amended as of 2007, to address issues of care and control in relation to mental health matters, particularly the application of the law in relation to compulsory treatment of mental health difficulties. The Act sets out the legislative responsibilities of pertinent professionals, time frames in relation to assessment and treatment and parameters and processes of appeal.

Mental Health Review Tribunals (MHRTs) The Mental Health Review Tribunal has the responsibility of hearing applications from those who wish to appeal against detention or more coercive applications of care under the MHA.

Mood disorders A class of mental health diagnoses that refers to a disruption or upset in mood. Common types of mood disorder include major depression and bipolar disorder.

Personality disorder This term describes a category of mental health disorders in which there is a pervasive and longstanding interference in self-concept, identity, impulse control, perception and mood with consequent disruptions to personal and social relationships.

Post-traumatic stress disorder A type of anxiety disorder that develops in response to experiencing or witnessing a severe trauma stemming from actual or threatened serious injury or risk to life. Symptoms include intense fear or helplessness and will be accompanied by flashbacks and recurrent intrusive images of the trauma. Responses may include hypervigilance, numbing and a persistent disturbance of a sense of safety.

Power of attorney A formal instrument by which one person empowers another to act on his or her behalf, either generally or in specific circumstances. In mental health contexts, service users would authorise a trusted party to make decisions on their behalf in relation to care.

Psychiatry The branch of medicine that assesses, diagnoses and treats mental health problems.

Psychopathology The study of mental disorders.

Psychotherapy An approach to treating mental or emotional distress through psychological methods such as talking or expressive means with a goal of uncovering and resolving earlier or more recent triggers and causes of distress. There are various theoretical and practice approaches including psychoanalytic, humanistic, cognitive and brief therapies among many others, which may be delivered in individual, couple, family or group sessions.

Psychotic disorders A class of mental health diagnoses that describes disorders in thinking, reality testing and social relationships featuring delusional beliefs and hallucinations and lacking insight. A common psychotic disorder is schizophrenia.

Psychotropic medication Types of medication prescribed to treat psychiatric symptoms. Anti-depressants and anti-anxiety medications are two classes of medication which are psychotropic.

Public Guardian, Office of A government body set up to help protect people who lack capacity through maintaining registers of lasting and enduring powers of attorney and overseeing the Court of Protection as well as supervising deputies who act on behalf of others through social services departments.

Responsible Clinician The Mental Health Act 2007 eliminates the restriction of this role to a physician. A Responsible Clinician (RC) is defined as the approved clinician with overall responsibility for an individual's mental healthcare. Responsible Clinicians may come from various professions, such as nursing, occupational therapy, psychiatry, psychology or social work. An approved clinician is one who has been delegated by the local authority to act in relation to the MHA.

Supervised community treatment This term refers to a feature of the Mental Health Act 2007 in which a community treatment order may specify conditions to which a patient is to be subject while the order remains in force. It may specify conditions only if the Responsible Clinician, with the agreement of the approved mental health professional, thinks them necessary or appropriate for one of the following: (a) to ensure the receipt of necessary medical treatment; (b) to prevent risk of harm to health or safety to the person in question; and/or (c) to protect others.

White Paper A document issued by a government department which contains detailed proposals for legislation. It is the final stage before the government introduces its proposals to Parliament in the form of a Bill. When a White Paper is issued, it is often accompanied by a statement in the House from the secretary of state of the department sponsoring the proposals.

Index

Added to the page number, 'f' denotes a figure and 'g' denotes the glossary.